DEEPER INTO THE HEART
OF THE ROCKIES

DEEPER INTO THE HEART OF THE ROCKIES

Selected Columns
from The Denver Post
1999-2012

ED QUILLEN

Edited by
Abby Quillen

Foreword by
Allen Best

Sidewalk Press

Eugene, Oregon

DEEPER INTO THE HEART OF THE ROCKIES

Published by
Sidewalk Press
Eugene, Oregon
E-mail: Sidewalkpress@gmail.com

Editor: Abby Quillen
Cover photo courtesy of Hal Walter
Author photo courtesy of Cayton Photography
Cover and interior design by Aaron Thomas with special thanks
to Bob Thomason

Publisher's Cataloging-in-Publication
Quillen, Ed.
    Deeper into the heart of the Rockies : selected columns from The
Denver Post 1999-2012 / foreword by Allen Best ; edited by Abby Quillen.
    p. cm.
    ISBN: 978-0-9899822-0-7
1. Colorado—Social life and customs 2. West (U.S.)—Social life and customs 3. United States — Social life and customs 4. American essays I. Title.
F781.3.Q55 2013   978.8'033

To the memory of Ed Quillen,
and to all the readers who made it possible
for him to do the work he loved.

Contents

Foreword

Allen Best

For more than a quarter-century, Coloradans had reason to smile two mornings a week. Some people probably grimaced, and that, too, is part of the story of Ed Quillen's phenomenal run as a columnist in *The Denver Post*. But I often found myself smiling, sometimes laughing out loud, enjoying the journey through Ed's allotted 750 words as he informed, analyzed and educated, using some topic of the day as his starting place but with no certainty of destination. I suspect the vast majority of those reading this passage will remember similar smiles, laughs and nods of appreciation. Mornings since his untimely death in June 2012 just haven't been as much fun.

Ed had many exceptional abilities. He read with the speed of a lightning bolt and comprehended nearly as rapidly. I first learned of this in July 1977, soon after I went to work for Ed as a reporter at the *Middle Park Times* in Kremmling. He couldn't have been more than twenty-seven, and I was twenty-five, but he seemed already to be a fully formed adult, wise to ways of the world that I still struggle to comprehend now, thiry-six years later. But that didn't make him staid. Exactly the opposite. He wore his red beard raggedy, rolled his own cigarettes with Zigzag papers, and guffawed and harrumphed with abandon, depending upon the occasion.

He was above all a family man, and one Tuesday evening, crunch time at that newspaper, I deposited a copy of a book called *Monkeywrench Gang* on his desk when I returned from the courthouse. He promised to look at it during supper with his wife Martha and their two young daughters, Columbine and Abby.

"Damned fine book," he said, or something to that affect, upon returning two or three hours later.

"Yes, Ed Abbey's first chapter is really a hoot," I might have replied, for that's what I thought was a good read in an hour's time. But Ed had read the entire book. He probably could remember passages of the book word for word. He had a mind like that. Even by his twenties, he had retrieved vast stores of knowledge from the universe. It was a rare treat to introduce him to an author, an idea or even a mere fact that was new to him. He was a prodigy.

Ed was above all an independent thinker. He tended toward liberal views, but you wouldn't want to bet the house on his stand on any particular topic. That's partly why he was such a good columnist. You never knew quite where he would end up. Nobody owned his thoughts. No ideology could completely claim him. He had prejudices, but they were shaped by facts and reasoning. He subscribed to certain mythologies, but they were deeply informed by his study of history, geography and life experience.

He was skeptical about the collateral damage of supposed good intentions. Institutions were almost always suspect. He fulminated early and often against the War on Drugs and the self-perpetuating, self-justifying agencies it spawned. Once formal public policy had declared certain drugs as enemies, then all manner of chicanery was authorized.

Schools and especially universities similarly were a source of skepticism and sometimes scorn. Although he saw great value in individual academics, he viewed their institutions as less motivated by intellectual inquiry than by financial self-interest. From the Ivy League on down to the paler imitations in the heartland, they were and are about elitism, not the democratic impulse.

As for cultural conformity, he had even less use. Libertarian in his instincts, Ed skewered these "right-thinkers," as he put it, often with his fictional confidante Ananias Ziegler of the Committee that Really Runs America. With family values deeply imbedded in his own existence, he could tolerate other lifestyles, other ways of living. What he couldn't abide were hypocrisies. He punctured those balloons with great skill.

Injustice, a companion of hypocrisy, was another gist for his rapier wit, as when a young woman who made significant mistakes unknowingly and indirectly contributed to the death of a police officer in Denver. The real defendant dead, Denver's legal establishment made sure the woman, Lisl Auman, would spend life behind bars. Ed saw through the hypocrisy and injustice of that, too, and was among a group of journalists – including another truth-teller, Hunter S. Thompson – who finally were able to achieve true justice. That was Ed at his best: comforting the afflicted, and afflicting the comfortable.

To a close friend, Ed once described himself as a "professional Coloradan." That pegs things. He had a detailed grasp of Colorado history and most of its component parts.

That history has warts, and he could describe them, but it also has epic passages, and Ed understood that element, too. He knew of the business titans, and accorded them their due, but his sympathies were with the blue-collar workers, such as dwelled in his own family roots and calloused hands.

He was also a geographer, intuitively understanding the complexities of life, the dependence of Denver and its suburbs on the various hinterlands: the farm towns of the great plains where he grew up, the mountain towns where he spent his adult life, and the rails that connected them, the itty-bitty places and the elbow-to-elbow density of Denver's Capitol Hill. Little bits of this vast knowledge would come out in his fifty-yard sprint through his essays.

Too, he could be funny. "I met an El Paso County Democrat once, and she said she'd introduce me to the other one the next time I visited Colorado Springs," he wrote in one column. He could work humor into an otherwise sober column and have a point to it. Other times, his humor was entirely acerbic, as was the case with his appellation of the "Stupid Zone," the place where people built homes that they shouldn't, especially in forested areas. Ed believed in living in town, and especially small ones. He understood Denver and the Front Range, but his voice was that of rural Colorado, especially Salida.

In this enterprise, Ed must be seen as the public figure of a team. Martha, his wife, was always his best editor and a key part of the intellectual fermentation that resulted in these sparkling and wry observations of our times. These columns are her columns, too.

It's a rare skill, being able to compress a history lesson, a joke, and a ton of critical thinking into 750 words. Ed rarely stumbled and never bored. He was remarkably consistent, with a run of column-writing in Colorado unrivaled in either duration or high quality. Ed left Colorado and the region a better place. His columns can still make us laugh, may sometimes make us angry, and, although sentimentality was never his mode of operation, a few might make you cry. Most of all, they'll make you think, and what gift can be larger than that?

Introduction

Abby Quillen

My sister has been attending law school for the last few years, and I like to joke that I've been attending Ed Quillen's finishing school. After reading at least a million of my dad's words, and then reading many of them again, and again, I've learned quite a bit.

For instance, in Colorado, water flows uphill toward money, and it's not smart, one might even say it's stupid, to build a house with a shake-shingle roof in a wildfire-prone forest. Also, to really understand Colorado, the West, national politics, or anything else, it helps to have a wide knowledge of history and literature, as well as real-life relationships with the laborers, lift-operators, cashiers, bartenders, and builders who do the work. Most of all, I've learned about dedication.

I stand in awe of my dad's devotion to his craft. For nearly as long as I can remember, he wrote one to three columns a week with no vacations, sick days, or sabbaticals. He spent his life mastering the short essay and, like many writers, he got better with age. The columns in this collection — the best from the height of his career — sparkle with his intelligence, wit and humor.

It's striking how many of them touch on issues in today's headlines. The topics my dad wrote about — the urban/rural divide, struggles over natural resources, the hypocrisy of politicians — rise time and again. Most of these columns are as prescient as the day he wrote them.

I wish my dad were here to write this introduction. He'd no doubt leave you guffawing and thinking about Colorado, life, politics, and the world rather than about him, as so many of these columns will. But it's my honor to curate some of his words into a form more lasting than newspaper archives. I hope you enjoy the collection.

Politics, Big and Small

M aybe there are such people who felt secure and innocent before September 11, but I sure don't know any of them. But even if they're annoying, the talking heads must be watched, especially now that they're applying spin, which comes in two forms: "act of terrorism" and "act of war."

WE LOST OUR INNOCENCE
A LONG TIME AGO
SEPTEMBER 16, 2001

IT SEEMED SURREAL at first, and in many ways it still does. The twin towers of the World Trade Center and the bulk of the Pentagon were mere images that I had seen only on television and movie screens; they were not real places in the sense that Mount Elbert or our state Capitol is a real place where I have walked and shaken hands with people.

For the first hour or two of Tuesday morning, attached to Cable News Network and its competitors, I felt like one of those people who believed that the 1969 moon landing never happened, that it was all part of some made-for-television spectacle designed to delude a gullible public. It finally started to seem real when the cameras got to people on the street who were fleeing from south Manhattan.

They weren't in military uniforms, and they weren't masters of the universe in their dress-for-success power outfits. They were in T-shirts and blue jeans, halter tops and shorts, with tattoos and nose rings and shaved heads and purple hair. They came in all known human colors and they spoke in accents that ranged from nearly incomprehensible to the Queen's English.

By noon, it sank in. They were my countrymen, and they had been attacked. These were real places with real people who sweated and swore and brawled and made babies and went about their lives, just like the rest of us. And they had been there. It wasn't a too-many-special-effects-and-no-plot Grade B disaster movie any more.

But maybe this seemed unreal because the talking heads were so much more sensible than they had been in the past. Not long after the Oklahoma City bomb exploded in 1995, the experts were assuring us that this was definitely the work of foreign terrorists. This time around, they weren't jumping to conclusions.

Nor was anyone saying this happened because the Ten Commandments weren't posted in classrooms. No Colorado politician got any airtime by blaming radical environmentalists who threatened national security by opposing oil exploration in national parks so we had to import it from the Mideast where the money flowed to terrorists. But watch long enough, and the stupidity will start to flow. The most galling phrase was "loss of innocence."

My house sits on land that was once claimed by the crown of Spain, as a result of bloody warfare led by conquistadors in the sixteenth century. It was then claimed by Mexico as a result of a revolution in 1821. In 1836, the Republic of Texas, born of bloodshed, claimed the same territory. The United States of America sent soldiers west in 1846 to take this land in a sanguinary struggle with Mexico. More soldiers came to expel the Utes during the following thirty-five years. After that there were labor wars at the mines, mills and railroads.

Just where in this chronicle of violence was this "innocence" that the talking heads said we had heretofore enjoyed?

Just where in America were there people who felt totally serene and secure before last Tuesday? Where were those people who didn't feel any need to worry about trigger-happy police kicking in the wrong door? Or the people who trusted their political institutions when a court went out of its way to interfere with a presidential election? Maybe there are such people who felt secure and innocent before September 11, but I sure don't know any of them. But even if they're annoying, the talking heads must be watched, especially now that they're applying spin, which comes in two forms: "act of terrorism" and "act of war."

If the conventional wisdom decides on "act of terrorism," then we're supposed to hold our heads high and go on about our lives, to show that the terrorists failed in their goal of disrupting our country. Those responsible will be arrested and tried through the normal channels of justice, or something close to it.

But if the commentary begins to settle on "act of war," then we're supposed to respond in precisely the opposite way: not normal life, but mobilization for a long war against invisible foes.

Civil liberties are generally curtailed during wartime. The same people who ran for office promising a smaller and less intrusive government will be beating the drums for internal passports and the monitoring of all personal communication. Those believed responsible for the initial attack, as well as anyone with any connection with them, will be bombed into oblivion. And of course there will be casualties on both sides, but presumably the talking heads who want war will find a way to be spared.

So as much as I'd like to ignore the talking heads, we've got to watch them. Whether they spin this as terrorism or war will make a big difference.

MASSACHUSETTS: A HOTBED OF RADICALISM
MAY 18, 2004

THE SUN ROSE TODAY. Also, Western civilization and our republic remain as strong as they were last week, before the Commonwealth of Massachusetts began issuing marriage licenses to homosexual couples.

This observation puts me in opposition to at least two Colorado elected officials who serve in Washington: Senator Wayne Allard and Representative Marilyn Musgrave, both sponsors of an amendment to the federal Constitution which would ban such unions. Musgrave, in particular, warns of dire consequences unless the federal government halts these Bay State marriages.

On the other hand, it puts me in the strange position of being in agreement with Vice President Dick Cheney. The topic came up during the 2000 campaign, and he responded with: "That matter is regulated by the states. I think different states are likely to come to different conclusions, and that's appropriate. I don't think there should necessarily be a federal policy in this area."

So, what are we to make of this? The opposing arguments come in several forms. One is that four un-elected judges on the Massachusetts Supreme Court are inflicting their radical agenda on the rest of the country, and it's time to restrain them.

The problem with this approach is that gay couples no doubt feel that our country is imposing a radical agenda on them. Our laws take away their right to decide whom to be with, whom to love and share a home with. Gay activists merely want the right to choose their own mates, to be responsible for one another, to share decisions, and insurance, and designate who will inherit their earthly goods.

And these do seem to be rights that heterosexual couples enjoy whether they've made good decisions or bad ones, and whether they're licentious, adulterous, abusive, selfish or just downright offensive. It's a matter of who gets to decide whom you will mate with — and nothing more. If someone wants to make that into a religious issue on the grounds that marriage is a "sacrament," then that's all the more reason that this is no proper business of the government.

Another argument, perhaps a potent one in an election year with a presidential challenger from Massachusetts, is that the Bay State is a hotbed of radicalism, and we should be suspicious of anything that emanates from it.

There is some historical truth to this. The American Revolution was born in Massachusetts as much as it was born anywhere, with the first battle at Lexington and the leadership of cousins John and Samuel Adams. Before the Civil War, the abolition movement (a fierce attack on American property and traditions) was based in Massachusetts. It was the only state that George McGovern carried in 1972.

But when it comes to marriage, Massachusetts has the lowest divorce rate in the nation. The national average in 2001 was 4 per 1,000 people; Nevada, Arkansas and Wyoming had rates over 6, and the Massachusetts rate was only 2.6.

So it's hardly a bastion of libertinism, even if some of its voters routinely re-elect Representative Barney Frank, who's liberal and openly gay.

The big argument is that if gay marriages are legal in one state, then they have to be recognized in all states, under the "full faith and credit" clause of the U.S. Constitution.

There is already a 1996 federal law that says that states don't have to recognize same-sex marriages. It hasn't been tested in court, but note that a "marriage license" is a license.

States appear to retain the option to honor or ignore other states' licenses. A Colorado driver's license will keep you from being cited for "failure to possess a valid driver's license" if you're pulled over in Wyoming or New Mexico, but a Colorado license to practice law does not automatically allow you to represent clients before the courts of those states.

So despite the rantings of Marilyn Musgrave and her allies, there's no certainty that Massachusetts weddings would affect Colorado at all. And even if it did, well, how is my marriage or yours thereby threatened?

The main effect of all this right-wing hand-wringing is political. It gives conservative candidates another issue. They can add to the list — abortion, flag-burning, raunchy TV, to name a few — when they're tossing red meat out to the faithful.

Then they can return to office and get back to the real business of rewarding their campaign contributors.

IRAQ UNLIKE WORLD WAR II
JUNE 6, 2004

LAST WEEK, COLORADO WAS HONORED by a visit from the Leader of the Free World, who stopped in Denver to raise $2.2 million for struggling Republican candidates, then spoke at the graduation ceremony at the U.S. Air Force Academy.

There, he compared the current war in Iraq to World War II, although the similarities escape me. The United States entered the war after Japan bombed Pearl Harbor on December 7, 1941. That was an act of war, and the U.S. Congress responded by declaring war against Japan on December 8. In Germany on December 11, Adolf Hitler honored a treaty commitment with Japan and declared war on the U.S.; Congress then declared war against Germany.

Also note that the 1941 attack came from Japan, and the U.S. went to war against Japan. Now observe that the 2001 attack came from Saudi nationals whose leader was believed to be in Afghanistan at the time, and that the major U.S. response has been against Iraq, which has no discernible connection to the September 11 attacks.

Also, the 1941 declarations followed the federal Constitution: "The Congress shall have power ... To declare War." Now see if you can find any declaration of war against Iraq by the U.S. Congress.

I'm too young to remember World War II — I was born five years after it ended — and even my parents were too young to see military duty. In grade school, I felt deprived on that account. On show-and-tell day, other kids would show up with "this here Luger pistol my dad took off a kraut he captured," and our house had no such souvenirs.

My parents talked about life on the home front during the war, though, especially rationing and recycling. Gasoline was limited to a few gallons a week, and you had to present ration coupons to buy sugar and meat. They saved bacon fat and empty toothpaste tubes, which were collected in every town, along with scrap metal. So I heard plenty about sacrifice on the home front then, as opposed to now, when the administration apparently asks us only to sacrifice our civil liberties in the cause of "protecting freedom."

As a boy, I loved to hear tales of adventure, and there was a World War II combat veteran in the Quillen family: my uncle Gene. He was five years older than my dad, and by the time I knew him, he was an Army major.

Like many WWII veterans, Gene didn't talk much about the war, but he saw plenty of it. He joined the National Guard in 1940 and got called to active duty a year later; his first assignment was guarding the railroad across Raton Pass.

Then he went to Officer Candidate School, which entitled him to the most dangerous job in the military — second lieutenant in charge of a small infantry combat unit, a duty which provides the approximate life expectancy of a fruitfly's. He fought in the Pacific: the Aleutian, Marshall, Philippine and Okinawa campaigns, and earned two bronze stars and a combat infantry badge. My brothers and I adored him when he visited, and we would pester him for war stories, hoping to hear how he'd led a charge against a Japanese machine-gun nest to take a vital island, or something like that.

But he always changed the subject. When I asked him about it a few years ago, he said that there had been a time in his life when he was "a professional killer," but it was in the past and he wanted to leave it there.

Fair enough. He was eighty-one when he died in Florida on April 3, and was buried at Arlington National Cemetery on April 26. No matter what they dedicate on the National Mall, he'll always be my World War II memorial.

And if our president needs to find historical parallels for the current operations in Iraq, there are plenty that fit better than World War II — say, the invasion of Mexico in 1846, or the "liberation" of the Philippines in 1898.

OPTIMISM AND THE CAMPAIGN
JULY 25, 2004

PERHAPS THIS TREND STARTED in early June with the death of Ronald Reagan. Pundits searched for good things to say about him, and often found "optimism" among his virtues. Shortly thereafter, someone important proclaimed that in all American presidential elections, the candidate who displays the most optimism will win.

Since then, we've been subjected to a barrage of commercials portraying John Kerry as an optimist and George W. Bush as a pessimist, or Bush as a sunny optimist and Kerry as a dour pessimist.

For instance, one spot started with a narrator who intoned, behind the image of a frowning Kerry, "Pessimism never created a job." Then comes our upbeat President Bush: "I'm optimistic about America because I believe in the people of America."

Does all this mean anything? You have to start with the premise that anyone running for president is an optimist, in the sense that he believes things can get better in the future — if he is elected, of course.

Nobody is going to campaign on "Our country is sliding downhill. Our economy is collapsing, most of the world hates us, disease and poverty are growing, more and more Americans are fat and lazy, and there's nothing we can do about it, and so you should elect me."

But how much optimism is appropriate? When Winston Churchill became prime minister of Great Britain in 1940, his nation's very survival was threatened by Germany, which was bombing London and threatening an invasion. Churchill did not talk about his optimism. He said his country faced an immense challenge and a hard struggle, and he had "nothing to offer but blood, tears, toil and sweat." In other words, he was honest with the British people about what lay ahead.

In this country, does the most optimistic presidential candidate always win? Four years ago, it was pretty much a dead heat. In 1996, well, just about anybody could sound more optimistic than Bob Dole, who came across as an old grump even though he had a marvelous sense of humor.

In 1992, Bill Clinton beat an incumbent by constantly pointing out that "We can do better than this" — certainly a more optimistic message than Bush the Elder grumbling about "Bozo and Ozone." But in 1988, Bush the Elder positively glowed in comparison to dour Mike Dukakis. And then we're back to Ronald Reagan, the Supreme Optimist, who got into the White House by defeating Jimmy "National Malaise" Carter.

So maybe there's something to the Greater Optimist Theory of Presidential Politics, at least in the past quarter-century. Go back much farther, and you run into people like Calvin "Looks like he was weaned on a pickle" Coolidge and Thomas "I tremble for my country when I reflect that God is just" Jefferson.

Given the current trend, though, we'll doubtless be subjected to more explanations coming from various spin doctors that detail how their candidate is the more optimistic fellow. But on a personal economic level, I'm worse off than I was four years ago, and so are most of my friends.

Even so, there might be grounds for optimism, based on what I learned from a printer about twenty-five years ago. He was in the habit of eating breakfast every day at Neil's Cafe, a diner in downtown Salida that closed long ago. To put it mildly, Neil's did not enjoy a reputation for excellent food. Just walking by the place could make your arteries clog, and the coffee made you wonder whether the creosote plant north of town had resumed production. So I asked him why he ate there every morning.

"It means I can handle whatever happens at the print shop that day," he explained, because "When you start your day at Neil's, you know the rest of the day has to be an improvement."

That seems like a possible reason to be optimistic; after the past four years, just about anything has to be an improvement.

RISE AND FALL OF INTELLECTUALISM
NOVEMBER 21, 2004

COMMENTARY SINCE THIS YEAR'S ELECTION, at least from liberals, alleges that the Bush victory, along with increased Republican control of Congress, represents yet another spate of "anti-intellectualism" in this country.

This seems odd, given that Bush is a graduate of both Yale and Harvard, two dens of intellectualism. Further, in recent years the GOP has boasted that it was the "party of ideas." Two of its leading lights in the 1990s, Georgia Representative Newt Gingrich and Texas Senator Phil Gramm, had been college teachers.

In politics, intellectualism goes in and out of fashion. President Dwight D. Eisenhower might have warned us about the "military-industrial complex," but he wasn't as witty as the man he twice defeated for the presidency, Adlai E. Stevenson.

Some intellectuals of the era found Eisenhower wanting, and as evidence they pointed to his fondness for Zane Grey westerns. They admired his successor, John F. Kennedy, and pointed to his fondness for Ian Fleming spy thrillers.

Having read both Grey and Fleming, I can't see either novelist as offering much more than entertainment — the characters are caricatures and the plots are predictable. Why one is more "intellectual" than the other escapes me.

But it was fashionable to be intellectual then, and Kennedy constructed an appropriate public persona. He flaunted his ghost-written books, and thus this fellow who loved Broadway show tunes appeared to cherish Bach concertos.

In more recent years, Americans have preferred the "regular guy" presidency, which explains why George Bush the Elder, a Connecticut blue-blood if there ever was one, let it be known that he liked pork rinds and the Oak Ridge Boys. If you look at American political history, it's little wonder that anti-intellectualism appears at intervals. Consider some of the theories that intellectuals have proposed.

Go back to the 1890s, and there was Social Darwinism: "survival of the fittest" should be applied to human society, and therefore it was right for the strong to prey on the weak. Government would be disturbing the natural order if it intervened on behalf of the weak, or even allowed the weak to organize to gain strength.

Should we be surprised that the "anti-intellectual" Populist Party arose to combat this? And was it "anti-intellectualism" or actually people of modest means organizing to protect themselves from rapacious millionaires and their experts who were happy to endorse any theory that justified greed?

A related intellectual fad was influential in the 1920s and '30s — eugenics. The idea was to improve the national character by selective breeding, and this led to everything from immigration restrictions ("inferior" types from southern Europe and Asia were excluded in favor of their betters from northern Europe) to compulsory sterilization in many American states. Opponents were criticized as being "anti-science" or "anti-intellectual," yet America is supposed to be a place where "all men are created equal" and deserve "equal protection of the laws." Eugenics eventually fell into disfavor because some German intellectuals used it to justify Nazi genocide.

In more recent times, very few dubious undertakings enjoyed more intellectual support than the Vietnam War in 1964. President Lyndon B. Johnson may have had his silent doubts as the escalation began, but certain intellectuals of the day, often called "the best and the brightest," were all for it.

They justified it on the basis of the now-discredited "Domino Theory." Among them were Walt Whitman Rostow, holder of a Ph.D. from Yale who had taught at Cambridge, and McGeorge Bundy, former dean of the faculty at Harvard.

Now, I don't think that this year's election represented a triumph of "anti-intellectualism." But even if it did, is that really a problem, considering some of the intellectual fads and currents of the past century or so?

OF COURSE BUSH CARES
SEPTEMBER 18, 2005

THE IMAGES FROM NEW ORLEANS, of people waiting for days on rooftops and freeway overpasses, inspired a benefit concert on national television on September 2. There, rapper Kanye West went off-script on the live broadcast to observe that "George Bush doesn't care about black people."

West was roundly denounced for that, and many have hastened to point out that George W. Bush is no racist. Others have stepped up to say that the slow response was based not on racial factors but economic status. That is, the federal government would have acted much more quickly to rescue wealthy people of any color; poverty, not race, determined the speed and scale of the response.

And they conclude that President Bush doesn't care about the poor. To buttress that assertion, they note that the president's first public statement of sympathy went to Senator Trent Lott of Mississippi, who lost one of his houses in Hurricane Katrina, not to some working family who lost everything.

But that's a superficial assessment. Further analysis shows that it's terribly unfair to President Bush. He cares about America, and America needs poor people.

We can start with a statement often attributed to Abraham Lincoln, the first Republican president: "Common looking people are the best in the world: that is the reason the Lord makes so many of them." The Bush variant would be, "Poor people are the best in the world: that is why we're making so many of them."

According to U.S. Census Bureau report on poverty, 37 million people were in poverty (12.7 percent) in 2004, up from 35.9 million (12.5 percent) in 2003. In 2004, there were 7.9 million families in poverty, up from 7.6 million in 2003.

In 2000, the year before Bush took office, there were 6.4 million families in poverty. The family poverty rate was 8.7 percent then; it's 10.2 percent now.

Why is an increase in poverty good for America?

Consider the Social Security system, which could be in financial jeopardy at some date in the not-so-distant future. The working poor pay into the system through a regressive tax — the rate is the same whether you make $12,000 a year or $90,000 a year, and the percentage actually drops after that.

If you're poor, your life expectancy is shorter. You don't live as long to collect the benefits. Thus the more poor people to pay in and die early without collecting anything, the more solvent the system. And a solvent Social Security system must be a good thing for America; why else would Social Security reform have gotten so much attention from our president?

There are, of course, many other benefits from poverty. It helps fight inflation because poor people are willing to work for less, thereby nipping the wage-price spiral in the bud. Earlier this month, the U.S. Department of Labor issued its annual National Compensation Survey. As a headline in the *Wall Street Journal* last Tuesday put it, "Most paychecks fell in 2004."

Thus inflation is being held in check despite the increases in energy prices. Low inflation means that bonds hold their value, and thus the coupon-clipper class stays comfortable — and we know how important that is to our country.

Nor should we forget that the lower American wages are, the less attractive our country is to illegal immigrants, and you don't have to be Tom Tancredo to agree that we've got some problems there. And poverty can help solve them.

New Orleans demonstrated that poor people tend to congregate in areas close to work with good transportation (they can't afford cars, and thus they pollute less while not contributing to urban sprawl).

These areas often make good industrial sites (for, say, toxic-waste incinerators). Because the occupants are poor, their real-estate is worth less, and thus land-acquisition costs are lower for American corporations. And who could be against reducing corporate costs?

Add all these considerations together, and you can see that it's a gross libel even to imply that George Bush doesn't care about poverty. He cares about America, and America needs poor people.

WILL MIERS MATTER?
OCTOBER 11, 2005

AT FIRST, IT WAS HARD TO KNOW how to respond to President George W. Bush's nomination of Harriet Miers, a Texas attorney with no judicial experience, to the U.S. Supreme Court. Chief Justice John Roberts holds a more prominent position, but he replaced William Rehnquist, a reliable conservative vote. Miers would replace Justice Sandra Day O'Connor, who has often been a swing vote in five-four decisions.

Thus Miers could change the balance of the court in a way that Roberts does not, and that has a lot of people worried — some because she would change the balance, and others because they're scared she won't.

But perhaps there's no good reason to be worried, one way or the other. For one thing, Supreme Court decisions may not be all that important anyway, and for another, how could the court get much worse?

Let's start with importance. Perhaps the most potent decision from the Rehnquist Court was Bush vs. Gore in 2000. But every thorough count of those hanging chads gave Bush a victory, so the Supreme Court decision was irrelevant. The Supreme Court did not change the course of history; at most it hastened it.

Go back half a century to the landmark decision by the court under Chief Justice Earl Warren (who also had no judicial experience before joining the court): Brown vs. Board of Education. It outlawed school segregation by race, and overturned the 1896 decision in Plessy vs. Ferguson, which had allowed racial segregation, so long as the "separate" facilities were "equal."

The decision changed the law, but not the hearts and minds of many Americans. That explains why Jonathan Kozol just issued yet another book which argues that American public schools are at least as racially segregated now as they were in 1954. So what did Brown really change?

Another big Warren Court decision was Miranda vs. Arizona in 1966. We know the drill from countless shows on TV: "You have the right to remain silent ... ."

Authoritarians might have bridled at the idea that the police had an obligation to inform suspects of their rights as American citizens, but criminals are still arrested and convicted. Indeed, we have more than 2 million people in prison in this country. Despite Miranda, and that bleeding-heart exclusionary rule that forbids the use of improperly obtained evidence, we lead the world in prison population.

Thus, if we look at the practical effect of major Supreme Court decisions, they don't seem nearly as momentous as they might have appeared at first.

As for the Rehnquist Court, can a Roberts Court be much worse? Under Rehnquist, it might well have been called the "Money Court," because that's the side that almost always came out on top. Consider two decisions from Rehnquist's last term. In Kelo vs. Connecticut, the eminent-domain case, the big money was on the side of the city so it could condemn property for a private development. You never hear of a municipal government condemning a four-star hotel so it can redevelop the site and sell it to ma-and-pa grocers, florists, booksellers, etcetera. It's always the other way around.

And guess which side the court was on? In the medical marijuana case last spring, the big money was on the side of the pharmaceutical industry, which does not want us using home-grown medications in lieu of buying its patented products. Again, we know which side the court took.

Go back to a Colorado case. We once made it illegal to pay people to gather signatures on petitions. It seemed a reasonable extension of the law that makes it illegal to buy votes on Election Day. But the Rehnquist Court found that this prohibition was a violation of the civil rights of millionaires. In the court's view, people with a lot of money to burn should be able to put anything they want onto a Colorado ballot.

Sure, I'd like to know what assurance James Dobson got that made him tell his right-thinking followers at Focus on the Family that they could trust Harriet Miers to do right by them.

But it may not matter. Miers probably can't do much damage to a court, and a judicial system, where the "Rule of Law" increasingly means the "Rule of Money."

JUST WHAT IS A FAIR MINIMUM WAGE?
NOVEMBER 1, 2005

THE U.S. SENATE has many important matters before it, ranging from a new Supreme Court nominee to a revision of the Endangered Species Act, and there's a proposal to increase the minimum wage, which has been $5.15 an hour since 1997.

This has received support from, of all places, Wal-Mart. Lee Scott, the company's CEO, said last week that "it is time for Congress to take a responsible look at the minimum wage" because "We can see first-hand at Wal-Mart how many of our customers are struggling to get by. Our customers simply don't have the money to buy basic necessities between paychecks."

In other words, if people don't have money to spend, they won't be enriching Wal-Mart. Cynics have pointed out that Wal-Mart's competitive position could be improved with a higher minimum wage. The company starts new employees at a rate higher than minimum wage, and the average Wal-Mart hourly pay is about $9.50 an hour. But the ma-and-pa shops often pay minimum wage. Raising that raises their costs, and makes them less able to compete with Wal-Mart. What should the minimum wage be? I've read that you're supposed to spend no more than 30 percent of your income on housing. If 900-square-foot "starter houses" are going for $150,000, the monthly payment on a twenty-five year mortgage will be about $1,100. That means a minimum wage of $19.75 an hour for a minimal house.

But there are other factors. When I got out of high school in 1968 and started paying attention to the prices of things other than record albums, the minimum wage was $1.40 an hour, and self-serve gasoline sold for 25.9 cents a gallon.

So an hour's labor in a laundry washroom bought 5.4 gallons of gas. An hour's labor at the current minimum wage buys about 1.9 gallons. To bring us to 1968 gasoline standards, the minimum wage should be about $14.50 an hour.

You could buy a car that ran, more or less, for $100 then. Judicious shopping for a clunker now might get one for $1,000. That's a tenfold increase, which suggests a minimum wage of $14 an hour.

In 1969, Martha and I rented a furnished studio apartment on Capitol Hill in Denver for $60 a month, utilities included. That cost forty-three hours of minimum- wage work each month. The same forty-three hours of minimum-wage work now would produce $220 for rent. The cheapest close equivalent I could find in yesterday's Post classified ads was $450 a month, and most were around $550. By the small-apartment standard, the minimum wage should be at least $12 an hour. A gallon of milk was $1. Now it's $3.50 or so, so lactic fairness would mean a minimum wage of $18 an hour. So it's hard to compare everything, but in general, it appears that a minimum wage of $12 to $15 an hour would restore American workers to 1968 standards.

There will be opposition to that, of course. Many economists argue that a higher minimum wage leads to the loss of low-end jobs and thus works against the poor. However, that argument always comes from economists who make much more than the minimum wage, and I've never heard it from anyone in a minimum-wage job.

We may be hearing much more someday soon, though, if the current push to make the Supreme Court look to the past continues. In 1923, the U.S. Supreme Court found that a federal minimum wage law was unconstitutional because it interfered with the employer's right to due process and the employee's right of contract. That was overturned in 1938, but these days, who knows how far back the court will go?

PAYING MORE, GETTING LESS
NOVEMBER 25, 2007

OUR STATE GOVERNMENT is looking at health-care reform, and it's also likely to be a major issue in next year's presidential election. And again we will hear dire warnings about the horrors of "socialized medicine."

As it is, about 45 percent of all American health-care spending comes from government at some level: local, state and federal. So the system we have is nearly halfway down the road to socialism.

American health care is also grossly inefficient. We spend about 16 percent of the nation's gross domestic product on health care, more than any other country. And if "you get what you pay for," then Americans" health should lead the world.

The common measures of public health are infant mortality rate, expressed in deaths per 1,000 live births, and life expectancy. At 6.3 deaths per 1,000 live births, the United States ranks thirty-third in the world, behind Iceland (2.9 infant mortality rate, and 83.4 percent of health-care spending comes from public coffers), Japan (3.2 and 81.5 percent) and Portugal (5.0 and 73.2 percent), among others.

As for life expectancy, we rank thirty-eighth, at 78.2 years, behind Japan (82.6), Iceland, Switzerland, Spain and Costa Rica (78.8). Thus many nations with "socialized medicine" spend less and get better results. They're more efficient, even though they lack "the discipline of the market."

As it is, 45 percent of our health-care spending comes from various public treasuries, and sixteen percent of our GDP goes to health care. That means that 7.2 percent of our GDP goes to "socialized medicine."

Ireland spends 7.1 percent of its GDP on health care, and it has "socialized medicine." It also has a longer life expectancy and a lower infant mortality rate.

If we were as efficient as the Republic of Ireland with its "socialized medicine," we could cover every American without raising taxes, meanwhile eliminating most private spending on health insurance, physicians, drugs, hospitals and the like. We'd have about $1 trillion a year to apply to other things.

Without having to support our inefficient health-care system, our industries would be more competitive in world markets (ask any American auto maker about this). Money would be freed for more productive pursuits, thereby improving our economy and our standard of living. Millions of Americans who labor in jobs they hate, just to have health insurance, would be free to move to work they enjoy, where presumably they would be more productive. And there should be a lot less litigation, since one major reason people sue is to recover medical costs.

So if there are health-care systems that are cheaper and provide better results while covering everyone, why aren't we moving that way?

Perhaps because the current system is huge. It includes insurance companies, HMOs, hospitals, clinics, billing departments, collection departments, specialized computer software developers, lawyers, claim examiners, drug companies, advertising agencies, all with an interest in preserving the current system, no matter how deep its flaws.

It's sort of like chattel slavery was before 1860 — an immense investment that was so much a part of the American system that despite its cruelties and economic inefficiency, only a few radicals could imagine eliminating it, even though most other civilized nations had charted a different course.

It took the bloodiest war in American history to change that. We ought to be able to do better in the twenty-first century.

WHO ARE THE OVERPAID PARASITES?
MARCH 6, 2011

SALIDA CAN'T BE THE ONLY TOWN where there's a joke that goes like this: "What's yellow and sleeps six?"

"A city truck."

And in this day of constant criticism of public employees in conjunction with the contentions in Wisconsin, there's plenty of vitriolic talk going around.

But when I think of public employees, I remember one fall evening a few years ago when the water line broke between our meter and the main in the street. Kevin Nelson of the city public works department came by and said they wouldn't be able to do much until daylight. But he talked to our neighbors and then rigged a hose from their outside tap to ours, so we'd have running water that night — something I didn't know was even possible. And then he came by later to make sure everything was working.

Ah, yes, those lazy, featherbedding, overpaid public employees. I recall a pregnant friend who went into labor in Greeley thirty years ago and started driving toward Boulder, where she'd made hospital arrangements. Her new

17

daughter arrived early and was delivered by a state trooper beside Interstate 25.

I don't think obstetrics are part of the state patrol job description. And I know that what happened next wasn't.

A few days later, she received a bassinet from that trooper, with a note that said something like this: "I've spent years scraping bodies off the pavement. Thank you for the opportunity to help bring life into the world."

Much more recently, I saw another public employee, an assistant at the local library, venturing out into a snowstorm with a bag of books. One regular patron, she said, had broken her leg and couldn't get out. So on her own time, she found some suitable books and was taking them to her.

Like any other good American, I have fantasies of winning the lottery or producing a best-seller, so that I could be rich enough to become a Republican and start demonizing the public sector. I could have my own vast estate so I wouldn't use public parks or public land. I'd have my own extensive book and magazine collection so I wouldn't need the public library. My own security force so I'd never need to call the police or sheriff. My own helicopter standing by, so I need not care whether the roads were passable.

But I don't think that's going to happen for most of us. We rely on public employees to provide our water and treat our sewage, to plow and maintain our roads, to instruct our children, to maintain our parks, patrol our streets, protect our food supply, to extinguish fires, to do scores of other things that we can't realistically do on our own.

Sure, there are time-servers in public employment, slackers who can always justify not doing whatever they don't want to do. And especially when times are tight, we have every right to demand efficient management and an honest day's work for an honest day's pay.

I suspect most public employees want to deliver an honest day's work for an honest day's pay. And I've seen many of them go well past that — teachers coming by on their own time with lessons for our sick kids; Denver firefighters helping my daughter when she locked her keys in her car one cold night; a game warden pulling my pickup out of a ditch along a back road. I could go on and on.

To put this another way, who does you more good? Those awful public-sector employees, or some $250 million-a-year hedge fund operator on Wall Street? Which one is an overpaid parasite? Who more deserves our torches and pitchforks?

TEN YEARS LATER, THE BAD GUYS WON
SEPTEMBER 11, 2011

OF COURSE I REMEMBER exactly where I was and what I was doing when the news arrived on September 11, 2001. At the time, we published a small monthly regional magazine, *Colorado Central*, and I had risen early that morning to get some pages for the October edition laid out so that we could head for the hills that afternoon. September, after all, is Colorado at its best, and we planned to get out and enjoy some of it.

So I was sipping coffee, fiddling with the page lay-out software and, as usual, corrupting my mind with vicious slanted liberal propaganda from National Public Radio's *Morning Edition*. The story was about a first-year teacher, whom they planned to revisit in the coming nine months. It was interrupted with an announcement that an airplane had flown into one of the World Trade Center towers in Manhattan.

That brought to mind something I'd read about a U.S. military plane hitting the Empire State Building during World War II. What had been the world's tallest building was still standing, so a hit by a plane didn't seem like a big deal. Plus, NPR went back to the teacher story.

All that changed in the next fifteen minutes or so, of course, as it became apparent that a civilian jetliner had been deliberately flown into a skyscraper.

I gave up on laying out the magazine and headed for the living room and CNN, where we saw another jet. Buildings fell and panicked people ran, and we wondered what it all meant.

In retrospect, it meant a great victory for people who hate America. To be more precise, there were people who hated the very idea of a peaceful, prosperous republic. And so they managed to get it to transform itself into a bankrupt security state that practiced torture and extraordinary rendition, a Patriot Act nation that betrayed the principles this country was supposed to stand for.

We spent billions of dollars and thousands of lives invading Iraq, partly on the dubious grounds that it was somehow connected to the September 11 attacks. Sleep any better at night on that account?

There were better grounds for invading Afghanistan in 2001. But we're still there, nearly ten years later, spending lives and money. Feeling any safer?

Most of what passes for political discourse these days concerns the growing national debt. Joseph E. Stiglitz, a Nobel laureate in economics, points out that these were the first wars in history to be financed entirely on credit.

He also noted that "Increased defense spending, together with the Bush tax cuts, is a key reason why America went from a fiscal surplus of 2 percent of GDP when [George W.] Bush was elected to its parlous deficit and debt position today."

There are other costs. Let's say the average American's time is worth $15 an hour. And said American has to get to the airport an hour earlier these days to participate in what some experts call "security theater" by being scanned and groped.

From June 2010 to May 2011, there were 727.6 million passenger boardings in the United States. That's 727.6 million hours of their time, and at $15 an hour, that's a yearly cost to Americans of nearly $11 billion that doesn't show up on anybody's books.

The list could go on, but by now it should be obvious that even if Osama bin Laden now sleeps with the fishes, the bad guys — the ones who hated a prosperous and peaceful republic — came out ahead as a result of September 11.

The Great Outdoors

Elms seem to thrive on kerosene, gasoline, rock salt, pickling vinegar and other traditional arbo-ricides. I feel safe in predicting that when NASA discovers life on Mars, it will be an elm.

URSINES SHOULD HOLD
HUMAN AWARENESS WEEK
MAY 1, 2001

OTHER PLACES MAY CELEBRATE National Bread-and-Butter Pickle Day or Adult Survivors of Childhood Month, but Colorado will be doing something a little different soon, with the start of Bear Awareness Week on Friday.

According to the Division of Wildlife, the idea is to make people more aware of how to prevent problems with Colorado's 10,000 or so black bears who are now emerging from hibernation.

But as a journalist, I have a duty to get all sides of the story, and so I wrangled an invitation to a recent meeting of the Ursine Liberation Front.

My guide explained that I was selected because our dog, a chow mix, "looks just like a small black bear."

"That tells us that you're tolerant and open-minded and don't just judge by appearances," the guide said. "You'd be surprised how bigoted some of your kind are — they automatically hate anything that is furry, walks on four legs and has huge teeth."

I just nodded — without explaining how my dog was a cute, cuddly little puppy when I first met it — and followed my guide across the river and up Cottonwood Gulch toward the Crater in the Arkansas Hills.

Eventually we reached the meeting site. Bear meetings are not nearly as organized as human meetings. I expected to receive a manifesto, or at least a list of non-negotiable demands, but instead they had questions.

"Why is it that you put food out for us, and then get mad if we get into it?" one young sow asked.

Patiently I explained that many humans just think they're emptying the garbage, and are just too stupid to recognize that they're actually putting food out for bears. Thus they don't expect bears to show up, and become quite frightened when some do.

Her friend had a question. "That food you put out really smells and tastes good," she said. "But the last time I got into some, this fellow came out and started yelling that old french fries and Hostess Twinkies were bad for me and I should go back up in the woods and eat berries if I knew what was good for me."

He was right, I explained.

"But if they're bad for us, aren't they bad for you, too? Aren't we both omnivores?"

Well, yes, fast foods and sweet treats aren't good for humans, either, I said.

"So why do you get to eat them and we don't? Just how can you expect us to be better than you are?"

Fortunately, while I was hemming and hawing, an old boar lifted his head. "Let me see if I've got this straight," he rumbled. "You keep moving into our territory, but whenever we move around in our territory, just going about our normal lives of eating and breeding and hibernating, we get accused of being invaders — when we haven't moved at all. Now, how can I be an invader when I haven't invaded anything?"

America works that way, I explained. Humans have a great power of imagination, and when they imagine that a given hillside will become an amenity-laden, gated, upscale real-estate development that is free of poor people, mountain lions and black bears, that's what they expect to be able to construct. Once the parcel is defined a certain way, then certain parties become invaders.

The old boar looked confused, but when I started to speak again, he cut me off. "Don't even try," he said. "I just don't understand why they market these parcels as being scenic and natural with lots of wildlife around, and then when some wildlife actually shows up outside their picture windows, they try to shoo us away, or even to kill us."

A matriarchal sow spoke up. "Your kind isn't fair at all. You'll identify so-called "problem bears,' and the second or third time they run into trouble, you execute them."

I nodded, and she proceeded. "We do the same thing. We identify "problem humans,' the kind that move into our territory and don't do a good job of keeping house. They leave birdfeeders and pet food outside. Some of them just set their garbage on the porch, or in an open barrel right next to the house. Or they leave food in their cars. They don't respect my strong maternal instincts and they get between my cubs and me.

"And I've tried and tried to teach these problem humans — first with some warnings, like trashing out their cars or spewing their inedible garbage all around. A lot of them will relocate after that.

"But some of them don't seem to learn. And so I don't see that we have much choice but to execute the "problem humans.' They've acquired bad habits, and they won't change."

The bears started yawning, which I took as a sign that they weren't yet fully awake for the season. I crept away, then tore off down the hill, hoping that I wasn't one of the problem humans.

TIME MAY NOT HEAL WOUNDS, BUT IT CAN TRANSFORM THEM
JULY 17, 2001

HOW LONG DOES IT TAKE for an act of vandalism to become an important part of our heritage, worthy of preservation?

That question occurred to me after reading a report last week about a graffito in the Indian Peaks Wilderness Area along the Continental Divide between Granby and Boulder.

It seems that one hiker happened upon two other wilderness visitors, a young man and woman. One of them was applying spray paint to a rock: "Roman + Ni" until they were observed and told to stop. The tagger apparently wiped the paint container free of fingerprints before handing it to the first hiker, and the couple took off.

The Boulder County Sheriff's Department has been trying to find them ever since. They could be charged with defacing property and, if convicted, be sentenced to up to a year in jail and a fine of $1,000.

Their aborted message was soon removed by sheriff's deputies, although there were some concerns that the cleaning chemicals might damage the moss and fungi on or near the afflicted rock. That raises the question of whether the environmental damage from cleaning the rock outweighed whatever environment damage was caused by the painting of the rock.

But this is a wilderness area, after all, and people don't venture into wilderness to see graffiti.

Technically, this spray-paint message wasn't graffiti. For one thing, "graffiti" is plural, and we're talking about only one message, so we should use the singular, "graffito."

For another, the word comes from the Italian "graffio," which means "scratching," not "painting."

And when it comes to scratching messages, Americans have been inscribing stones for a long time.

In the pleasant country around Fort Laramie, Wyoming, there's Register Cliff State Park. Wagon-train pioneers on the Oregon Trail were fond of scratching their names and other information on the relatively soft rock, and now it's part of our heritage, protected by law.

I've seen Register Cliff, and I enjoyed trying to read the 150-year-old graffiti, which was a lot more interesting than a natural sedimentary cliff. I've never seen Independence Rock along the Oregon Trail near Casper, which got its name because westbound settlers figured that if they reached it by July 4, they had a fair chance of getting across the far Western mountains before the snows fell and trapped them like the Donner-Reed party.

Independence Rock was where one James Nesmith recorded in his nineteenth-century diary, "I had the pleasure of putting the names of Miss Mary Zachary and Miss Jane Mills on the southeast point of the rocks," and he was not the only one. Farther along the trail, there's also pioneer graffiti on Register Rock in a state park near American Falls, Idaho.

The lithic literacy movement wasn't confined to the Oregon Trail. One branch of the Santa Fe Trail passed through Cimarron County, Oklahoma, located at the end of the panhandle (and famous among trivia buffs as the only county in America that borders four states: Kansas, Colorado, New Mexico and Texas).

The chamber of commerce there promotes Signature Rock and Autograph Rock as tourist attractions, even though they're just some old graffiti, and the sheriff would be looking for people who did the same thing now.

Those graffiti aren't nearly as old as the material promoted and protected throughout the Southwest: the Anasazi petroglyphs. No one seems to be able to decipher them. For all I know, they say things like "Maria the enchanted flute player loves John the killer of big elk," and it could be that any youngsters caught defacing the rocks 800 years ago were severely punished by the elders.

The impulse to mark our presence at some spot is an old one, and it continues. When I'm walking in the mountains and see a scarred aspen with an inscription like "JT + AC '79," I smile and wonder if they're still together.

There are people who do not find that charming. There was a group called "The Fourteener Cleaners," which went around removing summit registers from our highest peaks. In their view, a small piece of pipe stuck under some rocks was an artificial intrusion into what should be a natural environment. However, I never heard that the Cleaners wanted to obliterate the hiking trails up those peaks, and those trails are also "unnatural." For that matter, the whole concept of a 14er is artificial, since the determination is made by surveyors with hypsometric technology.

At any rate, if the spray-paint message in the Indian Peaks had survived, then at some point it would have ceased to be vandalism, and would have become worthy of protection as part of our cultural heritage, just like Register Cliff.

But when does that happen? Does it take a century, or just a decade? Somebody must have figured this out.

HOW DID LAWNS GET HERE?
AUGUST 27, 2002

ESPECIALLY DURING THIS DROUGHT, you seldom hear a good word about those thirsty bluegrass lawns that currently wither across the inhabited areas of Colorado. Even so, they have their defenders, and any day now, I expect to see a bumper sticker that says "I will give up my lawn when you pry my cold dead fingers off the nozzle."

Rather than delve into that controversy, though, we should ponder why we have lawns and lilacs. After all, they're not native to our high desert. They didn't just sprout. Somebody had to plant them and arrange for a water supply to maintain them. That's a lot of work.

So why would our pioneers go to all that trouble, especially when they had so much else to do back when they were defrauding Native Americans, watering railroad stock, promoting worthless mines, hustling federal subsidies, exploiting immigrant labor and exterminating the grizzlies?

When you read the history of many Colorado towns, be they in the mountains or on the plains, you see a pattern. The town site promoter (generally associated with a railroad subsidiary) acquires some land, subdivides it, and starts selling lots at inflated prices.

The first order of this land-office business is to snag a post office, but even before the first saloon or whorehouse gets off to a good start, let alone an opera house or schoolhouse, they're digging irrigation ditches that lead to the trees they're planting along the streets.

That's only part of the pattern, though. The bigger picture is that instead of adapting themselves to the landscape, the Colorado immigrants of 1860-1900 worked very diligently to adapt the landscape to themselves.

They didn't look at such plants as grew around here and find uses for yucca and prickly pear. Instead, they cleared fields and dug ditches and sowed the plants they were familiar with — wheat, barley, oats, potatoes, apples, peaches, etcetera. They didn't find a way to domesticate the bison that roamed the prairies and mountain valleys; they exterminated the bison and imported more tractable Herefords.

And when they built towns, they constructed their settlements to conform to their visions of what towns should look like. By and large, they were from the Midwest. That meant the railroad depot was at one end of the main commercial street (think of Union Depot at the bottom of Seventeenth Street in Denver). The streets were in a grid, rather than radiating from a plaza or village square.

They planted trees and lawns to make the place look more like the Iowa or Illinois that they came from, places that get forty inches of precipitation a year instead of fifteen. Further, they didn't plant native flora — they planted the familiar varieties, the bluegrass and maples and all the rest.

And to bring this vision to completion, they built expensive waterworks to "make the desert bloom." This was all for aesthetics — to create a Midwestern environment of tree-shaded walks and lawns and gardens, an aesthetic that traces back to soggy old England.

The New Mexico colonists who got here a little earlier had their own visions of how towns should look. The plaza with the church, not the railroad depot, was the focal point. Rather than build frame houses that needed extensive heating systems, they used thick adobe walls fabricated from local mud. Rather than install yards with lawns for greenery, they built sheltered courtyards so that the harsh sun and wind wouldn't desiccate their plants.

If the pictures I remember from my Sunday-School books are accurate, that was also the architecture of the Levantine deserts — houses of sun-dried clay constructed as little fortresses with small courtyards within, rather than set amid the verdant fields and forests made possible by large-scale irrigation projects.

A competent cultural historian could probably trace this architecture from the eastern Mediterranean across North Africa to Spain to the New World where it blended easily with Pueblo construction along the Rio Grande, but I just have to guess that this is how it happened.

At any rate, if Colorado towns and cities had been built with Mideastern architecture, rather than Midwestern, then our communities probably wouldn't be suffering from a drought, since we wouldn't be using nearly as much water because we wouldn't have yards with lawns and trees.

But then, I look at my own domicile. Without the shade from the water-wasting trees, the house would be beastly hot, so I'd likely need to install air conditioning. If there were no trees and gardens along the sidewalks, with their shade and evaporative cooling, walking would be so unpleasant that I'd end up driving more.

In other words, we might save water by adopting a different architecture, but there would be other costs, like rebuilding most of the state so that every residential block looked something like Bent's Fort.

You can adapt to the desert, or make the desert adapt to you. The founders of modern Colorado took the latter course, and we're still trying to make it work.

KEEP THE HOME FIRES BURNING
NOVEMBER 25, 2003

NOW THAT SOME SERIOUS WINTER HAS ARRIVED — along with high natural gas prices, which must please that industry and its subsidiaries in the White House — many Coloradans are responding in a perfectly sensible way: They're taking a serious look at heating with wood.

We once lived in a house with a fireplace, but no stove. What they tell you about the negative heating value of an open fireplace is true: A crackling fire radiates some heat, which you can feel if you're within a yard or two of the flames, but the fire actually sucks warm air out of the house and sends it up the chimney. The result is a net loss. Burning wood in that circumstance makes as much sense as burning $20 bills.

Then we moved to a different house in 1989. It came fully equipped with two wood-burners: a 1924 Universal range in the kitchen and a 1979 Vermont Castings Resolute in the living room. Neither saw many fires in the latter 1990s, since wood heat is dirty and a lot of work, and natural gas was quite affordable in those dismal days before Dick Cheney started implementing a national energy policy.

Then came one gelid morning a couple of years ago. Natural-gas bills had arrived the day before, and they went into the triple digits, causing "sticker shock" in our household and many others. There was a line at Gambles downtown — we were all buying things like dampers, stove black, ash rakes, flue thermometers, chimney brushes, pokers, splitting mauls, whatever it took to get those idle wood-burners back into operation.

Since then, our parlor stove has operated almost constantly from October into April. And here are some useful pointers, gleaned from experience:

Have your chimney cleaned at least once a year, preferably by a professional sweep whom you can blame if it isn't done right. Wood smoke generally contains some combustible material that hasn't yet combusted. When this stuff encounters cool chimney walls, it can accumulate.

If it is not removed from the flue, eventually it will ignite. This spectacular event is called a chimney fire. It sounds like a freight train indoors, and outdoors, the roiling smoke is dark and vile. We had a chimney fire once, and I don't know anyone I hate enough to wish one on.

Clean out your stove as seldom as possible. Small, hot embers can linger for days in ashes, which means that there's a possibility of a loose spark every time you move the ashes. Minimizing stove cleaning minimizes this possibility — and besides, stove cleaning is a tedious and dusty chore well worth all the procrastination.

A new stove-lid lifter may be impossible to find — no store here had any, and my Internet searches came up empty. You may be able to find one in an antique store; if that's too pricey, a brake spoon will do the job.

No matter what you do with stove pipe, it won't fit perfectly, and it will cut and pinch you several times in the process.

Attitude is important. Do not look upon the daily wood preparations as chores, but as wholesome exercise. Other people pay to go to gyms, whereas you're saving some money and building your body as you hoist heavy chunks of wood onto the block, cleave them, then pick up the pieces that have flown every which way.

To maintain a fire through the night, drink a quart of water before retiring. You'll thus be up several times, and you can feed the stove then.

Ignore complaints from environmentalists. They're right that wood smoke is a pollutant. However, as we learn every summer, our forests inevitably burn and produce great clouds of pollution. So if we're going to suffer from smoke anyway, why not get some use out of the wood first?

And one warning: The greatest threat from using renewable solid fuel is what my neighbor Mark Emmer calls "wood-stove narcolepsy."

It works like this: On a cold afternoon, you bring up the wood, then rejuvenate the fire. You're tired from the woodpile exercise. You observe the household cats, all sleeping near the stove. The urge to imitate them is impossible to resist. Work that should have been done does not get done, which probably explains why high natural-gas prices and a sluggish economy often go hand in hand.

Forget about global warming
September 4, 2005

Even before Hurricane Katrina demolished New Orleans last week, I read that the intensity of this particular tropical storm could be explained by global warming.

After all, hurricanes are gigantic heat engines, and if the ocean surface is warmer, then there's more heat to power the hurricane. Thus the wind blows faster and more rain falls than otherwise would have.

Of course, just about every natural disaster in the past decade, at least, has been blamed on global warming. Our five-year drought might have resulted from shifts in the jet stream brought about by global warming. The tsunami of last December might have been aggravated by a slight rise in sea level caused by global warming, which is melting the glaciers. A hard winter could also be the result of global warming, since it's supposed to make for more climatic extremes.

And if that's not sufficiently dismal, try sorting out politics of global warming. If you're a liberal, you most likely believe in it, presumably because hundreds of scientists say it's happening, and it fits with an apocalyptic vision of catastrophe because we trashed the environment.

If you're not a liberal, you probably don't believe in it, presumably because it seems impossible to gather enough information from enough places over a sufficient period, and then construct a model that will accurately predict climatic changes. Or you've got an apocalyptic vision that has nothing to do with climate change, but rather with a decadent culture that inspires divine wrath.

When we get to the science, about the only thing everybody agrees on is that the average ocean temperature appears to have risen slightly in the past century.

Why? The global warming explanation is that our consumption of fossil fuels (coal and oil) has risen greatly during that period. These fuels contain carbon, and when they're burned, they produce carbon dioxide, an odorless gas. It's also a "greenhouse gas." In a greenhouse, light enters through the glass. Some of that light energy is used by the plants inside, and some becomes heat. The heat cannot pass easily through the glass, and so it gets warmer inside. On a global scale, carbon dioxide works like the glass — it lets light through the atmosphere, but deters heat from radiating back out into space.

That's the theoretical explanation for global warming, which supposedly makes the oceans deeper and snowpacks thinner. This could be hard on people who live near sea level, and those who live at high altitudes and depend on snow for a livelihood, like ski-resort operators. But it could make northern areas, now too cold for agriculture, into productive farmland.

So the effects of global warming are not entirely dire. But it still may be a big problem. The solution that is generally offered is to burn fewer fossil fuels, so there will be less carbon dioxide in the atmosphere. Also, we should plant more trees, because they inhale carbon dioxide and exhale oxygen, thereby reducing the concentration of one greenhouse gas.

Let's take global warming out of the picture for a moment. Is it a bad thing to plant trees? Are trees evil? In general, would it hurt us to have more trees? Can we not make use of those trees after they have matured?

As for petroleum, is it good for our country to be sending billions of dollars each year to countries whose residents hate us? Is it a productive use of our time to be commuting for hours every day because we've built sprawling metropolitan areas that rely on cheap gasoline? Is it good for public health to construct environments where walking and bicycling are dangerous or impossible? Is it smart to rely so heavily on a diminishing resource?

Is our nation secure when one storm can cause substantial economic damage because it affects petroleum production, transportation, and processing facilities?

The responses that we're supposed to make to global warming, like planting trees and coming up with better energy sources, are things that we should be doing anyway. So it doesn't really matter whether global warming is real or not. The solutions are good for our health, our economy and our future.

BIG GAME AND BIG PROBLEMS
MARCH 6, 2007

THE FIRST TIME I SAW DEER inside the Salida city limits, it was a charming anomaly. Some muley had wandered into town and would doubtless wander out, and wasn't it wonderful that we lived so close to nature and all that. But that was years ago, and now, to say you saw some deer in town is about like saying you saw a fire hydrant or a realty office.

Visitors are sometimes impressed, though. Back in the 1990s, I was chatting with the director of the local chamber of commerce on a December afternoon, and she said she didn't have a good answer for a Virginia tourist who asked her how the town arranged to have all those reindeer running around just before Christmas, adding to the holiday spirit, for he would like his own town to host a similar promotion.

Alas, our mule deer do not return to the North Pole after Christmas. They're around all year, trotting across streets and devouring gardens. And there's no way to handle them that is going to please everyone.

Consider the "don't do anything" approach, which means leaving the critters alone to be fruitful and multiply. Deer are woefully ignorant of traffic regulations. They bolt out into the street. They get maimed or killed, and every year, about 200 motorists nationwide die as a result of collisions with deer.

Further, deer can be deadly all on their own. They can stomp, gore or bite pedestrians. Numbers are hard to come by here, but it has been known to happen. Martha came home quite shaken on a recent evening. She'd been walking the dog along the railroad tracks when a doe came out of the brush and threatened to charge her. "I didn't know what to do," she said, "because I sure couldn't outrun it."

The deer ended the standoff by taking off after the dog, who had bravely decided to run away. The dog returned in a few minutes without the deer.

Another danger is that where there are deer, there are mountain lions. The people who think it's mellow and cute to have Bambi in the yard may not feel the same way about pumas, but one inevitably leads to the other. There's an excellent book about this relationship in Colorado, *The Beast in the Garden: A Modern Parable of Man and Nature*, by David Baron.

He points out that as deer multiplied on Boulder's open space, the state Division of Wildlife proposed hunting to thin the herd. Boulderites opposed that, so cougars moved in. And cougars have killed people.

Other cities have been more broad-minded than Boulder. In the San Luis Valley, Alamosa just hosted a special hunting season to thin its troublesome municipal deer herd. One deer wandered into a house in October, a buck shattered a bank window in December, and at least a dozen deer charged through a crowd at a football game last fall.

The hunt was held at the golf course. The city required hunters to pass a marksmanship test. Only two muzzle-loaders passed, and they got no game, but the archers killed eleven deer during February.

Did it reduce the problem, though? Persuade the deer to migrate to safer ground? "No, not really," according to the woman I talked to at city hall on

Monday. "When I was driving to work this morning, there were six deer that bolted across the street in front of me."

Deer, of course, aren't the only troublesome large herbivores. An Estes Park correspondent tells me that members of the growing elk herd have figured out how to climb the steps to her deck, which "comes as a shock" since she and her husband had felt safe there for years.

Reducing the elk population will be tricky, since it's illegal to hunt in nearby Rocky Mountain National Park, a haven for elk — which are also a major tourist attraction, especially during bugling season.

In Salida, deer were rare twenty-five years ago, but dogs ran all over town. The city cracked down on dogs, and now we have deer. That inverse relationship seems to hold in Leadville, where the local newspaper carries many dog complaints, but few if any complaints about deer.

But turning the dogs loose brings its own problems, sometimes lethal. In 1977, a toddler was killed by roaming dogs in Summit County.

It appears that we will have trouble no matter what we do about the big game among us. And if we don't do anything, we'll still have trouble. I'd rather not have to carry a .357 to walk to the post office, just in case a deer-attracted cougar wants some dietary variety, but it may come to that.

CALL ME A SKEPTIC
MAY 15, 2007

THERE IS A DIFFERENCE BETWEEN skepticism and denial, except when the topic is "anthropogenic global warming." Then, if you're skeptical, you're "in denial" and must be on the payroll of Big Oil.

"Anthropogenic" comes from Greek roots, and means "human-caused." "Global warming" means a rise in the Earth's average temperature, leading to the shrinkage of glaciers, a rise in sea level, hotter summers, etcetera.

The theory holds that humans have, in the past century or two, produced "greenhouse gases" which trap more of the sun's radiant energy in our atmosphere, thus causing the planet to be warmer than it would be otherwise. There are several such gases, among them water vapor, but the main culprit is carbon dioxide.

Just about everything we burn is a compound of carbon and hydrogen, and when they unite with oxygen, they give off energy while producing water vapor and carbon dioxide. Plants consume carbon dioxide and solar energy, and produce carbon compounds that we can eat or burn for energy.

What perturbs this cycle now is "fossil fuels" like coal and oil, whose combustion may be producing more carbon dioxide than the cycle can handle. Thus the increased carbon dioxide in the atmosphere, which seems to correlate with rising temperatures. But carbon dioxide can come from other sources, like undersea volcanoes and animal respiration, so it's difficult to be precise.

Further, correlation is not causation. The rooster's crowing does not make the sun rise. So while the theory of anthropogenic global warming is plausible, there's no way to prove it — short of finding several Earth-like planets and varying their carbon-dioxide levels, then watching the results. That's an unlikely experiment.

In a recent report of the International Panel on Climate Change, more than 600 scientists from more than forty countries all agreed that there is anthropogenic climate change.

But you can have near unanimity among scientists on a given topic and still be wrong. If you had surveyed geologists a century ago, about 100 percent would have agreed that Earth's continents had been fixed in place since the planet cooled.

In 1912, a German scientist named Alfred Wegener proposed a theory of "continental drift." Most geologists thought he was crazy, but over time it became the modern theory of "plate tectonics."

Nearly every physicist of the nineteenth century believed in "luminiferous ether," a postulated substance that filled the universe and provided a medium for the vibrations of electro-magnetic radiation. They also believed that time proceeded at the same rate under all circumstances, that the dimensions of an object would not change with its velocity, and that energy could come in as small a quantity as you might desire. Then came quantum mechanics and the special and general theories of relativity, and those theories are the foundations of modern physics.

We don't have to go that far back. In grade school, I learned about he marvels of modern science, among them DDT, a chemical which would soon eliminate insect-borne disease from our planet with no adverse side-effects. Then came Rachel Carson's book *Silent Spring*, as well as the discovery of resistant mosquitoes. We're a lot more careful about pesticides these days, and few if any scientists promote any chemical as a panacea.

Another memory from grade school concerns swamps. Back then, the science textbooks assured us they were nothing but useless breeding grounds for pestilence. Today we call those swamps "wetlands," and we protect them rather than fill them.

So to say that a vast majority of scientists agrees on something doesn't make it true, whether it's luminiferous ether or anthropogenic global warming. The scientific process means our understandings will change as a result of experiment, criticism, discussion and analysis. Anthropogenic global warming may be our best explanation at the moment, but that doesn't mean it's true, and it should be questioned and criticized, not taken on faith.

In the meantime, the things we're supposed to do to combat global warming — reduce emissions, use more renewable energy like wind and solar, improve efficiency, grow more food close to home, walk more and drive less — are all things that would make us a more prosperous, secure and healthy society. In other words, they're things we should do anyway, whether global warming results from our emissions or variations in solar radiation. So why can't we just do them?

WHEN THE ASPEN FAIL IN HIGH COUNTRY
SEPTEMBER 25, 2007

ONE BENEFIT OF LIVING IN THE MOUNTAINS is that you become an expert on what must be a major contributor to the build-up of atmospheric carbon dioxide that causes the Arctic ice cap to melt and the sea level to rise, thus imperiling life as we know it.

I refer, of course, to the changing color of aspen leaves, a spectacle which inspires myriads of metro residents to drive around the mountains this time of year, burning much gasoline in the process. Those aspen viewers often spend some money in little mountain towns, thereby easing the local transition from "summer when you might make a little profit" to "seven or eight very slow months."

Around Labor Day every year, I start getting inquiries: "When are the aspen going to be at their peak this fall?"

We used to figure about September 17, an easy date to remember in Salida because it's also the average date of the first killing frost. But as of yesterday, a week later, there has been no frost in town and few surrounding aspen have changed colors.

I check them every morning when I walk the dog along the river and railroad tracks just east of town. Along the way there are several panoramic views that spread from the Sangre de Cristo range to Monarch Ridge and north along the Sawatch Range to Mount Harvard.

When the aspen change, great golden bands and patches glow on the mountain flanks. But it hasn't happened yet.

Several theories have been advanced. These days, just about every untoward event gets blamed on global warming, and so if the climate is warmer, then the trees should stay in summer form longer.

While global warming may explain some changes in the scenery (for example, old tourist books say the Angel of Shavano snow formation peaks around July 4, and in recent years it's more like Memorial Day before the angel melts away), it doesn't explain the aspen. The color change is not brought about by a decrease in temperature, but by the diminishing hours of sunlight.

In a sense, the leaves don't actually change color. The tree responds to decreased daylight by halting its production of chlorophyll, the green chemical of photosynthesis that turns sunlight, air and water into plant material. When the chlorophyll fades away, the yellow carotenoids that were present in the leaf all along become visible.

This year, though, a lot of the local chlorophyll is refusing to fade away even though the days are still getting shorter.

Some locals have theorized that the Sudden Aspen Decline Syndrome, observed with dying stands in the San Juan Mountains, could have moved north. But there's no real evidence for that.

The most logical explanation is that we had more moisture than usual in July and August, with thunderstorms on many afternoons. According to Ann Ewing at the local U.S. Forest Service office, the wet conditions encouraged the growth of an "aspen leaf blight fungus," which smites the leaves just as they're about to shut down for the year anyway.

"Basically, the leaves will just turn black and fall off, instead of turning yellow," she said, adding that "It doesn't seem to hurt the tree, though."

On an excursion to Breckenridge a dozen days ago, I noticed a few golden aspen around Leadville, so I called a friend there yesterday for an update. He said the display still hasn't peaked, and the yellow doesn't seem as vibrant this year, "but it still should be a pretty good show by the end of the week."

Our aspen do seem to be acting up: mysteriously dying in the San Juans, refusing to change colors in the central mountains, changing later than usual in the highest country.

This could hurt tourism, but there may be a way around it. We know that people will come to the mountains and spend money to see trees that have changed colors. And when I was in Summit County earlier this month, I saw thousands of trees that had been a rather monotonous gray-green now displaying a diverse panoply of red, yellow and orange needles.

So if the aspen are failing us, we should quit complaining about the pine bark beetle epidemic that produces colorful needles, and instead start promoting it as yet another glorious natural spectacle to admire and cherish, well worth the trip up from the city.

HOW ABOUT AN UN-ARBOR DAY?
APRIL 21, 2009

THIS WEEK OFFERS TWO QUASI-HOLIDAYS that seem related: Earth Day tomorrow, and Arbor Day on Friday.

So far as I know, Arbor Day is the only national celebration that originated in our neighboring state of Nebraska. Anyone who's driven across the Sand Hills (Martha's elder sister once taught in Springview) will understand why Nebraskans felt a compulsion to plant trees.

Our small Salida yard has plenty of trees: lilacs, plums, apple, maple, juniper, even a Colorado Blue Spruce. Indeed, we have too many trees; elms have sprouted beneath the front fence next to the sidewalk. After the sprouts grow big enough to be noticed, they're impossible to remove.

Cut off everything that shows above ground, and within a week there's a forest of sprouts. Attacking the root cluster with a shovel and a Sawzall appears to stimulate growth. Elms seem to thrive on kerosene, gasoline, rock salt, pickling vinegar and other traditional arboricides.

I feel safe in predicting that when NASA discovers life on Mars, it will be an elm.

Thus, I would gladly celebrate an "Un-Arbor Day," devoted to the removal of unwanted volunteer trees that attack fences, foundations, sewer lines and sidewalks. The mayor could issue a proclamation, the city public works department could offer assistance, and the CSU Extension Service could conduct workshops.

There must a way to defeat the evil elms before they take over and sequester all the carbon dioxide in the atmosphere for themselves, thereby launching an era of Global Freezing.

Which brings to mind Earth Day, and how best to celebrate it tomorrow. Once I was invited to speak at Earth Day in Alamosa. Nobody remembers a thing I said because I followed Peggy Godfrey, the cowboy poet from Moffat, who's so funny and entertaining that you never want to appear after her.

Further, it just doesn't seem right to make a 170-mile round-trip in a fossil-fuel-burning vehicle just to celebrate protecting the environment. At least for me, it doesn't, but then again, Al Gore jets around for the same purpose, in much the same manner that Phyllis Schlafly used to fly around the country telling women to stay home.

But it is hard to chart a green course. For instance, it's supposed to be more environmental to use existing stuff rather than subject our planet to the rigors of building new stuff.

I tried that once when building a computer. I'd found a junkbox deal (four for $10) on some forty-gigabyte Seagate SCSI hard drives. They offered ample capacity for the day. And why consume more materials and manufacturing energy with a new drive?

I had to modify the case to hold the beast — it was "full-height," or about three inches high, and 5.25 inches wide. It weighed 6.5 pounds. After I navigated the mysteries of parity, wide-SCSI vs. ultra-SCSI, device IDs and the like, the drive worked fine, although I could swear that the lights dimmed every time I booted that computer.

Obviously, spinning all the weighty platters in that old drive consumed a lot more electricity than a little modern hard drive uses to store much more data and deliver it faster.

But which is the greener course overall? Using the power-pig old drive until it dies, or buying an abstemious new drive with greater capacity and speed?

Questions like this are hard to answer, and I've never seen them addressed on an Earth Day. But hey, the music is usually pretty good at an Earth Day rally, if you can hear it over the noise of the portable generators.

Fallacy of the carbon footprint
August 20, 2009

Reading Chuck Plunkett's article about the "Prius Effect" in Sunday's *Post* inspired a thought experiment.

In essence, the article argues that as automobiles become more fuel-efficient, their "carbon footprint" (the amount of the greenhouse gas carbon dioxide produced per passenger mile) correspondingly shrinks. Indeed, it shrinks below the carbon footprint of light rail, whose streetcars are generally powered by electricity produced from coal.

Calculating a carbon footprint can be exceedingly complicated. My winter woodstove burns biomass from the current carbon cycle, rather than fossil fuels from some ancient carbon cycle, so presumably it's wholesome. But the cordwood is generally cut with gasoline-powered chainsaws and hauled to town with gasoline-powered vehicles, all with carbon footprints.

Then you need to get into the manufacture, shipping and maintenance of the cast-iron stove, the wood-cutter's trucks and tools, the ratio of dead wood (emits carbon dioxide as it rots) to recently live wood (absorbing carbon dioxide before the tree was felled) in the wood pile, the amount and source of the electricity used by my little wood-splitter — reckoning all this could take weeks, and the numbers could change with every cord.

So to avoid all that work, let's get to the thought experiment. Posit an extremely energy efficient automobile that has no carbon footprint. For our purposes, we can imagine it runs from rooftop solar panels or batteries charged by nuclear power plants or, for that matter, pixie dust. The point is that it is cheap to run and does not consume fossil fuels.

All our transportation problems are thereby solved, right? Not exactly.

1. Cars need roads, and roads need maintenance, everything from snow removal to rebuilding bridges as they decay.

Traditionally, we've paid for that with fuel taxes, and without fuel to tax, there would have to be another method. We could go to toll roads built and operated by private entities, or some sort of Big Brother system based on mileage and vehicle weight, or perhaps funding from general tax revenues.

Thanks to reduced driving and better fuel economy, we've already seen the start of "creative highway financing" from our General Assembly.

Instead of taking the honest and sensible course of making the public case for a gasoline tax increase to meet a highway funding shortfall, the legislature raised auto registration fees, which have at best a tenuous connection to highway wear and tear. More unfair taxes loom.

2. Our thought-experiment Imaginary Green Car doesn't pollute and it has no carbon footprint. But as noted, it will use roads. And the more of them on the road, the more congestion, gridlock and general aggravation.

Thus there will be a demand for more freeways and more lanes on existing freeways, as well as wider streets to handle the traffic. More space devoted to roads means less space available for productive enterprise.

Meanwhile, a light-rail corridor has a much smaller physical footprint, even if it does have a carbon footprint in our thought experiment.

3. Where do we park all those cars? About 30 percent of the typical American city is paved either with roads (see above) or parking lots. More cars mean more need for paved parking, which has pernicious effects ranging from urban "heat islands" to polluted and intensified storm-sewer runoff.

So even if we could build cars with no carbon footprint, that wouldn't come close to solving urban transportation problems. The carbon footprint may be the fashionable tool of analysis these days, but it can obscure as much as it illuminates.

REPLACE EARTH DAY WITH BINGE DAY
APRIL 21, 2011

EARTH DAY IS FRIDAY, and as a loyal resident of Earth, I want to celebrate properly.

I may have already found the wrong way to celebrate. In 2003, I was invited to speak at an Earth Day rally in Alamosa. Being rather immodest, I accepted.

But my 170-mile round-trip drive must have damaged the ozone layer or accelerated global warming or otherwise worsened whatever we were worried about eight years ago. The gathering in Cole Park was pleasant, but there were generators growling and smoking to provide electricity for the amplifiers. This didn't strike me as especially Earth-friendly.

And when my stage turn came, I followed Peggy Godfrey of Moffat, who's a cowboy poet or cowgirl poetess. However you describe her, she's a great performer. I felt like the local garage band that somehow ended up appearing after the Rolling Stones. Peggy is a hard act to follow.

This was clearly not an appropriate Earth Day commemoration for me. But what would be?

To find out, I called the greenest person I know, my daughter Abby in Eugene, Oregon. She has a big garden and keeps chickens. She and her husband, Aaron, don't own a car; Aaron bicycles twelve miles to his teaching job. Abby's always on the lookout for local foods and gentler ways to run her household — for instance, she washes her long brown hair with baking soda and vinegar instead of commercial shampoo.

(I should point out that we did not raise Abby to turn out this way, as we had a car but no chickens. It's a choice she made after graduating with honors from the University of Colorado Denver with a degree in history.)

"So how do you plan to celebrate Earth Day?" I asked Abby, expecting to hear that she'd be at a big rally in a downtown Eugene park.

"I know some people who are driving clear up to Vancouver, B.C., for an Earth Day festival." She laughed at that irony. "But for us, it will be pretty much the same as any other day. I'll feed the chickens, gather eggs, tend the garden, take Ezra (their three-year-old son) for a walk, hope he naps long enough for me to get some writing done — what I do most days."

Abby's got the right idea here: If you care about the environment, forget about Earth Day trips and celebrations, and live simply every day. When you think about it, focusing on the environment once a year doesn't make much sense, especially when that celebration often involves burning a lot of fuel.

But there does seem to be a basic human need for annual celebrations, and to that end I propose a yearly Binge Day.

On the other 364 days of the year, we would live simple green lives with local food and drink. We would walk, bicycle or ride public transit to get around. We would eschew gaudy imported novelties, fad electronics destined for quick obsolescence and other trashy food, goods and geegaws.

In other words, we would live prudently and sensibly, following adages like "Waste not, want not." The global economy might contract on that account, but it seems to be doing that anyway.

On Binge Day, though, we could pig out on champagne and corn-fed prime rib. We'd rent a Hummer or an Escalade to drive to the shopping mall for an orgy of conspicuous consumption. We'd ignore the recycling bins and just toss our abundant trash in a barrel. And after the once-a-year Binge Day blowout, we'd go back to living sensibly.

Add it up, and Binge Day should be about 364 times better for the environment than Earth Day.

The Rural West

We have been getting plenty of immigrants and, truth be told, it can be hard to adjust to them. For one thing, there are language problems. They do not speak as we do. Few of them know a "widow-maker jack" from a "come-along," or even a "mule" from a "burro." If you refer to "my beater," they think you're talking about a kitchen tool rather than your vehicle. And when they speak, we have trouble understanding that a "Black-Berry" is an electronic device rather than something to eat. Then there's the culinary problem. Before the immigrants came, you could sit down in a diner and order a "cup of cof-fee." But now there are dozens of ways to order coffee, none of them simple. When I hit my afternoon slump and just want some liquid caffeine because a siesta would be incon-venient, I do not want to have to ponder espresso, cappuc-cino or mocha latte. Yet the immigrants have forced such decisions on us.

STRUGGLING TO UNDERSTAND
THE LATEST LINGUISTIC NUANCES
JULY 6, 1999

SINCE THERE ARE SO MANY OF THEM, and because I suffer from a disorder known as "compulsive reading," I found myself poring over the real-estate advertisements in a recent newspaper.

It wasn't *The Denver Post*, which groups these messages into special sections so that I can leap right to them if so inclined. Instead it was *The Wall Street Journal*, which humbly bills itself as "the most important newspaper in the world."

Next to a consumer review of mail-order running pants (I told you I was a compulsive reader), the *Journal* offered a page and more of Colorado real-estate advertising. There was a time, when I was more actively involved with mountain newspapers, that I could translate real-estate prose into standard English. In fact, I once joined with a colleague (B.J. Plasket, now of the *Longmont Times-Call*) to produce "The Buyer's Dictionary of Colorado Real-Estate Terms."

For instance, "ski out your door" meant "the county doesn't plow the road in the winter."

"Easy monthly payments" was a short way of explaining that "the last four buyers failed to make their balloon payment," and "lots of amenities" translated to "in most of the world, running water and electricity are amenities."

We had collaborated on it for some now-defunct magazine in Breckenridge. The editor glanced at it, suggested that we examine her most recent edition and count the number of large advertisers who would be offended by our prose, and told us not to let the door hit our rumps on the way out.

Our prose remained unpublished, and the manuscript has long since entered some landfill.

This time around, I found new and unfamiliar terms.

There was a "ski-in exclusive" whose "Interiors draw on the traditions of European craftsmanship." Note that the interiors are not constructed by Old World artisans — the cabinets and closets just draw on that tradition, just as my columns, whatever their quality, draw on the traditions of Montaigne and Mencken.

One common phrase was "walkout-site." Since I've never seen a home site that someone couldn't walk out of, I wondered why anyone would promote this as something distinctive.

"That means it's next to a golf course," a knowledgeable friend explained. (While I'd like to thank him publicly, he made it clear that while he enjoyed fame as much as the next guy, his real priority was continued employment at a local realty firm.) "Walkout means you can stroll right over to the seventeenth green."

"But why would anybody want to live next to a golf course?" I asked. "Wouldn't errant balls fly into your yard, where they could break things or hurt somebody? What about the poisons the use to grow perfect grass in this desert? And the noise from the maintenance equipment? Isn't it bad enough to put up with arrogant yupscale swine during the workday, without having them walk by your house all the time?"

"If you want one of those houses, you won't mind being around them," he said. "And being next to a golf course is like being 'surrounded by public land,'" he added. "It's a guarantee that you'll always have that open space instead of neighbors, who might be of the wrong color or social class.

I moved on. "Why would a house have nine bedrooms and thirteen baths? Is this being marketed to people who have a medical condition that could be cured with Kaopectate?"

"No, it's just a status thing," he said. "The rule is that the modern mountain manor must have at least as many baths as bedrooms, and more is better. I think that regulation was adopted in 1993 — it replaced the old rule that the square footage of the exterior redwood decks had to exceed the interior floor area."

He translated some other phrases. "Nestled in the pines" means "will have to be evacuated the next time there's a forest fire anywhere in that county," and "gourmet kitchen" means "lots of high-tech stuff that your live-in cook, a non-documented worker who doesn't speak English, won't know how to use."

I asked if there was any difference in the quality of the views, variously described as great, stunning, awesome, or dramatic. "No, they're all pretty much the same. Really, it's hard to have a bad view in Colorado — even out on the plains, you can talk about vast vistas or supernal horizons. We used to draw the words out of a hat, but now we have a computer generate them.

So all Colorado views are great?

"Unless you can see one of those fabulous, charming and exquisite houses that we sold to somebody else. For some reason, that ruins the view."

PERHAPS WE DO NEED AN OFFICIAL END OF SUMMER
SEPTEMBER 12, 1999

ON TELEVISION NEWS LAST WEEKEND, there were several stories about the Labor Day holiday, some of which called it "the official end of summer."

We seem compelled to stamp "official" on all manner of things: an official language for a state, an official candy bar for the Olympic Games, an official beer for a stadium, an official newspaper for the fan, an official misleading account of a government raid, to name a few.

But an "official end of summer"? Perhaps naively, I thought that had been settled long ago, at least in the northern temperate zone, by ancient astronomical observers who recorded the sun's course across the sky — particularly its rising and setting points on the eastern and western horizons.

There were intervals when the point appeared not to change for several days, as though the sun was resting before switching directions between north and south. These became known as "solstices," from the Latin "sol" for sun, and "sistere," to stand.

A solstice occurred in late June and late December — twice a year.

The ancients observed other times when the hours of sunshine matched the hours of darkness. This event came to be known as an "equinox," from the Latin for "equal night." We have two each year, in late March and late September.

My references do not say when or how these celestial events became associated with the onset of terrestrial seasons, only that it happened: Winter starts with the winter solstice, spring with the vernal equinox, summer at the summer solstice, and fall at the autumnal equinox.

So if there's a truly official end of summer, it must be the start of fall, and the autumnal equinox occurs this year at 5:31 a.m. MDT on September 23 — more than a fortnight after the TV journalists proclaimed the "official end of summer."

Perhaps this isn't fair, though. I have long argued that the traditional calendar with four seasons does not fit well in the mountains of Colorado.

Some argue that there are only two seasons: "winter" and "company."

But others allow a "summer." In the higher places, like Leadville, you'll hear things like "I sure hope summer comes on a weekend this year so I can get out and enjoy it." Legend has it that Leadville is the only place where an Independence Day baseball game was canceled on account of snow, but I've also heard the same story about Silverton, and I've never seen any documentation for either.

Perhaps because Salida offers a more clement climate, I have proposed seven official seasons: Ski Season, Mud Season, Tick Season, Tourist Season, September, Big-Game Hunting Season and then Firewood Season before Ski Season returns.

Further, in my scheme, the season of "September" would be set aside for residents as a reward for putting up with Colorado during the rest of the year. No tourist-oriented events could be scheduled or promoted, all chambers of commerce and visitor centers would be closed, and gas stations would be allowed to sell out-of-county aspen viewers only enough fuel to get home.

Our legislature could keep this in mind if it ever considers an Official State Calendar, and could then also formally enact Southern Colorado Standard Time: "Things happen when they happen," so as to preserve what's left of the pleasant, relaxed atmosphere in the better portion of our state.

Let's return to the end of summer, which was informally signified by the start of school, which came after Labor Day during my youth. It was still that way when my kids were in school here — the professional educators would propose starting school earlier, and a large body of parents would always object.

But Salida schools started in August this year, and they weren't even close to being the earliest. That distinction apparently went to the Jefferson County schools, whose opening received considerable coverage on account of a media desire to wring yet another story from the April Columbine High School shootings.

Those poor kids had to go back to school in the middle of August. They missed several weeks of the vital education we used to get in late summer — the hydrology segment of floating down irrigation ditches on inner tubes, the botanic exploration of farmers' fields for ripe sweet corn that could be grabbed, the literary joy of checking out half a dozen books from the library and returning them the next day for another load because we had lots of time to read.

If August 16 has become the de facto start of fall in Colorado's most populous county, summer in the metro area is even shorter than it is in Leadville. Maybe the Legislature does need to declare an official start of Colorado fall, before summer vanishes altogether.

THE REAL CRITERIA FOR DETERMINING THE BEST RURAL TOWNS
OCTOBER 24, 1999

IT WAS KIND OF HARD TO BELIEVE. After all, just a few years ago, some candidate for statewide office wanted to illustrate what could happen if his economic development program was not adopted. He ran an ad with a photo of decay and dilapidation and asked if people really wanted Denver to turn into a ghost town like the one in the picture.

The picture had been taken in Salida. Last week, I saw another published picture taken in Salida. It was in *Sunset Magazine*, where Salida was no longer an avatar of ghost-townhood, but instead among twenty-four places featured as "The West's Best Cities."

At least, I think it was Salida. I knew all the people who were quoted, but the Sunset Salida was "in the San Juan Mountains three hours southwest of Denver."

You can't even see the San Juans from Salida, much less claim to be in them. The Sangre de Cristo range, the longest in the Rockies, starts just south of town. The arid Arkansas Hills rise on the east. The Sawatch Range, highest in the Rockies, looms to the west.

But no San Juans. Over the years, I've concluded that our Sawatch Range lacks the charisma required of a modern Colorado range, and so writers try to eliminate it.

Thus when an Air Force bomber crashed in the northern part of the Sawatch Range in Eagle County near New York Peak, we heard about "the New York Range." Frequently the Collegiate Peaks (Harvard, Yale, Princeton, etcetera) in the middle of the Sawatch Range get extended so that the entire 120-mile stretch is mistakenly called the Collegiate Range.

And then there's the *Sunset* writer, John Villani, who continues to put Salida in the San Juans (he's written about us before), rather than along the Sawatch Range.

At least he didn't put us in the San Luis Valley, as many UFO writers do. The San Luis Valley offers enchantment, ethnicity and more cosmic vortices than any spot north of Sedona, Arizona.

But our depression to the north, the Upper Arkansas Valley, is a mundane and prosaic zone with nary a cosmic vortex in sight. One major economic activity involves making big rocks into little ones — either at mines and quarries before the Reagan regime, or at prisons since then.

Even so, Salida has been "discovered" quite often in recent years — *Snow Country*, *Men's Journal* and *Vintage Motorcycles* come to mind — and it makes various lists of "Great Outdoor Towns" or "Wonderful Art Towns" and the like. Since I'm not in the business of touting real-estate here, it would suit me fine if Salida were neglected, since the process is so destructive.

First the place gets discovered by a writer or two, who extol its down-home authentic nature, uncorrupted by industrial tourism and the ensuing hordes. That leads to more publicity and more tourists, which attracts the attention of chains and franchises. The ma-and-pa cafes and motels get replaced by national brands. Whatever unaffected charm the place had is gone, but by then the writers have discovered a new place to trash by putting it on a list.

Of course, I'm a writer, too, and I like money as much as the next guy. So I've been tempted to produce a list of "The Best Rural Towns to Live In," based on these criteria:

Average nap time of a dog lying in the middle of Main Street.

The probability that the bartender is the only person in the saloon with a steady job.

No home mail delivery. People have to go to the post office every day to get their mail, which means they can keep up on local gossip and thus feel involved in the community.

Size of the police department. Ideally, there isn't one, and the sheriff's office is at least twenty-five miles away, although there's a resident deputy known for his low-key and friendly ways.

Number of resident eccentrics pointed out to visitors — people like "the town drunk," "the village idiot," "the guy with all the junk in his yard" and the "cat lady," a widow in an old frame house with at least twenty felines wandering in and out. Every settlement has these, but in the towns that make the list, everybody knows who they are.

Certainly there are many other factors — a high average age of the town's pickups, an abundance of cranks and troublemakers, a wide variety of housing that ranges from teepees and trailers to an old mansion or two — and this information would have to be gathered and collated. That sounds like too much work, so the good towns are probably safe from me.

And perhaps there's another safety factor. For all I know, *Sunset* might have been trying to help Salida by putting it in the San Juans, thereby sending pilgrims to South Fork or Durango.

Why bother to learn the Colorado dialect?
November 28, 1999

An article in the Post last week explained that many newcomers to Colorado try hard to fit in by buying SUVs and driving on six-block errands, but give themselves away by their speech. Just why anyone would want to sound like a local is hard to understand. If you're a potential newcomer, Colorado woos you with tax breaks and expanded highways. Then Colorado takes you for granted while it uses your money to recruit more people to congest your neighborhood.

My best advice, as a forty-nine-year resident, is to sound like you're rich and from Orange County, looking for places to build a private airport and a twenty-seven-hole golf course surrounded by a gated enclave where lots start at $750,000. You'll get a hearty welcome, even if you say "Call-oh-RAW-do" instead of "Collor-ADD-o."

Not all people will take this advice, though, and over the years, I've noticed some peculiar pronunciations. The weirdest came one night on the TV news about fifteen years ago. The announcer, a new arrival, began a segment with "Two people were aboard a small airplane which crashed this morning in Cone Joss County."

Martha turned to me. "Ed, you've lived in this state all your life. Where's Cone Joss County? I've never heard of it."

Neither had I. After some mental struggle, I realized that the announcer must have meant Conejos (pronounced "Koh-NAY-hohs") County.

But if we use the Spanish pronunciation for Conejos, why not for Salida? We were supposed to, according to a local newspaper of 1880: "For the benefit of all concerned, we will say that the word is pronounced Sah-lee-dah." And for the past 119 years, it's been locally mispronounced as "Sah-LIE-duh."

Much the same holds for Buena Vista, which should be "BWAY-nuh VEE-stuh," but is instead pronounced "BEW-nah VIS-tah," except that people usually shorten that to "Buny." (Mayor Clint Driscoll has recently decreed that the proper spelling is "Bjuni" with an umlaut over the u.)

Neither Salida nor Buena Vista, despite the Iberian names, represents a legacy of the conquistadors. The only documented Spanish visit was one trip in 1779 by Juan Bautista de Anza, and while his place names often remained elsewhere, the one he applied here didn't stick.

As place names, Salida and Buena Vista represent what New Mexico writer Stanley Crawford called the leading commercial dialect of the American Southwest: Real-Estate Spanish. It's the dialect that produces names like Table Mesa, Lake Laguna and Cerro Heights.

In Colorado, Poncha Pass is a boundary. Given a Spanish-looking place name, pronounce it Anglo if it's north of the pass like Salida or Buena Vista. If it's south, like Conejos or Costilla, use Spanish pronunciation.

This doesn't cover everything. Monte Vista is usually just "Monty" and the final vowel in "Del Norte" is seldom pronounced.

However, those towns were originally Anglo developments, just like Salida and Buena Vista, rather than Hispanic villages like San Luis ("Sahn Lweese" rather than "San Louie," and in good Coloradese, San Luis Valley is pronounced "the Valley" while other depressions get specified, as in "South Park" or "Wet Mountain Valley.").

Thus, a guide to the proper Colorado pronunciation of Spanish place-names would have to indicate whether the name came from Real Spanish or Real-Estate Spanish, and I suspect that most Coloradans, be they new arrivals or fifth-generation ranchers running for office with that as their major qualification, don't care.

Nor would such knowledge help with Ute names like Saguache and Uncompahgre, or French names like Laporte and Cache La Poudre, or a Quecha name like Cotopaxi (locally pronounced "PAX-ee," except that the road heading south is the "Cotopaxi Cut-off"). You would not learn to pronounce the Purgatoire River as the "Picketwire."

Also, pronunciation isn't the only way newcomers reveal themselves. If you really want to sound like an established peckerwood Coloradan, here are a few hints:

Never refer to "Copper Mountain." Always call it "Wheeler Junction."

In Cañon City, call the main drag "River Street" rather than "Royal Gorge Boulevard."

The entire sprawl from Fort Collins south to Castle Rock is known as "Denver," and then there's "the Springs."

And as I pointed out earlier, there's no good reason to learn these things. You'll get treated better if people think you're rich and from somewhere else and very interested in buying property in Colorado, no matter how you mispronounce it.

WHO ARE OUR WORST DRIVERS?
SEPTEMBER 30, 2003

FOR YEARS I AGREED with the state troopers who have told me that Colorado's worst drivers, taken as a category, are skiers. I first heard this from a trooper who had been transferred to Grand County in the 1970s from the plains; before his prairie stint, he had worked in the mountains.

He said he was happy to be back in the mountains, except that "Now I'll have to deal with skiers again. They drive in the worst weather, when anybody else would stay home, and they're in a hurry, so they take awful chances."

I agree. When you see somebody passing on a snow-packed blind curve in a low-visibility blizzard, that car almost always boasts a loaded ski rack.

However, people drive in Colorado for many other recreational reasons. Vehicle roofs boast mountain bikes and kayaks, pickup beds carry all-terrain vehicles and dirt bikes, trailers contain those and more. So it may be that skiers are no longer the worst drivers.

But if they aren't, who is?

A Denver cab driver who e-mails me on occasion would probably say that people like me — small-town motorists who aren't familiar with city ways — rank near the top in the "when you see one coming, find another road" category.

I'm sure he's right. Urban drivers expect each other to be aggressive, and there I sit, unwilling to pull onto a street if any other cars are in sight. Even if I know where I'm going, often I don't know if the exit lane is on the left or right, so I'm straining to see signs while poking along in the middle lane, backing up traffic. And when I get there, well, speedy parallel parking is not a skill one develops in Salida.

The cabby's complaint was that since the state quit issuing license plates that identify a car's county, he has trouble spotting hick drivers until it's too late. I advised him that if the windshield is cracked and the vehicle has not been washed since the administration of Bush the Elder, then it comes from the Colorado hinterlands.

There, the skiers might indeed be the worst, but they have competition. Rigs with bicycles on top are pretty well behaved when they're westbound on a Friday afternoon or Saturday morning, but when they're headed back to the city on Sunday afternoon, they can't get there fast enough, so there's a lot of stupid passing.

This is a popular white-water area, so we see many spewts with kayaks or similar small vessels on top. The drivers seem to have a problem like mine in the city: They know there's a river access up there somewhere, but they don't know exactly where, so they tend to speed up and slow down at odd times.

Since few places have as little flat water as Colorado does, I've never understood why boats are popular here, and I really hate being stuck behind one headed for Blue Mesa when I'm going up Monarch Pass on the way to Gunnison. But the boaters are in general good drivers, even on the downhill side.

The same holds for hunters: Despite the stereotypes, they drive sensibly, to and from camp. Anglers aren't quite so angelic, since they're often looking for places to pull over and fish, especially during the May caddis-fly hatch. So they speed up and slow down, and they're not looking at the road as much as they should.

Until last weekend, I never would have put "aspen viewers" on a "Colorado's worst drivers" list. We attended a nephew's wedding in Arvada, and on the way down to civilization Friday afternoon, I saw more bad driving — mostly stupid passing — than I have ever seen in any other three hours of my life.

That is the most common hazard, according to Orville Wright of Broomfield, a retired state patrol captain. About twenty years ago, he was in charge of a five-person accident-prevention team that intensely worked certain stretches in the foothills and mountains.

After "bad passes," he wrote me, the most common violations were "following too closely, speeding, DUI, impeding traffic and driving on the wrong side of the road." Aside from the DUI, that's pretty much what you find on mountain roads when leaves are changing.

So perhaps aspen viewers, rather than skiers, are the worst drivers in Colorado.

INFLUX OF IMMIGRANTS HITS SALIDA
APRIL 4, 2006

ASIDE FROM THE "MARCH MADNESS" that continued into April, all anyone seems to want to talk about these days is immigration. Salida and Chaffee County have been growing in recent years, and this is not a result of a rising birth rate. We have been getting plenty of immigrants and, truth be told, it can be hard to adjust to them.

For one thing, there are language problems. They do not speak as we do. Few of them know a "widowmaker jack" from a "come-along," or even a "mule" from a "burro."

If you refer to "my beater," they think you're talking about a kitchen tool rather than your vehicle. And when they speak, we have trouble understanding that a "BlackBerry" is an electronic device rather than something to eat.

Then there's the culinary problem. Before the immigrants came, you could sit down in a diner and order a "cup of coffee." But now there are dozens of ways to order coffee, none of them simple. When I hit my afternoon slump and just want some liquid caffeine because a siesta would be inconvenient, I do not want to have to ponder espresso, cappuccino or mocha latte. Yet the immigrants have forced such decisions on us.

Further, it used to be simple to order "meat and potatoes" as in "burger and fries" or "sausage and hash browns" or "sirloin and baked." Now those items are a small portion of the menu if they're there at all. The immigrants have encouraged our eateries to offer organic muffins for breakfast, garden-fresh salads for lunch and braised boneless free-range skinless chicken breasts for dinner. Immigration has made it hard to find real food here, because these people insist on keeping their bizarre culture after moving to our country.

My teacher friends tell me that the immigrants have made their work harder. In the pre-immigration days, parents were pleased if their offspring learned to read, write and handle numbers. Since this wave of immigration began, teachers are supposed to worry about "fostering individual self-esteem" and "implanting holistic refusal skills."

They have also messed up the local housing market. When they buy in town, they bid up prices so that local workers can no longer afford local housing. When the immigrants build in the countryside, they construct gated ghettos where they become isolated from our mainstream society, and presumably attempt to maintain the customs and culture of their homelands rather than learn to assimilate with us.

The effects don't stop there. My plumber recently explained that he was getting out of the repair end of the business. "I can work on clean, new construction for $50 an hour," he explained, "or crawl around in the cramped grungy cellars in the old part of town for half that. Which would you rather do?"

Thus do the immigrants burden the local economy, by forcing long-time residents to pay more not just for plumbers, but also for carpenters, glaziers, masons, roofers, electricians, auto mechanics and computer technicians.

Immigrants also cost us as taxpayers. Several studies have demonstrated that the immigrants' rural developments provide only about seventy cents in tax revenue for every dollar they cost in public services — road maintenance and plowing, ambulance service, fire protection, sheriff's patrols and the like.

And yet the federal government, which refuses to halt this costly immigration, offers precious little assistance to our strapped local governments. Local taxpayers get stuck with the tab.

And politically, there isn't much we can do about it. Every time the county tries to pass a new master plan designed to discourage the immigrant enclaves and encourage the immigrants to live in town and participate in our society, the powerful immigrant-support bloc of developers and real-estate agents manages to defeat it.

Granted, these immigrants really haven't taken jobs away from locals. Since about 1980, there haven't been any jobs here to take. But there are certainly times when I, and some of my friends, wish that our government would do something about the growing problem of suburban immigration into rural Colorado.

SILT STILL HAPPENS
MAY 14, 2006

DESPITE A PLEA FROM ONE RESIDENT, it appears that the town of Silt, which sits about seventy miles west of Glenwood Springs, will keep its humble name. The matter came up last week at a town board meeting after Town Trustee Doug Williams, in the hope of improving the town's image, had proposed a hearing.

Most people spoke against a name change. Only one favored it, Joyce Esgar. "The name is degrading," and a new name "would increase the value of our property." She added that "For this beautiful country, it doesn't do it justice. When you tell somebody you're from Silt — and it never fails — they say, 'Silt? You mean dirt?' I think a pretty name would be better."

From a real-estate marketing perspective, she has a point. Property values would doubtless rise if it were rechristened "Grand Mesa Vistas" or "The Estates at Dry Hollow Creek." I should note, though, that many of us enjoyed the "Silt Happens" bumper stickers that circulated a few years ago.

However, Silt shares a problem with many other Colorado towns: What do you call its residents? Siltans? Siltites? Silters?

This issue came up in Leadville earlier this year when the editor of the *Herald-Democrat* wanted to resurrect "Leadvillian," which charmed her after she discovered it in a nineteenth century paper. But when she surveyed readers, most preferred the more prosaic "Leadvillite," although there were a few supporters of "Leadhead."

Around here, some places are simple in this regard, as in Salidan, Buena Vistan and Alamosan. But others are tricky. Nathropians and Villa Grovillians sound good, but I have no idea whether they're correct, and it's hard to come up with even a good guess for a Saguache resident.

Elsewhere in our state, at least in Unofficial English, Lamar does best in this regard with "Lamartian," although the "Montroids" of Montrose and the "Durangutangs" of Durango also deserve recognition.

So Silt has a problem there. And it's not as though towns don't change names. I've lost track of whether a Silt neighbor is currently Grand Valley or Parachute. Hot Sulphur Springs was once merely Sulphur Springs, and Winter Park was West Portal.

Salida began in 1880 as the South Arkansas railroad station. The South Arkansas post office then was near present-day Poncha Springs. This post office was named Arkansas, and it was all so confusing that the residents begged the railroad for a new name. They got it, complete with the correct pronunciation ("Sah-LEE-dah" in a newspaper of the time), and began mispronouncing it immediately, a tradition that continues to this day.

But if we're going to talk about new names for Colorado places now, Silt is way down the list. For instance, there's Colorado Springs. There's no convenient term for a resident, since the term "Dittoheads" embraces people far beyond the city limits. The five-syllable name is a mouthful, and even the vernacular short version, "the Springs," is totally inaccurate, since the namesake springs are actually in Manitou Springs. The "Springs" name was a hustle to attract more real-estate buyers to what had been known as "Fountain Colony."

Consider Denver. Out here in the hinterlands, it does not mean "the city and county of Denver." A "run to Denver" could mean an expedition to anywhere from Castle Rock to Fort Collins. We could keep the convenient "Denver" name for that expanse. The city proper could be dubbed "Auraria" — the name of an early competitor on the other side of Cherry Creek, and one that would fit well with other metro place names that start and end with "A," like Arvada and Aurora.

This shouldn't hurt real-estate values. As for Silt, there are many other Colorado locales whose prosaic names do not inspire $500,000 lot prices:

Punkin Center, Crook, Stringtown, Poverty Gulch, Smeltertown and Yellow Jacket, to name a few.

We should cherish such names, and come up with a few more, if they really do depress the real-estate market — it may be the only way to provide affordable housing these days.

WARMER THAN TABERNASH
JULY 18, 2006

BACK IN MAY, some people proposed changing the name of Silt, a small town west of Glenwood Springs, because a new name would "increase the value of our property." The town trustees wisely left it at Silt.

But the desire to use nomenclature to inflate real-estate prices never rests, and it struck in Grand County last week. A resident of Fraser proposed dumping its municipal motto, "Icebox of the Nation," and replacing it with something less frigid. "I think there are a lot better amenities that highlight the area rather than "It's cold," said Kirsten Laraby, who works for a company building high-end homes.

She talked to Joyce Burford, a town trustee who is marketing director for the local chamber of commerce, and so tomorrow night, the town board will discuss changing the motto.

Back in the 1970s, Martha and I survived four winters in Grand County, all of which is colder than a banker's heart. We lived in Kremmling, whose motto was "Sportsman's Paradise." It was also known as "the Banana Belt of Middle Park" because when it was a balmy thirty below in Kremmling, it would be thirty-five below in Granby ("Dude Ranch Capital of Colorado"), only twenty-five below in Grand Lake ("Snowmobile Capital of Colorado"), and a hard forty below in Fraser.

Old-timers assured us of two facts: Winter nights were even colder when they were kids, and Fraser wasn't even the coldest spot in Grand County. That distinction belonged to Tabernash, a couple of miles down the road. It was a helper station in the days of steam locomotives, and giant mallets would leak steam as they waited for a train to assist up to the Moffat Tunnel. The leaking steam would instantly condense to ice when it hit cold metal, and freeze the driver wheels to the rails. Men would have to apply blow-torches in fifty-five-below January nights before the locomotive could move.

Just how true those stories were, I never learned. And Tabernash did not have an official weather station, so there was no hard climatic data. But Fraser could probably change its motto to "Warmer than Tabernash" without objections from Tabernash. That wouldn't help sell real-estate, though. "Ike fished here" is more promising, but that was back in the days when the Denver Water Board allowed water to flow in Fraser-area streams. Everything else that comes to mind is pretty generic and would fit just about any mountain area suffering from an invasion of People of Money.

Fraser did inspire a suitable slogan for the Gunnison Country, though. My friend and colleague Allen Best, then living in Fraser, joined me and a daughter one February afternoon for a cross-country ski trip over Old Monarch Pass. We got slowed considerably by deep powder, and he came close to losing half a dozen toes as icicles clinked on our beards. Thus was born "The Gunnison Country: Where People from Fraser Go to Catch Frostbite."

That's hardly a marketer's dream, though, and I'm having trouble finding appropriate slogans in Colorado.

Salida is "The Heart of the Rockies," which shouldn't hurt real-estate sales. On the other hand, it inspires obnoxious tourist questions like "If This is the Heart, Where's the Armpit?" It also leads to institutional names like "Heart of the Rockies Regional Medical Center," which is such a mouthful that people just say "the hospital."

Nearby Poncha Springs is "Crossroads of the Rockies." That's attractive to commercial developers, but who wants to build that dream retreat next to a busy crossroads?

Saguache is the "North Gateway Thru the Prosperous San Luis Valley." I once asked Dean Coombs, publisher of its newspaper, just where this "Prosperous San Luis Valley" might be, since "prosperous" hardly fits the one we know and love. "You have to go through Crestone and become enlightened," he explained, "and then you'll be able to visualize a prosperous San Luis Valley." So there's another slogan not of much use in adding value to local property.

I figured that some Colorado town must have devised a motto which would help sell high-end real estate. So I called the Colorado Municipal League, hoping there was a statewide list of slogans. But they don't keep one.

Besides, Colorado doesn't have a shortage of pricey amenity-laden real estate. It has a shortage of affordable housing. So perhaps we should search for municipalities with down-home, price-depressing slogans like "Home of the World's Hungriest Mosquitoes," "Land of the Double-Wides" and even "The Nation's Icebox."

An official state sport
June 3, 2007

ALTHOUGH IT'S HARD TO BE SURE about these things, Colorado may lead the nation in official state symbols, which range from the greenback cutthroat trout (state fish) to the stegosaurus (fossil), and include a mineral, rock and gemstone, as well as an insect, dance, flower, tartan, bird and two songs — one added just this year.

So far, we have managed without an official state boondoggle (Animas-La Plata?), official state horror (Ludlow? Sand Creek?) or official state Super-fund Site.

However, there is a movement to add an official state sport: pack-burro racing.

The impetus comes from Edith Teter Elementary School in Fairplay. The high school teams there are the Burros. There's a monument to Prunes, a sixty-three-year-old burro that died in 1930, on Front Street in Fairplay. And it was in Fairplay that pack-burro racing began in 1949.

Contrived folklore has it that the sport began with nineteenth century gold rushes when prospectors would race with their burros (also known as donkeys, asses, Rocky Mountain canaries, Equus asinus and "what Jesus really drove") to the courthouse to file their mining claims.

But pack-burro racing actually started as a gimmick because the merchants of Fairplay wanted to attract more tourists to the fourth annual Gold Days celebration.

They worked with Leadville, over on the other side of 13,179-foot Mosquito Pass. The first race was on July 30, 1949. It started in Leadville, crossed the highest pass in North America, and ended at the Prunes memorial, 22.9 miles away. The winner, with a time of 5:10:42.2, was Melvin Sutton of Como, with his burro Whitey.

For four years, the races started in Leadville and ended in Fairplay. Leadville merchants noticed that money-spending spectators tended to hang around the finish, not the start, and so, in the interest of fairness, the towns alternated as start and finish.

In the 1970s, Leadville and Fairplay each began to hold their own race to the apex of Mosquito Pass and back. Races have since been added at Buena Vista and Cripple Creek, as well as Georgetown, Idaho Springs and other towns that vary from year to year.

The rules specify that the runners may carry (or push, pull, or drag) the burros, but the burros cannot carry the runners. In honor of the prospecting heritage, each burro must bear a pack saddle with gold pan, pick and shovel. For more, check out www.packburroracing.com.

Should this be our official state sport? I'm prejudiced, of course, because some of my best friends, as well as one of my daughters, have run these races.

Beyond that, though, this is the only competitive sport indigenous to Colorado. It began for good indigenous reasons (more money in little mountain towns). It's open to any willing runner (you can borrow a burro). Women do well in the sport (Barb Dolan of Buena Vista has won the Triple Crown many times).

There could be a political problem, though, because the donkey is the symbol of the Democratic Party, and Republican elephant racing has not caught on in Colorado. But we could embrace that, with Democrats in charge at the statehouse now and the national convention coming next year.

Or one might point out that one of our most prominent pack-burro racers, former legislator Ken Chlouber of Leadville, is a staunch Republican. And further, modern outdoor Democrats seem to prefer the upscale llama to the humble working-class burro. So the partisan angle might be moot.

Either way, pack-burro racing would make a fine official state sport. It's either that, or we continue the quasi-official state sport of designating yet another official state symbol.

Family Matters

In 1968, my folks moved to Longmont, where my dad managed the Model Laundry. I worked there off and on before my brief Army career in 1972. Upon my discharge, it was my understanding that I had something like a constitutional right to twenty-six weeks of full unemployment benefits while I pretended to look for work. So I went to the state Job Service office, next door to the laundry on Main Street, to sign up for my paid vacation. The woman looked at my name, then made an announcement. "Your dad said you'd probably be by. He said to send you next door. He needs a washman, and you can start this morning.

SOMEDAY, PERHAPS, SHE'LL GET HER GOOD NAME BACK
MAY 2, 1999

THIS IS A FAMILY MATTER, of sorts, so if you want to skip this and move on to discourses about relevant matters of public import, no one will blame you. There's only so much time on a Sunday, and we have nuclear waste shipments, a war in Yugoslavia and a dozen people running for the presidency.

As you may know, Martha and I have two daughters, both now in college. The younger one is named Abigail and goes by Abby, and seems to like her name just fine.

Our older daughter has one of those offbeat names that hippie parents sometimes inflict on their children. Even so, she managed with it until the events of April 20. Her name is Columbine.

Naming children is one of those parental decisions I had hoped to avoid by having a son whom I could christen "Edward Kenneth Quillen IV." That never happened, and so decisions had to be made back in 1975.

It isn't easy. You've got a defenseless newborn child, and you're putting a name on it — a name that can affect the grades your child gets in school, the child's social standing in the American caste system, your child's self-image.

There are names you like the sound of, but they're associated with people you don't. You may even like the people, but not enough to have them think you named your children after them. Other names that sound attractive turn out to have dreadful meanings — it's a tough job.

We lived in Kremmling then. Kremmling seemed like a pretty obscure place, but an old-timer told us that Zane Grey had set one of his westerns in the Kremmling area. Naturally, we had to find the book — *The Mysterious Rider* — and we read that its heroine was named Columbine.

Since that's the official state flower, it was a familiar word, but we'd never thought of it as a name before. We mulled it over, and decided that if this baby turned out to be a girl (in those days, you waited until delivery for such information), then we'd name her Columbine.

It seemed apt in many ways. To some degree, we were "flower children" who had escaped to the mountains of Colorado, and the columbine is the archetypal Colorado mountain flower. Its Latin roots mean "dovelike" (one part of the flower supposedly resembles a dove), and the dove is the symbol of

62

peace. And it was the name of the heroine in the only novel ever set in Kremmling, where she was born.

Even better, it wasn't one of those "Moon Child of the River" constructions often seen in little mountain towns. It was even listed in a couple of those name-your-baby books. So we weren't stepping too far from the customary bounds of acceptable nomenclature.

Since the name is a mouthful, we figured that a nickname might evolve — perhaps "Colly," like the heroine of the book. But she always preferred the full Columbine, even though it meant some teasing in junior high and high school.

And when that daughter was introduced, people would often comment, "My, what a pretty name."

Until April 20, anyway. Whenever I hear a phrase like "hatred produces a Columbine" or "the Columbine tragedy," my paternal instincts take over and I want to shout to the world that "Columbine isn't a tragedy. She's an intelligent and energetic young woman, an honor student who speaks three languages. Find some other name for this horror."

In conversation, I've begun referring to the massacre site as "Stateflower High School." Otherwise, I feel as though we named her something like "Chernobyl" or "Wounded Knee."

Last week, I asked her how she'd been handling it.

"For the first time in my life, I'm embarrassed to give out my name," she said. "Always before, people might have thought my name was a little weird, and if I wasn't in Colorado, I'd need to explain that it was the state flower back home in the mountains.

"But now, when I say my name, people act like I'm trying to play some sick joke on them, like I made it up just to see the horrified look on their faces."

The main reason for our conversation last week, though, was to continue making arrangements to attend her graduation from Western State College in Gunnison Saturday.

Since I'm a world-class slob, Columbine was concerned that I'd show up in dirty T-shirt and faded blue-jeans, and she made some suggestions.

But despite my assurances to her about appropriate attire, I'm giving serious thought to wearing a T-shirt — one I saw on TV the other night. A man was wearing it at Clement Park, and it said "Proud Columbine Parent."

FIRST YOU HIDE IT FROM YOUR PARENTS, THEN FROM YOUR KIDS
SEPTEMBER 7, 1999

EVER SINCE THE PURITY POLICE seized power a few years ago, and especially since questions about Texas Governor George W. Bush's youthful blood chemistry began to circulate, we have been exposed to "What Baby-Boomer Parents Should Tell their Children about Their Own Salad Days."

I've been fortunate, since my reputation is such that there is very little in my past which could damage it.

Granted, there are some potential embarrassments — a job application at IBM, brief service as a director of the Kremmling Area Chamber of Commerce, occasional wearing of a tie when I had a day job, removing a junked car from my yard without a court order, but those are easy to explain.

It's harder to be honest when encountering old classmates. They are often quite complimentary: "Gee, Ed, everybody else sold out to be a corporate drone, but you haven't really changed since you got sent to the office for putting out an underground newspaper."

The truth is that I was eager to "sell out" if anyone made an offer. But no one ever did, presumably because I wasn't worth much in the great American marketplace. To avoid humiliating myself in response to those compliments, I generally just smile and change the topic.

To get back to parenting, those friends from days of yore can be a major source of embarrassment for a Baby Boomer parent, so one good way to reduce the number of annoying questions from your children is to move far away from where you went to high school and college.

That helps, but it doesn't totally eliminate the questions. And it isn't always drugs that children ask about.

For instance, there are many events that seem rather recent to me, but which now appear in school history books, like Woodstock and the Vietnam War.

My kids were disappointed when I confessed that I wasn't at Woodstock, and neither was their mother, and further, as far as we were concerned, there wasn't any music on earth worth three days of rain, mud and brown rice.

As children will do, they compared us unfavorably to a local family whom I'll call the Aquarians. Through the 1980s, Mr. and Mrs. Aquarian wore tie-dyed T-shirts, drove a florid VW Microbus, and often took their children, even during the school year, to Grateful Dead concerts.

"Why do we have to go to school? Why can't we go on fun trips all the time like the Aquarians?" The best answer I could muster was "Because I don't make my living by selling beads and candles to nomadic Deadheads. I have to stay home and write."

Vietnam was easier to answer. I explained that I avoided the draft as long as I could with a college deferment, in the hope the war would end before I got the greetings.

That didn't work, so I spent seven weeks at Fort Leonard Wood, Missouri, before the Army and I finally agreed on something — that I wasn't military material — and sent me back to Colorado with an honorable discharge. I also explained that if my father had been wealthy and powerful, he could have pulled some strings to get me into a National Guard or reserve unit, so that I could run for high political office someday. I presume that the Bushes and Quayles also explain this to their children.

The drug questions do come up, since our schools have programs like D.A.R.E. that encourage children to take an interest in drugs.

If our government followed its own constitution, I would explain then what is or was in my bloodstream or yours would be nobody's business.

But then I'd talk about the real world. "If the social workers ever think that you've touched a forbidden substance, they'll grab you at school, hold you in a little room with a counselor for hours until you tell her what she wants to hear, and then put you in a foster home.

"And if the cops suspect there are drugs in our house, a whole bunch of them will come over some night. First they'll kill our dog. Then they'll kick in the doors. They'll trash the house. They might even shoot us when we're lying on the floor, terrified.

They'll confiscate what little we have in the way of cars, money and other assets that we might have otherwise used to pay a lawyer."

That accurate answer satisfied their curiosity, but for some reason, both our daughters now have serious attitude problems about the American political and judicial systems.

So, I don't really know how we Boomer parents should answer. Lying is wrong, but the truth, at least to date, hasn't produced any children who appear likely to follow lucrative careers so that they can support us in elegance during our sunset years.

THOSE SQUISHY LIBERAL KIDS' TALES
DECEMBER 11, 2001

THESE ARE HARD TIMES and I've been looking for more writing work. I may have found an opening: fabricating scripts for productions for the children of America's right-thinkers.

Eric Bolling, an intrepid investigator at Fox News, recently interviewed Dan Gainor of the Media Research Center, and thus was America informed that the new Muppet movie is a liberal plot designed to make impressionable children hate oil companies and capitalism.

This is just the latest worry from these folks. Jerry Falwell attacked a Teletubby for somehow advancing the homosexual agenda. James Dobson had problems with SpongeBob SquarePants.

The Christian Coalition hit at *Twilight*, not because it was stupid, but because "it's just not natural for young people to idolize a vampire."

Maybe it isn't natural, but wouldn't idolizing a powerful blood-sucking creature make kids feel more favorable to capitalistic corporations like Goldman Sachs?

Never mind. When I ponder this, I realize that the right-thinkers have a point. It's been years since I read to my children, but as best I can remember, if the stories had messages, they promoted squishy liberal ideals like fairness, cooperation and tolerance.

I never encountered any stories suitable for the children of America's right-thinkers. A story where, say, most of the kids get together to beat the tar out of the new kid who's "different." Or the one with everyone cheering at the death of a character who didn't have health insurance. Or shooting the brown-eyed kid who tried to get into their gated community. Or maybe a story where the cool kids had fun mocking the kid who couldn't afford the newest styles, and Newt Gingrich could lead them in chanting. "Get a haircut."

I'm looking forward to writing plots that involve privatizing those evil government schools. Or chronicling how heroic kids went to war to save their wholesome lunch-time French fries from being replaced by decadent green beans. Maybe I could have a science teacher who failed to promote Intelligent Design with sufficient enthusiasm get shouted down by brave children, who then moved down the hall to perform the same service for an English teacher who insisted teaching Shakespeare's play *Macbeth*, with its mention of witchcraft.

You're just not going to find that kind of stuff in *Curious George*, and so it's clear that the stuff we put before our children does not convey the vital values of intolerance, xenophobia and greed. However, the right-thinkers also seem to have missed an important fact: Kids don't always get the intended message.

For instance, there's the chase scene in Disney's *Cinderella* movie where the mice are pulling the pumpkin coach as a rapacious cat pursues them. Obviously, you're supposed to root for those cute little rodents.

Except we'd had some mouse problems at home, which inspired the acquisition of a cat. Thus our 4-year-old daughter Abby stood on her seat at the theater years ago, shouting, "Go cat go! Eat those dirty mice!" It was rather embarrassing.

Among the stories I read to our daughters was "Three Billy Goats Gruff." I mentioned to Martha that I remembered the story from my own childhood, and had always rooted for the trolls. They had to eat, after all.

Martha pointed to the illustration in the book. "A bunch of unemployable guys smoking their pipes while loafing under a bridge, looking forward to a barbecue — no wonder they were your heroes, Ed. That's pretty close to your life's ambition some days."

In other words, no matter what message you're trying to impart, kids are clever enough to draw their own conclusions, and maybe the right-thinkers should find something besides Muppets to worry about.

SINGING THE WEDDING-TRIP BLUES
JUNE 1, 2003

FINALLY I GOT TO SEE THE SOURCE of many Colorado water problems. Less than a fortnight ago, we flew to Eugene, Oregon, for the May 24 wedding of our younger daughter, Abby, to Aaron Thomas. On the way into town from the airport, I saw immense fields of what looked like never-mowed lawns gone to seed.

The appearance was not deceiving. That's exactly what I saw; according to the local boosters, Lane and Benton counties in Oregon produce 95 percent of the grass seed sold in the United States.

Eugene gets about thiry-six inches of rain each year on average; we average less than half that much. Their summers are milder, too, with an average July high of eighty-one degrees; Denver's is eighty-seven, which means more evaporation. Little wonder that it takes so much water development to make alien bluegrass feel comfortable in Colorado.

Oregon has a reputation for strong land-use controls, and Eugene has a reputation that makes Boulder look like a citadel of free-market capitalism. Thus I was surprised, as we came into town, to see land-use planning that resembled Broomfield the Generica of isolated cookie-cutter housing developments, big-box stores, strip malls and the like.

But once we got into the older part of town, where Abby and Aaron live, Eugene looked more rational. Lots are small, the narrow streets are rigged for bicyclists and the sidewalks are wide. Every three or four blocks, there's a small market that sells everything from greeting cards to wine, and they get plenty of pedestrian business.

Downtown was an easy ten-block stroll, and thus on Memorial Day we could practice some traditional family values and walk to the railroad depot, where we boarded a comfortable train for Portland to meet the Hays family (old college friends) of Seattle for lunch and some urban exploration before returning that evening.

It was simple and civilized; the Amtrak Cascades train has hydraulic equipment to keep the cars level on curves, so the ride was smooth as we traversed the 124 miles in two and half hours. Naturally, anything that sensible is endangered in this era of diminished state budgets. Oregon is hurting so bad that the public schools were ending their sessions weeks ahead of schedule - so the train may not run for much longer, even though it seemed quite popular.

As for our other travel, I was pleasantly surprised. Our planes ran right on schedule, we did not undergo intensive searches and the Transportation Security Agency people were all polite and friendly.

The only hassle was at DIA. We used "Economy Parking," which means catching a shuttle van to the terminal — or more precisely, to the second level of a parking garage next to the terminal, followed by an elevator ride and a long walk with heavy luggage to the check-in area. Getting out is a similar travail.

Since everybody else — taxis, limos, rental-car shuttles, etcetera — gets to use the convenient upstairs doors next to the check-in and pick-up areas, this can't be on account of security. My guess is that it's a way to punish people who aren't spending enough at the airport. As for the marriage, my new son-in-law has good Colorado roots. Aaron grew up in Georgetown. His father mucked at Climax for years. A great-great-grandfather helped build the first telegraph line into Denver.

Aaron played washtub bass in a jug band, and once worked at the Mercury Cafe in Denver, where he met Abby when she was attending CU Denver.

Aaron manages a coffeehouse, which seems to be a common fate for English majors; Abby, with a history degree, is the chief records clerk at a medical clinic. Given Oregon's high unemployment, they both feel fortunate to be working full-time.

Their wedding, a small family affair, was outdoors in a city park that was bright with blooming rhododendrons despite the gray sky. Martha and I both gave the bride away, then stepped away to brush away a few tears.

An event like a wedding makes you wonder what kind of world we leave to our children. Five years ago, I felt pretty good about our legacy. Our air and water were cleaner than ever in my lifetime.

The United States was generally at peace, and the economy was growing. The national debt, a burden to any generation, was going to get paid off. And now the national government is careening toward bankruptcy, most of the world fears and mistrusts the United States, and our environmental protections are under serious attack.

What Hunter Thompson called "cheap-jack hustlers" are back in charge with a vengeance, and even if tears aren't an effective response, sometimes they're all that's available.

FATHER'S DAY IN THE LAUNDRY
JUNE 19, 2005

ON FATHER'S DAY, it is traditional to write about those wonderful times you had playing catch with Dad, about how he always came to your games and school events.

Not for a moment of my life have I doubted that my father loved me and cared about me, and yet I can remember playing catch with him precisely once. His eyesight was bad, and he had so much trouble judging trajectory that he once got hit in the head at a bowling-pin toss in Kremmling.

My Dad ran a laundry and went to work at 5:30 six mornings a week to fire the boiler so there would be steam when the crew got there, and he stayed at the laundry till 5:30 p.m. He didn't have a lot of time or energy for my ball games or school productions, although he attended a few.

My Dad did take my brothers and me hunting and fishing, and sometimes we camped in the mountains. But mostly I felt close to my Dad because

I worked with him, starting in 1964 at age thirteen on the sorting table in the laundry.

In the laundry, I acquired many skills, which have been utterly useless since then. In the past thirty years, I have never had to thread pipe, re-cover the rollers on a flatwork ironer, rod the flues of a boiler, rebuild a steam valve after grinding the seat, or lace a flatbelt.

It is, however, hard to express the sense of competence I felt after he taught me how to make my own soap for a nasty washroom job. Some restaurant customers used gunny sacks to clean their grills, and every so often they would send these stinking, grease-laden "grill wipes" to the laundry.

The trick was to follow the old home recipe for soap. Start with tallow (the bacon and hamburger grease caught in the cloth). Add lye (known as "hot alkali" in the washroom), and apply heat (superheated steam) while stirring (the rotation of the washing machine). If you did it right, suds would appear in the froth of the washing machine, and your home-generated soap would build up and clean the greasy jute bags.

When that's one of the high points, you know that a washman's job doesn't offer much excitement. But there was a time at the laundry in Longmont when I saved my father's life.

I was in the washroom, tending to the Saturday afternoon chore of cleaning 600 pounds of "shop wipers" — the red rags that mechanics use. They were so filthy that they took about three times longer to wash than the usual stuff, like motel and hospital linens, so they always got put off until the end of the week.

Dad was in the boiler room, working a set of clamshells to pull crud (mostly fragments of wipers and stringy mops) out of a sewer manhole. He leaned down to pull at some recalcitrant object and then slipped.

Eventually I heard a muffled "help, help" from the boiler room, went back to investigate, and saw a pair of kicking legs sticking out of the floor. As soon as I stopped laughing, I pulled him out, realizing that if one of my washing machines had drained while he was stuck there, he would have drowned.

It's not that I wanted to be in that laundry then. My dad and his father had the Crystal White Laundry in Greeley, where I began working. In 1968, my folks moved to Longmont, where my dad managed the Model Laundry. I worked there off and on before my brief Army career in 1972.

Upon my discharge, it was my understanding that I had something like a constitutional right to twenty-six weeks of full unemployment benefits while I pretended to look for work. So I went to the state Job Service office, next door to the laundry on Main Street, to sign up for my paid vacation.

The woman looked at my name, then made an announcement. "Your dad said you'd probably be by. He said to send you next door. He needs a wash-man, and you can start this morning."

My Dad, my brothers and I spent a lot of time together - working, going out for coffee, fixing cars, talking about machinery. We seldom had bleachers or an auditorium between us. You get to know people by spending time with them.

There are a lot of ways that fathers can be fathers without ever tossing a ball.

Happy Father's Day to the other Ed Quillen, the respectable one.

A WALK DOWN THE AISLE
SEPTEMBER 20, 2005

PROCRASTINATION IS ONE OF MY MAJOR TALENTS, and for the past month or so, I've had the perfect excuse for delay. Every time some-body has asked why I haven't yet done something I was supposed to do, I have replied, "My older daughter's getting married on the seventeenth, and until that happens, it's real hectic here. I'm doing the best I can, but I'm sure you understand."

And of course, they do. Despite all the talk of the decline of traditional family values and how they can be restored just by electing sanctimonious right-thinkers who will give their campaign contributors the keys to the public treasury, weddings are still a pretty big deal.

Wedding customs do change, though. For about as long as I can remem-ber, the father walked the bride down the aisle. Now it's more sensible: Both mom and dad can make the walk with their daughter.

So it came to pass that at the Rotary Amphitheater in Riverside Park on Saturday afternoon, Martha and I stepped down the path with our Colum-bine. A few minutes later, County Judge Bill Alderton, wearing his robe of office over a snap-button shirt, blue jeans and cowboy boots, pronounced her married to Brad Goettemoeller. (During the weekend, I learned that the trick to remembering how to spell it is that every third letter is an "e.")

Until the spring of 1999 and the massacre at Columbine High School in Jefferson County, the usual response to her name was "Oh, what a pretty name." I joked that it was an old Ute phrase which meant, "My parents were hippies in the mountains," but the name actually came from Zane Grey, more or less.

We were living in Kremmling when Martha was pregnant with her, and one of the local old-timers said that Zane Grey had spent some time in Middle Park long ago, and that one of his Westerns resulted from the visit. I made further inquiries, and found the book, *The Mysterious Rider*.

It did take place near Kremmling, mostly at a ranch up the Troublesome, and the heroine's name was Columbine. I knew it as our state flower, of course, but had never thought of it as a person's name until I read the novel. It seemed pretty and appropriate, and Martha and I decided that if the impending baby was a girl, we would name her Columbine.

(In those days, prospective parents generally did not learn the sex of the offspring until delivery. And if the baby had been a boy, I was ready with Edward Kenneth Quillen IV - not very creative, I grant, but easy and traditional.)

Columbine and Brad both grew up in Salida. They sort of knew each other even though they were three years apart and ran with different crowds. Brad was a football star while Columbine was often in trouble for ditching pep assemblies. One of Brad's best friends was Nate Ward, and Nate's little sister Sara was our daughter Abby's best friend for years.

Brad's father, Jack, owned a shoe store and would occasionally drop by the newspaper office to complain about something or another that appeared in *The Mountain Mail* when I was its managing editor. However, I was forced to admit to Jack last weekend that I had no specific recollections of his appearances, because, alas, visits by people complaining about the newspaper were not so rare as to be memorable.

Brad went off to college - Mines and CSU - and then a job with Hewlett-Packard before he ventured into the dot-com boom just before it burst. He's back in it now with web-page design, search-engine optimization and the like.

After high school, Columbine went to Iceland as a Rotary exchange student for a year, then to Western State in Gunnison. She seems to have inherited one of my deficiencies: working 100 hours a week to keep from working forty. She tends bar, makes jewelry and guides river trips.

That would make her a fairly typical Salidan, but she and Brad are buying a house in Bend, Oregon. Abby and her husband, Aaron Thomas, live in

Eugene. Abby keeps telling me that I'd like Oregon: "It's a lot like Colorado, except it has trees and water and Democrats."

Maybe I'll find out someday. But for the time being, I'm just a happy father, glad that young people still have enough faith in each other to join together and face the future.

THE DANGERS OF VACATIONING
MAY 7, 2006

YACHATS, OREGON — The Pacific Ocean is across the street as I write this. As nearly as I can tell, the "c" in "Yachats" is silent and the place is pronounced "Yah-hots." There's no point in making fun of Beaver State orthography, not when we have "Saguache" with a silent "g."

The idea was to take a vacation in the traditional American way — that is, mooch off friends and relatives. We flew to Seattle to visit some old college friends, Bill and Jan Hays, who have for years visited us on their trips to Colorado and often invited us to see them on Puget Sound.

Denver was overcast and misty when we left that Friday; Seattle was warm and clear, with Mount Ranier shimmering in the distance. Of course I had to point out that Ranier, at 14,410 feet, would not even be the highest mountain in Chaffee County, let alone Colorado. Bill, of course, countered that our 14,420-foot Mount Harvard did not start at sea level, and thus Ranier was a much bigger and better mountain.

Saturday, the weather was more like what I expected — raw, wet and windy — as we took a ferry to Whidbey Island, where we saw some truly vicious water at Deception Pass. These passes, like ours, are gaps in the terrain, although theirs allow boats to pass — sometimes. Bill said he'd once spent six hours anchored in a sailboat waiting for the proper tide.

He also said this was wonderful weather, bracing and invigorating. I felt especially invigorated at a warm saloon that served fried clams and steamed mussels.

The plan was to get from Seattle to Eugene, Oregon, where our daughter Abby lives, by the comfortable Cascades train. When we made the plan, we told Abby that the train would arrive at 8:45 p.m. She laughed.

"Something will go wrong. I'll figure midnight."

She was right. Our train stopped at the Olympia/Lacy station (named Centennial, or something like that), and it stayed there for two unscheduled hours. Somewhere down the line near Centralia, they told us, a trespasser had been hit and killed by a train, and we had to wait for the coroner to complete an investigation.

Didn't sound like more than a ten-minute job to me, but the day was pleasant, and wandering around the park at the depot was a big improvement on being stuck on a runway. Abby was only thirteen minutes off on her estimate, made weeks earlier, of the arrival of Amtrak 507 in Eugene. It pulled in at 11:47 p.m.

Our other daughter, Columbine, lives in Bend, Oregon. Our girls had decided that we should all rent a beach house along the coast, since Martha loves salt water, and our home in Salida is about as far as possible from the tides.

After driving for several hours, we were established in a comfortable small house in Yachats. Out the big front-room windows, I could watch the waves rush to the shore and break up on the dark rocks as birds swirled about. We could relax.

Well, not exactly. We live in a society that believes in warnings, just in case you're not worrying enough. I headed for the rocky beach below the bluff, only to encounter a sign that said "Danger: Bluff drops off. Falling hazard."

At the next trail to the sea, it was "Danger: Bluff unimproved for beach access." There were no "improved bluffs" nearby, so I took my chances. I'm used to unimproved terrain.

But I was not accustomed to the topic of the next warning. "Sneaker waves cause many deaths each year on the Oregon coast. Small children, or even adults, are often caught by an unexpected wave and are quickly carried out to sea by the undertow. Stay clear of driftwood near the surf and never turn your back on the ocean."

So I sat on a bench at the top of the bluff and enjoyed the view. I might have seen a gray whale, spouting on her way north for the summer. After a pleasant hour of beach-watching, I rose and then noticed the sign on the back of the bench: "Tsunami Hazard Zone: In case of earthquake, go to higher ground or inland."

Well, I do plan to return to higher ground. After all these warning signs, I need to return to work to be able to relax and quit worrying.

Rear entertainment system? Bah
November 21, 2010

Usually I have a book or magazine at hand when watching TV, so I can read during the ad breaks. Thus I can skip the encouragement to waste money on a Windows 7 PC, and avoid any compulsion to ask my caregiver for some new panacea with side effects that range from drowsiness to necrosis.

But occasionally an ad slips through my filters. This one was for a crossover SUV that had a "sweet rear entertainment system" to the delight of one boy, whereas the deprived kid in the back seat of the other vehicle had to put up with three hours of his parents lamely singing "Angel of the Morning."

I can't say I remember my parents singing anything for more than a few minutes on a Sunday afternoon ride, but I did learn that certain pop songs of yore, like "Mairzy Doats," were just as nonsensical as the ones I listened to. "Wooly Bully," anyone? During this time of year in the late 1950s around Greeley, the sugar-beet harvest was in full swing. The railroads were so busy that they put their moth-balled steam locomotives back into service and I learned to spot the plumes of coal smoke from miles away so we could race to see some magnificent machinery, like the Great Western's No. 90, hard at work. That's way better than a sweet rear entertainment system.

On trips to the High Plains, which may seem like the most boring part of our planet, my dad would point out the ruins of an old farmstead. On the slope behind, he'd trace the contour of a one-time ditch. He'd point out that below the ditch, the land had been cleared of sagebrush for plowing and a crop that eventually failed, or else the farm would not have been abandoned.

I learned to see that land in a whole new and tragic way; one of the saddest sites was Dearfield, the failed African-American agricultural colony. On a drive from Greeley to Denver on U.S. 85, my mom recalled her first such trip after moving to Colorado from Wyoming. Every time she spotted a substantial farm, she said, "I asked your dad what town it was, and he was mystified at first." But to her, they looked like towns, for they were larger than Wyoming settlements like Bill and Dull Center.

We all played a car game to find all the letters of the alphabet on roadside signs. I had the ending down pretty well if we were stopped at a railroad crossing for a freight train. Almost always, I'd spot a Burlington boxcar with "Way of the Zephyrs" painted on the side, which covered W, Y and Z. The X I'd get from the cross-buck that marked the tracks.

My daughters also suffered from similar childhood deprivation. They read roadside historical markers and learned to spot old mines and railroad grades. We had a musical car game. You'd end a piece of song lyric on one word, and the next player had to pick up with that word from another song:

"House of the Rising Sun"; "Sunshine, Lollipops and Rainbows"; "Rainbows and What's on the Other Side," etcetera.

They haven't complained, and neither do I. The lack of a rear entertainment system meant learning more about the world around you, rather than watching some lame DVD for the eighteenth time.

There have long been concerns about how families seldom eat dinner together any more, and now families are being discouraged even from taking rides in each other's company, what with that sweet rear entertainment system.

The American Way of Life

In a country run by oil men, walking is a profoundly subversive activity. Walk half a mile to the store, and you're just wearing out some cheap sneakers produced by exploited labor somewhere in Asia. Drive, and you're supporting American wars to control oil resources in the Middle East. Plus the immense auto industry, and the insurance industry, and the associated litigation industry, to name a few.

There's no comfort in any of the proposed remedies
April 25, 1999

The news arrived here Tuesday afternoon when Martha decided to take a break and watch the tube in the living room for a while.

From my desk in the back of the house, I heard her shout "You (many expletives deleted), what school is it?" Unlike me, Martha hardly ever swears at journalists on the screen, so this sounded serious. I went to the living room.

"What's the problem?"

"Some maniacs with guns and bombs are inside some school in Denver," she said, "and all they show us is bricks and roof, like we know what every school building in the metro area looks like so that we can identify it at a glance." Our younger daughter, Abby, attends the University of Colorado at Denver, and for all we knew, we were looking at a building on the Auraria campus.

"They must have said where they are," Martha muttered, "but they seem to assume that everybody's been watching for the past hour, and ..."

She didn't have to finish the sentence, and even though we were 150 miles away, we got to join the legion of fearful parents for a few minutes that dismal afternoon, until finally a helicopter shot established that we weren't looking at Auraria.

We must not have been the only ones who were alarmed, because a crawler soon appeared at the bottom of the screen with the location and other pertinent information. Relieved but still horrified, we settled in for the duration. Inevitably, the discussion, both in the media and in the household, turns to "What can be done to make sure nothing like this ever happens again?"

And the inevitable answer is "Realistically, nothing."

Consider the proposals that have been offered.

• Tighter gun laws. Much of the carnage resulted from bombs, which gun laws would not affect. Much of the shooting was done with shotguns, and shotguns will be accessible in any society that allows bird hunting.

• Looser gun laws, specifically teachers with concealed weapons. Maybe, but by all accounts, the school was a hell of bomb smoke, spouting sprinklers and general confusion — that is, the "fog of battle" that can produce casualties from "friendly fire." Armed people inside the school might have saved lives, but they might have made things worse, too. There's no guarantee here.

- Metal detectors at the door. In this case, they were shooting as they entered, and what difference would a metal-detector alarm have made, or a challenge from whoever was operating the detector?

- Reducing access to information. For one thing, the Internet is impossible to censor. For another, even if the Internet didn't exist, any half-bright kid can visit the library for an afternoon and figure out how to make black powder at home in his spare time, and take it from there.

- Reducing access to potentially destructive materials. Try to imagine how our society would do that with gasoline, propane and miscellaneous stuff at the hardware store. To put this another way, society devotes billions toward drying up the supply chain (specific chemicals at that, rather than the wide range of potentially destructive items) for meth labs, and crystal meth is still widely available.

- Early identification and treatment of alienated kids. I was one of the alienated in high school — the strutting jocks were the hot stuff, and the rest of us were pretty much peons. It was the same when my daughters were in high school. The exalted jocks "represent the school," and their bullying gets winked at.

Colleges are by and large the same — the highest-paid person on the state payroll is a football coach. Nor is it much different in the "real world" — look at whom society exalts and where the endorsement dollars flow.

Changing this would require a social upheaval beyond imagination. Most of us find other ways of dealing with our alienation from such a society, but how many counselors do we want to hire to treat "kids who aren't into the rah-rah stuff"?

And how do we differentiate between the merely disaffected and the truly dangerous? Adolescence is a time of exaggerated expression, when an outrageous statement might be a "warning signal," and it might be just posturing.

Add it up, and no answers appear. The U.S. Secret Service devotes every possible resource to the protection of the president of the United States, and I've read many statements from its agents that there are no guarantees that they could stop a suicidal and determined maniac.

Two suicidal and determined maniacs launched a reign of terror Tuesday afternoon. Like millions of others, I would like to take comfort in saying "We can take steps to keep this from ever happening again."

But there isn't any comfort. There's only some personal relief, and an inability to find words to express sorrow.

THE SHOCK OF RESPECTABILITY
JANUARY 28, 2003

THAT THE ROLLING STONES are now rather mainstream and respectable is like seeing Republicans in leathers and driving Harleys. It happens in plain sight, but it totally contradicts the impressions and attitudes acquired in one's formative years, and so it's hard to believe.

The Stones will play in Denver Saturday night, but I won't be there. The last Stones concert Martha and I attended was at Hughes Stadium in Fort Collins in the summer of 1975, just before our first child was born. We also owned a newspaper then, and in retrospect, that concert might have represented a transition.

We went with my old friend Rex Ewing, who was worried about getting back to LaSalle in time to tend his horses. Martha and I were worried about our newspaper, as well as the prospect that she might go into labor during the 170-mile drive back to Kremmling. The daily concerns of adult life seemed to overwhelm even "the greatest rock 'n' roll band in the world," and it's been pretty much that way ever since.

But it was fun while it lasted. When I was in high school, musical attachments were such that you could get in a fight by announcing you preferred the raunchy Rolling Stones to the sweet little Beatles.

Most of that differentiation was the contrivance of publicists at the time, although we kids didn't know that. Once the Beatles were positioned as adorable and harmless moptops singing about love, a clever London entrepreneur named Andrew Loog Oldham figured there would be a niche for an opposite image — thuggish louts projecting menace while singing about lust and alienation.

Oldham was quite successful in his image-building. When I was in college, one frequent topic of conversation at parties was, "Whose parents had the most violent reaction to the Rolling Stones?" There were tales of the TV getting unplugged when the Stones performed on Ed Sullivan, of 45s and LPs getting smashed by parental hammers, of stereos getting pulled out of bedrooms.

My own parents were country-music fans, so they didn't single out the Rolling Stones. As they saw it, all rock 'n' roll was inferior to Hank Williams, and doubtless they figured my collection of Stones records was just some adolescent phase that would fade away. But it didn't. In the fall of 1969, rumors circulated that the Rolling Stones, now that they didn't have Brian Jones and all his legal problems, were going on a U.S. tour and they would play in Colorado.

Then the wild tale was confirmed, with hip FM deejays telling us that the Stones would be playing at Moby Gym in Fort Collins on November 7. Of course I desperately wanted to go, but I was in Greeley, which was something of a backwater in those days — no place in town sold tickets. I drove to Fort Collins and Denver to learn that every outlet was sold out, and resigned myself to missing a show by the band I most wanted to see.

Just a couple of days before the concert, a guy walked into the college newspaper office and said he wanted to put in a classified ad — he had two extra Stones tickets to sell for their face value of $6 apiece. I almost leaped over the desk to catch him and his tickets ahead of everybody else. We had great seats for a great show. Many bands worry that their opening acts will upstage them, so the warm-ups are bad. Not the Stones — that night it was Terry Reid, then a promising young British rocker, followed by blues legend B.B. King, and then the opening riff of "Jumpin' Jack Flash." Every so often, I run into someone who was also there, and we can talk about it for hours.

I had always presumed it was a law of nature that kids would rebel against their parents' musical taste, so I was quite surprised when our daughters were teenagers. Instead of making fun of Dad's Lame Music Collection, they did something even more annoying — I'd have to go their rooms to find my Stones tunes. They even went, all on their own, to a 1994 Stones concert in Denver.

That was nearly nine years ago, an eternity in pop culture, and the Stones have been at it for more than forty years. A few years ago, Keith Richards was asked if he would ever retire. "Why in the world would you stop doing what you like to do?" he replied. "If we ever do a tour and nobody turns up, then I go back to the top of the stairs where I started. I'll just play to myself."

They're still playing, despite all the drugs and arrests and internal disputes. They haven't made a decent album since "Exile on Main Street," but there's a good song every so often, and it appears they've proved one thing: If you stick with anything long enough, mainstream respectability eventually follows.

PEDESTRIANS SUBVERT AMERICAN WAY
MAY 18, 2003

FOR YEARS, PUBLIC-HEALTH PROFESSIONALS have been warning about the dangers of obesity among Americans, and last week they even produced some financial figures. A study published on May 14 by the peer-reviewed journal "Health Affairs" said that medical spending caused by obesity and overweight Americans amounts to about $90 billion a year, or about 9 percent of total medical spending in this country.

What makes this a public issue is that "Medicare and Medicaid finance approximately half of these costs." Obesity is connected with "diabetes, cardiovascular disease, several types of cancer, musculoskeletal disorders, sleep apnea and gallbladder disease."

That's quite a list, and a fair pile of money. Plus, it's a lot of people: "More than half of Americans are either overweight or obese."

Since the report authors are scientists, they have to use neutral politically correct terms, which are based on the "Body Mass Index." This is calculated from your weight and height. I'm five ten and weigh 178 pounds, which gives me a BMI of 25.5. Anything over twenty-four (167 pounds) is "Overweight," and thirty and beyond (209 pounds) is "Obese."

I'm not a scientist, and so I'll use a common term: Fat person. I'm a fat person, though I'm making progress. I was close to the Obese zone at the beginning of the year, and then I decided to do my best to walk for at least an hour every day.

Thanks to Salida's geography, I didn't have to set aside an hour. This town was laid out in 1880, before there were cars, and it's about the same size as it was a century ago with many enterprises remaining downtown. So the old part of town, where I live, has good sidewalks, and most of life's necessities lie within a few blocks.

The common errands — post office, bank, groceries, library, office supplies, etcetera — turn into part of my pedestrian hour. The remaining minutes are usually easy to make up.

I sleep better, work smarter and eat less. We save money — not just on car costs, but at the store, since we're more cautious in our purchases when we have to carry them home, rather than haul them home.

To give proper credit, part of the inspiration came from a neighbor, Denny Daley. Our paths don't cross often, so I didn't recognize him the last time I saw him — he'd lost about 100 pounds.

I asked about costly designer diets and expensive gym memberships, and he said it was much simpler and cheaper. He and his wife had opened a store in Poncha Springs, five miles away, and he walked to and from work every day. That was it.

So there's an easy way to reduce the number of fat people in America, and I had visions of writing a book proposal and getting rich and famous as a health guru.

Then reality entered the contemplations. In a country run by oil men, walking is a profoundly subversive activity. Walk half a mile to the store, and you're just wearing out some cheap sneakers produced by exploited labor somewhere in Asia. Drive, and you're supporting American wars to control oil resources in the Middle East. Plus the immense auto industry, and the insurance industry, and the associated litigation industry, to name a few. Further, you're getting exercise without paying to use a gym or fitness center. And if walking does improve your health, then you're not spending money on physicians, nurses, specialists, laboratory tests and the like; medical spending is 13.2 percent of the nation's gross domestic product, and so thousands of jobs must depend on fat people.

There's even more subversion if routine pedestrianism got popular. People wouldn't want houses on big lots in distant suburbs — they'd want to live within convenient walking distance of stores, schools and jobs. Smaller house lots means lower water consumption for the yard, and that's a threat to the water developers.

It would also mean more small stores and fewer big ones. Immense shopping malls and big-box chain outlets — that is, anything with a parking lot measured in acres — would lose favor, and our municipal governments might even stop subsidizing them with tax and utility abatements. Their profits and stock prices would drop, and that could cause panic on Wall Street.

So while this pedestrian stuff works pretty well on a personal level in a small town, it would be irresponsible of me to recommend it on a national basis. America needs us to be fat; indeed, our current way of life relies on driving more and walking less — unless you're paying by the hour to use a treadmill, of course.

THE LOGIC OF RESPONSIBILITY
SEPTEMBER 26, 2004

SO FAR THIS MONTH, two university students in Colorado have died after drinking too much alcohol. Many people think this means that somebody should do something to prevent future tragedies like this, but what?

The law does not appear to be much help here. It is already illegal to drink alcohol in Colorado if you are under twenty-one. One student was eighteen and the other nineteen, so they were already breaking the law, as were the people who provided them with alcohol.

Sure, there will be calls for new and improved laws with stiffer penalties. But if the current laws are not enforced, why should we think that stricter laws would be enforced? And if they could be, it would doubtless take more law-enforcement personnel, which means higher taxes.

What form would a new law take? The only effective one that comes to mind is making it a felony to be in the same room where a minor drinks alcohol, and thus require everyone to check every ID, just to be on the safe side.

However, it is hard to imagine even our legislature passing something like that, and even if that were the law, there is always the problem of the fake ID.

During my college days, I sometimes checked IDs at the door of a 3.2 joint (back then, eighteen-year-olds could drink 3.2 beer in Colorado, a practice that ended a few years ago when our legislature bent over for the federal government). Since the Weld County Sheriff's Department was always looking for an excuse to close these dens of iniquity and rock 'n' roll, I was quite conscientious.

Once you passed the ID test and paid the cover charge, your hand was stamped so that you could come and go. Sometimes a person would get stamped, then go outside and give his ID to someone who resembled him, who would then come through.

One night, after a name started to get too familiar, I got to the microphone just before the band resumed after a break, and asked, "Will the real Gloria Gonzales please stand up?" Three young women headed for the door.

As the failure of Prohibition demonstrated, not even amending the U.S. Constitution, let alone passing a mere state law, will keep people from drinking alcohol if they choose to do so.

There remains, however, the question of individual responsibility. In the two recent Colorado cases, one had been participating in a fraternity initiation, and the other was party-hopping. Both are voluntary activities. Now we encounter a logical problem. If we assume that eighteen-year-olds are of sufficient intelligence to know when they are drinking too much, then it follows that they are old enough to drink.

If we assume that eighteen-year-olds lack that knowledge, then it follows that neither student is responsible, and we should find some other party to blame — for example, beer ads, the fraternity system (both were found dead in frat houses), a "party school" social environment, aggressive marketing by retail liquor merchants, to name a few that I have seen recently.

Logic demands one or the other.

Logic, however, has nothing to do with how America runs, especially in this regard. According to the National Institute on Alcohol Abuse and Alcoholism, about 350 Americans die every year from accidental alcohol poisoning. In all of recorded history, not one person has ever died of a marijuana overdose.

So guess which substance is illegal.

That begs the question, though, since the law already forbids minors from drinking themselves to death. Perhaps we need a new attitude. Drunken driving decreased as a result of social pressure from slogans like "Friends don't let friends drive drunk."

And perhaps, around America's fraternity houses, where young people are supposed to learn to care of one another, they could post slogans like "Friends don't let friends pass out and die."

Hiding it from the kids
April 10, 2007

Somewhere in this great land of ours there must be an organization called the Society to Keep Children from Seeing Things. Not that I have been able to find its headquarters or identify its officers, but it does seem to be an active outfit that emerges from time to time.

The most recent outbreak has come in Littleton on account of plans to honor a local war hero, Navy SEAL Danny Dietz, with a statue in Berry Park. Before we get to that, however, we ought to recall some earlier outbreaks.

About four years ago, state Representative Ted Harvey of Douglas County ventured into a Virgin Records store, and was shocked to find "blatant triple X-rated covers right there at eye level for any five-year-old to see."

Children must be protected from viewing this, he decided, and so he sponsored a bill which would have made it a crime "in displaying in a commercial establishment any materials that are harmful to minors, to fail to take commercially feasible measures to prevent the display of the materials to minors."

Harvey went into some detail as to what was harmful to minors. Suffice it to say that images of body parts used for the natural production and feeding of children are images that are harmful to children, according to Harvey.

The protection racket popped up again last year in Loveland, where there was a statue called "Triangle" by Kirstin Kokkin. It had three people — a man and two women — none with clothes on. Two were standing, their feet together, as they leaned back and held a third high in the air between them.

It was about as sexual as a high-wire act at the circus, and the sculptor said it symbolized the interdependence of people, rather than anything sexual.

But "If you look at it, it's pretty clear the intent of the statue is sexual," said one detractor, Dan Danowski, who wanted it moved because it could be harmful to children who might pass it on the way to nearby schools. Nowhere could I find the specific damage children might suffer from exposure to a statue, though. Perhaps we should consult the Greek and Italian authorities as to how they heal the children damaged by their statues.

Now we get to Danny Dietz. He grew up near Berry Park in Littleton. He was part of an elite fighting unit, the Navy SEALS. The twenty-five-year-old was killed in Afghanistan on June 28, 2005. He and three other members of his unit were ambushed by guerrillas. Severely wounded, he fought for forty-five minutes, providing cover so one of his team members to escape. Posthumously, he received the Navy Cross.

His statue, with him holding an assault rifle, is scheduled to be dedicated on the Fourth of July at the park.

And some parents don't like that. "If I've got a four-year-old at the playground, I feel it would be a threatening image that would frighten her," said Emily Cassidy Fuchs, who has opposed the location.

In my experience with my own four-year-olds, back in the day, they can get quite frightened by things that shouldn't scare them, like the Bogey Man that haunts bedrooms when the lights go off at night, and they don't get frightened by things that should scare them, like the river along Salida's Riverside

Park during peak runoff. In other words, there's no logic connected to what scares four-year-olds, so it's hardly a basis for sane public policy.

Further, if statues of soldiers with guns are unfit for the eyes of children, then it's time to cancel school tours of our state Capitol. Out on the grounds there is a statue of Joseph P. Martinez, a Coloradan who won the Medal of Honor for bravery during the Aleutian campaign in World War II. He's holding a rifle.

So also is the bronze figure of a generic Union soldier facing south. He's flanked by two bigger guns — Civil War cannons. Old artillery appears in broad daylight elsewhere in Colorado — I pass a cannon in a park on every excursion to Cañon City or Gunnison, but I haven't seen any accounts of terrified children in those cities. Indeed, sometimes I see kids playing on the cannons.

Obviously, the Society to Protect Children from Seeing Things has a lot of work yet to do, which unfortunately means that it is not likely to vanish anytime soon.

THE QUEST FOR VILLAINS
APRIL 24, 2007

ONE DAY I WAS STANDING IN LINE at the local post office, behind a guy whom I did not know but had seen around town. He wore a heavy belt that held a couple of knives, a big wallet on a chain, another chain to a bundle of keys and, as I noticed with this proximity, a small pistol.

Should I have been worried because he might pull the gun and start shooting? Or relieved because if someone else "went postal" that morning, he was ready to defend us by shooting back?

As our simmering handgun debate intensifies after the Virginia Tech rampage last week, that's a question with no good answer. (As for the armed fellow at our post office, he got to the counter, picked up a package, and went about his business.)

Sure, it is possible to construct a plausible scenario wherein an armed student or teacher brought Seung-Hui Cho down early and saved a couple of dozen lives — although in that case, of course, we would not know how many lives were saved.

It is also easy to construct another plausible scenario: Half a dozen armed students and faculty, all shooting back at Cho, with lead flying every which way, causing plenty of "collateral damage" before the police show up and start shooting, too. The casualties number in the dozens.

So who can say which is the more likely scenario? I cannot. From the pro-gun side, I read that the shooter knew that Virginia Tech was a "gun-free zone," so he could plan his rampage with the serene confidence that no one would be able to shoot back. But he could not have been sure that he would not encounter a campus cop somewhere along the way, or another student who figured rules were for other people.

The anti-gun side argues that it's just too easy to buy handguns in America, and Cho's mental-health problems should have been flagged to prevent his gun purchases. And the truth is, no matter what was on his record, he would have been able to procure weapons if he wanted them. After all, America has been conducting a "war on drugs" since about 1970, and just about any substance you can imagine is still being sold and consumed.

And if buying pistols had been too difficult, he could have rigged propane bombs, or gone after some nitrogen fertilizer and diesel fuel, and killed even more people.

The most intelligent response a public official ever made to these horrors came from Representative Tom Tancredo after the Columbine High School shootings in 1999, which occurred in his congressional district. Initially, he did not say that school prayer, or posting the Ten Commandments on classroom walls, or putting all illegal immigrants in concentration camps would prevent future mass murders at schools. He just said he had no idea what society could do to keep this from happening again.

One notion in circulation today is "blame the media." It's appealing. Often I'm embarrassed by my line of work when I see herds of journalists amid a forest of boom mikes with the satellite trucks in the background.

This time, the argument goes to NBC, which received a packet of material from the shooter and aired some of it. That's just giving the shooter the notoriety and the platform that he wanted, isn't it? So why accommodate the desires of evil people?

But our inner sense of narrative works something like this: There's a serene place, and then the bad guy enters and the action starts. In other words, there wouldn't be a story without the bad guy.

The Bible would be only one chapter without the serpent in the Garden of Eden. Greek mythology would be much simpler if Pandora had not opened that box back in the Golden Age. Knights would have been superfluous without dragons and ogres to put damsels in distress.

I suspect that has something to do with how our minds are wired. If NBC had not aired the material, we would be speculating about motives and background and all the rest.

We're fascinated by villains — but when we have a real one, why do people insist on looking for others, be they gunshop owners or television networks?

MEMORIES OF 1968
DECEMBER 16, 2007

WHAT IS IT WITH 1968? It made the cover of *Newsweek* recently and got two hours on the History Channel last week. As long ago as 1978, it inspired a TV documentary that I remember watching, so for at least three decades, it's been seen as a pivotal year.

Historians are fond of that. One of my favorite excursions into American history is *Year of Decision: 1846* by Bernard DeVoto.

The year 1968 got its own chapter in William Manchester's *The Glory and The Dream: A Narrative History of America, 1932-1972*, and the title of the chapter was "The Year Everything Went Wrong."

The first time I can recall thinking about 1968 was in the fall of 1962 when I was starting seventh grade at Evans Junior-Senior High School in Evans, Colorado. Our home-room teacher told us we had to pick a class song, class colors and a class flower for our "Class of 1968," which seemed impossibly far into a remote future.

When that year arrived, Evans High was no more; school consolidation had put us at Greeley West High, and if we had a class song, class colors or a class flower, I don't remember them.

I do remember that 1968 got off to a dismal start. On January 23, North Korea seized the U.S.S. Pueblo, a ship that gathered electronic intelligence, along with its crew. This got plenty of attention, especially in Colorado, since the ship was named for one of our major cities.

A week later, the Viet Cong launched the Tet Offensive in South Vietnam, over-running much of the country and reaching the gates of the American embassy in Saigon.

What made 1968 especially cruel, as I recall it, were those moments of hope that were then dashed. In March, Senator Eugene McCarthy of Minnesota, the anti-war candidate, got 42 percent of the vote in the New Hampshire primary, and at the end of the month, President Lyndon Johnson announced he would not seek re-election.

So the awful Vietnam War was going to be over and the draft would end. The Cold War looked to be ending too, with the "Prague Spring" in Czechoslovakia. It was possible to feel hopeful for a few days in the early spring of 1968, and as an idealistic high-school senior, I was optimistic for about a week. What a wonderful, exciting world we were about to enter.

Then came the assassination of the Reverend Doctor Martin Luther King on April 4, followed on June 5 by the shooting of Senator Robert F. Kennedy. The police clubbed and gassed anti-war protesters in Chicago that summer, and Soviet tanks rolled into Prague to keep the Iron Curtain in place. Richard Nixon was elected president with a secret plan to end the war within a year, and it remained a secret.

My family's business, the Crystal White Laundry in Greeley, went under that spring. I moved with my parents and brothers to Longmont that summer, but returned to Greeley for college that fall. What had seemed so permanent — the house in Evans that my dad had built when I was a toddler, my grandmother next door, the laundry — had all changed. The year 1968 would have been tumultuous for me even if the rest of the world had been tranquil and serene.

Thus it's hard to be objective about how 1968 fits into American history. But if I had to come up with something, it would be this: Running as an independent candidate for president, George Wallace got forty-six electoral votes from what had been the Democratic "Solid South." Republican strategists noticed that and started pandering. The Party of Lincoln became the Party of Dixie, and American politics haven't been the same since then.

LIFE, LIBERTY, GRATITUDE
JULY 5, 2009

YESTERDAY, WE CELEBRATED the 233rd anniversary of the Declaration of Independence, which must be the most successful document ever produced by committee.

One must grant that this particular committee — Benjamin Franklin, Robert R. Livingston, Roger Sherman, John Adams and Thomas Jefferson — boasted an abundance of intellectual horsepower. It was Jefferson who wrote the Declaration, with the rest of the committee proposing a few changes before it was submitted to the Continental Congress in Philadelphia, which made more changes.

One might wonder how the Declaration would fare if it fell into the hands of a modern committee:

"When in the Course of human Events ..."

(Clearly specist, elevating "human" events above sylvan or cetacean events. Lose the "human.")

"... it becomes necessary for one People ..."

(To say "one People" deliberately obscures our diversity. This should refer to our glorious mosaic or perhaps a rich tapestry.)

"... to dissolve the Political Bands which have connected them with another, and to assume among the Powers of the Earth the separate & equal Station ..."

("Separate and equal" sounds too much like "separate but equal," which has bad connotations. Let's rephrase this.)

"... to which the Laws of Nature and of Nature's God entitle them ..."

(Why "Nature's God" instead of just "God?" This might appeal to treehuggers and secular humanists, but it could alienate parts of the market we need to reach.)

"... a decent Respect to the Opinions of Mankind ..."

(We're the United States of America. We don't pander to the "Opinions of Mankind." Delete this fuzzy-thinking internationalism.)

"... requires that they should declare the causes which impel them to the Separation. We hold these Truths to be self-evident, that all Men are created equal, that they are endowed by their Creator with inherent and unalienable Rights, that among these are Life, Liberty & the Pursuit of Happiness ..."

("Pursuit of Happiness" sounds libertine. We should stick with John Locke's formulation of "life, health, liberty or possessions.")

(Agreed on possessions, though we should change that to "property." But proclaiming an unalienable right to health could lead to socialized medicine, so cut that.)

(If right to Liberty is unalienable, how can anyone be imprisoned, no matter how heinous the crime? We need to scratch this, too.)

(When does right to Life take effect? Fertilization, quickening, breathing, reaching of age of majority? We need precision here.)

"... That to secure these Rights, Governments are instituted among Men, ..."

(Too much about Rights. What of public duties and responsibilities?)

"... deriving their just Powers from the Consent of the governed; that whenever any Form of Government becomes destructive of these Ends, it is the Right of the People to alter or abolish it, & to institute new Government, laying its Foundation on such Principles, & organizing its Powers in such Form, as to them shall seem most likely to effect their Safety & Happiness. ..."

(This is sedition. We definitely need to dial back a few notches.)

Back in the day, Jefferson was perturbed by the revisions that came from his fellow committee members, as well as "these mutilations" made by Congress.

But for a committee, they did a good job. To put it another way, can you imagine a modern congressional committee with something so inspiring and enduring?

Wal-Mart health care
July 26, 2009

In any conflict, it's good to know what the enemy is thinking, so I found the Republican talking points on health-care reform.

Here's one: "We cannot allow politicians and special interests to stand between patients and the care they need. The American people deserve the freedom to choose the health care that is best for their families."

But politicians already "stand between patients and the care they need," as with the war on drugs, which removes medical decisions (such as the treatment of chronic pain) out of doctors' and patients' hands.

As for those special interests affecting health care, it's hard to watch TV without seeing an ad about some newly discovered ailment that needs instant and vigorous treatment and the advice to "ask your doctor about Xylobetazine" followed by the caution that "side effects may include nausea, flatulence, incontinence, hypoxia, cardiac dysfunction and cerebral necrosis." Is the maker of Xylobetazine not a special interest? Is it not trying to affect health care?

But I don't hear many Republican complaints about these affronts to their talking points. They also state that "a government takeover of health care ... would have devastating consequences for families and small businesses."

To examine the extent of this devastation, consider the country the Republicans love to hate, France, with its horrible government health care.

The average life expectancy at birth in France is 80.9 years. Here it's 78.1. The French infant mortality rate is 3.4 per 1,000 live births. Ours is 6.7.

The French spend 11.1 percent of their gross domestic product on health care. We spend 15.1 percent. In annual dollars per person, they spend $3,248 and we spend $6,071. We pay considerably more to get shorter life spans and more dead babies. Talk about devastating consequences.

But the GOP derailed President Harry Truman's national health insurance plan, proposed in 1945, as well as President Bill Clinton's effort in 1994.

So I wouldn't bet against the Republican opposition this time, no matter how persuasive President Barack Obama might be. But I have read that Wal-Mart, America's largest private employer, supports a national health-care plan. And if we don't get one, perhaps Wal-Mart could step in with its own plan, offered to the public. The company has an immense infrastructure in place, with 4,269 retail units scattered throughout the country. In general, the stores are open for extended hours, thereby allowing people to come in without taking time off from their paying jobs.

So why not a Wal-Mart health care plan, based on a clinic in every store? The service would be rather spartan — for example, waiting in line rather than making appointments — but if you're in a Wal-Mart, you're used to being in line anyway.

To lower costs, physicians could be imported from India and China. Therapies would range from herbs and acupuncture to traditional American pharmaceuticals. Unlike the federal government, though, Wal-Mart would use its buying power to drive drug prices down, down, down. Wal-Mart also has the clout to negotiate great deals with hospital chains — or to open its own hospitals if they balked.

So, if we can't do it the French way, Wal-Mart could do it the American way, with a coverage plan offered to the public that featured no-frills service, ruthless competition and relentless cost-cutting. You know, "Save money, live better."

WHO CARES ABOUT INDEPENDENCE, RIGHT?
APRIL 24, 2011

MAYBE THIS WILL BE THE YEAR that we forgo celebrating Independence Day in the United States, since it's becoming quite obvious that millions of Americans have no desire to be independent of Great Britain.

This surfaced last fall when a right-thinker named Dinesh D'Souza published an article in *Forbes Magazine* — which used to enjoy a decent reputation — explaining that our duly elected president, Barack Obama, could be understood only if we realized that he suffered from an anti-colonial view of the world.

Another right-thinker, disgraced former House Speaker Newt Gingrich, picked up on that. He told *National Review*, a conservative journal, that Obama "is so outside our comprehension, that only if you understand Kenyan, anti-colonial behavior, can you begin to piece together" his actions. "That is the most accurate, predictive model for his behavior."

Obama was twenty-six years old the first time he visited Kenya. But his father was a Kenyan, and Kenya spent much of the twentieth century as a British colony before gaining independence in 1964 following violent struggles which included the Mau Mau rebellion.

Now, I'm not going to hold Kenya up as a model republic. But I would like to know why it is considered abhorrent for Americans to oppose British colonialism.

As best as I can recall from school history classes, this nation was founded in 1776 in opposition to British colonialism, and fought a bloody war for seven years to be free of British colonialism.

Our seminal document, the Declaration of Independence, is a lengthy indictment of British colonial practices, ranging from trade policy to King George III having established "a multitude of new offices, and sent hither swarms of officers to harass our people, and eat out their substance."

Thomas Jefferson wrote that. Other opponents of British colonialism included George Washington, Alexander Hamilton, John Adams and Benjamin Franklin, to name a few. And yet modern right-thinkers, if D'Souza and Gingrich are typical, tell us there's something un-American about opposing British colonialism.

Maybe those are just rantings that no reasonable person would take seriously. But our popular culture suggests otherwise. These days it's really hard to escape from the breathless coverage of the impending April 29 wedding of His Royal Highness Prince William to Catherine Middleton.

Every time I encounter something about how the Coldstream Guards band will play along the procession route, or the exquisite design of Kate's wedding dress, or the details of the tiered wedding cake, I think "Wait a minute. Didn't we fight a war so we wouldn't need to care about the doings of some distant decadent aristocracy?"

I felt the same way in 1981 when Prince Charles wed Princess Diana, followed by the adventures of Duchess Sarah Ferguson, and then the affair of Charles and Camilla, Duchess of Cornwall — why should anyone, especially an American, care about any of this folderol?

But care we do, if our magazines, newspapers and television programs are any indication of what matters to us. While we have established some homegrown dynasties like the Kennedys, Rockefellers and Bushes, we're still enthralled by the House of Windsor. You end up wondering why we shoot off fireworks on July 4, when it's obvious that we really don't want to be independent. Even though our constitution forbids titles of nobility, we still swoon for dukes and princes.

So it's come to this: To be good Americans, we need to forget why America was founded.

Words, Words, Words

Maybe I'll get thrown out of the Guy Club for this confession, but when I was devouring juvenile novels by the armload forty years ago, I preferred Nancy Drew, especially the early ones, to all the other series. Sure, the Hardy Boys were okay, but they were also too cozy with the local police, who in my experience believed that boys could help solve crimes in only one way — by confessing.

A GOOD DECISION THAT COULD HAVE BEEN STRONGER
APRIL 14, 2002

SOMETIMES THE BEST READING lies between the lines, and by that process, last week's decision by the Colorado Supreme Court provides some insight into the twisted minds that conduct the War on Drugs in this country.

This tale started on March 13, 2000, when agents of the North Metro Drug Task Force looked through the trash from a mobile home in Adams County that they had been monitoring. They found evidence of drug operations, as well as a mailing container from the Tattered Cover Book Store addressed to one trailer occupant. The envelope bore invoice and customer numbers, but did not indicate the contents.

The task force got a search warrant and searched the mobile home on the next day. Inside the master bedroom, they found a meth lab, various other items, and two books about how to make meth.

Even though they had their suspicions, the police did not know which person, of several possibilities, actually occupied the master bedroom and presumably cooked the meth.

But there was the mailing container in the trash, plus the books. If they could get the bookstore records, to show that he books had been ordered by a certain person, they'd have a better case — or so they said.

What they were really doing was something else. Their true purpose was not to gather evidence to convict someone of a crime. Instead, they were trying to harass a bookstore that sold material they didn't approve of. And if they had succeeded, bookstores in the future might well decide that no matter what the Bill of Rights says, it would be too much trouble to fill certain customer orders.

How do we know this was harassment instead of a good-faith search for evidence? By reading between the lines of the state Supreme Court decision.

The court observed that the police had many other ways to establish who was making crank. "The master bedroom in the trailer appears to have been a typical bedroom containing clothes, furniture, papers, and other personal objects. Clothes and shoes could have been examined to see if the sizes matched. Objects could have been fingerprinted. The bed and flooring could have been examined for hair or other DNA samples. There are numerous witnesses that the City likely could have interviewed."

In other words, the police had plenty of evidence to gather and examine by the usual methods, but instead decided to harass a store for selling the wrong kind of book.

For further evidence that this was their true purpose, observe the process they followed.

The usual method would be to ask for the records, and if that didn't work, to subpoena the records. And upon receiving the subpoena, the Tattered Cover could have either complied or contested it in a hearing before a court.

But instead of requesting a subpoena that might have led to a hearing, the task force went shopping for a prosecutor who would request a search warrant. The Adams County district attorney's office properly refused. So the task force went to Denver. If Bill Ritter, the Denver District Attorney, has any sense of shame, this fact has escaped public notice, so his office requested and got a search warrant from a judge who should have known better.

In general, you don't get to contest a search warrant. This makes sense; for example, if the trailer occupants had received notice of the search warrant and the opportunity to contest it, they likely would have destroyed the evidence.

But the Tattered Cover wasn't a suspect, and there was no reason to fear it would destroy the relevant records. The search warrant was just another way to harass places where people might buy books that don't bear the North Metro Drug Task Force stamp of approval.

Fortunately, the Tattered Cover had attorneys at hand when Ritter's forces appeared with the warrant, and that led to last week's Supreme Court decision.

The court did not grant an absolute right to privacy concerning book purchases. It did say that law-enforcement agencies should first exhaust other means for gathering evidence, and then go through an "adversarial hearing," rather than just get a search warrant.

And when the request was based on the content of a book, as it was in this case, then the hurdle should be high, because our state constitution guarantees that "every person shall be free to speak, write or publish whatever he will on any subject."

Since police officers and prosecutors take oaths to support the constitution of the state of Colorado, and here they acted purposefully against our constitution by harassing a book seller (for example, they didn't pursue other evidence, and they sought a search warrant instead of a subpoena), I wish our Supreme Court had addressed a proper punishment for these scofflaws — for example, does deliberate subversion of our constitution constitute treason, and if so, would the death penalty be appropriate?

Despite that bleeding-heart omission, though, it was a good decision. If liberty means anything, it should mean that you can buy any book you want without ending up on some police list.

NANCY DREW WASN'T JUST FOR GIRLS
JUNE 9, 2002

IT WAS WITH BOTH SADNESS AND IRRITATION that I read of the recent death of ninety-six-year-old Mildred Benson of Toledo, Ohio. Under the pen name of Carolyn Keene, she wrote the first Nancy Drew novel, and went on to write twenty-three of the first thirty installments in that series.

My sadness at her passing was just that, but the irritation came from the news accounts of her death. Every one I read said something like "generations of girls enjoyed reading Nancy Drew books."

Maybe I'll get thrown out of the Guy Club for this confession, but when I was devouring juvenile novels by the armload forty years ago, I preferred Nancy Drew, especially the early ones, to all the other series.

Sure, the Hardy Boys were okay, but they were also too cozy with the local police, who in my experience believed that boys could help solve crimes in only one way — by confessing. Also, I lived in land-locked Colorado, and the Hardy Boys spent way too much time on or near some saltwater bay for me to identify with their adventures.

It's getting hard to remember any of the others that I toted home from the city library. There was a Mel Martin series about high school baseball players that probably inculcated moral lessons about the virtues of sportsmanship, which were a staple of the athletic tales of John B. Tunis.

I could swear that there was another baseball series about a major-league team called the Blue Sox, loosely based on the New York Yankees of my boyhood (the Yankees had a pitcher named Whitey Ford, the Blue Sox had Wilcey Lord, that sort of thing), but my nosing around the Internet produced no evidence, not even of how Wilcey should be spelled.

There was also a series about astronauts, with the Cold War carried over into plasma-ray battles between capitalists and socialists about mining the asteroid belt. No names leap to mind from that, but I also remember a whodunit series that featured an ace reporter, Whiz Walton.

None of these, though, was a tenth as good as Nancy Drew. She was smart and spunky and her blue roadster was even cooler than a '57 Chevy Nomad wagon. And I'm not the only guy who thinks this way; every so often the subject of juvenile literature comes up when we're keeping some brewery in business, and always it turns out that Nancy Drew was everybody's favorite.

Among people my age, that is. When our own daughters started reading for pleasure as they became teenagers, we suggested *Nancy Drew*, which they tried. Times have changed. They thought that Nancy's friend Bess was a useless priss, while her tomboy friend George was a lesbian who added nothing to the story line and was probably there just for diversity — when Martha and I had been of that age, we didn't even know what lesbians were, let alone diversity.

Our daughters preferred modern series like *Sweet Valley High* and *The Babysitters Club*, and didn't much care for *Nancy Drew*. I found out why when I read one of theirs — the series had been updated, even the early ones, and the charm left when Nancy no longer drove her blue roadster.

At any rate, Nancy wasn't just a favorite of girls — a lot of us boys enjoyed her adventures. But the widespread belief that the series was read only by girls illustrates one problem with the publishing industry: It doesn't know much about its audience.

Mildred Benson wasn't the only "Carolyn Keene." The publisher had a stable of writers who used that name for Nancy Drew books. The practice continues; about fifteen years ago, Martha and I were "Jon Sharpe" — there were several Jon Sharpes who helped produce a new adult Western every month for the *Trailsman* series about the adventures of Skye Fargo circa 1859-61.

One year we wrote seven of them. We also fought a lot with the editor. Anything that even hinted that there was a Civil War erupting back East was generally taboo, because Westerns actually sell best in the South, and they don't like to be reminded that they were on the losing side.

We got a copy of one installment that some other Jon Sharpe had written. It had Fargo forted up with a wagon train, fighting off the circling Apache (very unlikely that any such thing ever happened, but it's a staple of Western fiction), and the spent brass shells began to pile up.

I told the editor that they didn't use brass cartridges on the frontier in 1860, that the bullets and powder and priming caps were all loaded separately into Skye Fargo's revolver and carbine.

"Oh, who cares?" he responded. "They just read these things in truck stops, you know."

It had been my experience that if you needed to find experts on the history of American firearms, a bunch of guys drinking coffee at a truckstop would be about the best place to start, and I feared the *Trailsman* series would lose all credibility under an editor who knew so little about his audience.

And that, I fear, is probably what happened to *Nancy Drew* after Mildred Benson quit serving as a Carolyn Keene. Benson's tales were great reading for 12-year-olds — even twelve-year-old boys. She knew that, even if nobody else there did.

GREAT BOOK BEHIND "TROY"
MAY 23, 2004

NEARLY 20 YEARS AGO, I interviewed local author Steve Frazee, who died in 1992, for *The Denver Post*'s book section. In the 1950s and '60s, Frazee wrote novels, on topics from juveniles to contemporary humor, but mostly he wrote westerns.

At the time of that interview, some purification lobby was whining about violence in entertainment — and violence is the heart of the western. Steve laughed. "It's always been in our stories. Look at the *Iliad*. Homer spilled more blood in a chapter than I did in my whole career."

Steve could bring characters to life in just a paragraph or two. Eager to learn some secrets of the writing trade, I asked how he did it. "I stole it from Dickens," he said.

I pressed for an explanation.

"You could call it 'being influenced by,'" he said. "Your writing is influenced by what you read. Consciously or unconsciously, you'll imitate. So you should always read the best — Shakespeare, Cervantes, Dickens, Homer. That's the best way to write better."

That's as good a piece of writing advice as I ever got, and it inspired me to read the *Iliad*, which has currently returned to popular culture as the 2,700-year-old book behind the movie *Troy*. In theory, I had read it in a 1969 college humanities class; in practice, I had faked my way through with *Classic Comics* and *Cliff's Notes*.

How best to read the *Iliad*? Doubtless in the original ancient Greek, but most of us will need a translation. The original is poetry, but dactylic hexameter and English aren't a good fit. So find a prose translation. After trying several, I settled on the old Penguin Classic translation by E.V. Rieu.

Don't try to read it in one sitting. This epic was made for many nightly installments from a bard at a campfire. At the time, my daughters still wanted a bedtime story, so I read them a piece of the *Iliad* every night over several months.

Going slowly, we had time to look up everything we didn't understand, from greaves (baseball catchers wear them, though they're usually called shin guards now) to Grecian goddesses. The kids loved the *Iliad* — a tale of violence and magic and human passions from the sordid to the sublime. And as Frazee had predicted, I learned much about literature from Homer.

This may be the greatest war story ever (Shelby Foote based his Civil War trilogy on the *Iliad*), and Homer was on the Greek side. Yet he never dehumanizes the enemy; the noblest warrior, Hector, is a Trojan.

Most of Homer's characters are soldiers, but almost always, he makes them more than just swords and shields. When they die, they're someone's son or husband. There's a vineyard back home which will never be tended again. Even though they delight in battle, Homer tells the cost.

The cost gets clear in an unforgettable scene with Hector, his wife Andromache and son Astyanax on the wall of Troy. The child doesn't recognize his father and is frightened, until Hector removes his crested helmet. And then Hector must choose between duty to family and duty to country. Homer isn't afraid to address the moral complexity of life, and it adds immeasurably to what appears, at first, to be just a tale about a bunch of guys fighting a long time ago in a place far away.

Whether you see the movie or not, you ought to read the book. Although it should be required in every American school, as one of the foundations our literature, the pecksniffs of both the left (violence and the objectification of women) and right (it's totally pagan, and there's the homosexual relationship between Achilles and Patroclos) will ensure that it's never on a public-school curriculum in this country.

So read it yourself, or even better, read it to your kids. It's about blood and guts and fate and valor and treachery — the unsanitized stuff of life and death. And it's a great story.

BOULDERESE: IT'S NOT JUST IN BOULDER
JULY 27, 2004

COLORADO HAS ENJOYED an official language since 1988, but the state government has never gotten around to publishing a dictionary of Colorado Official English.

That's probably just as well, because the dictionary would have to include a special section dedicated to the Boulder Dialect of Official Colorado English. The most recent distinction between Boulder English and the language we use in the less enlightened portions of our state appeared last week.

In the past months and years, there have been allegations and investigations concerning the recruiting of athletes to the football program at the University of Colorado. The charges included rape, underage drinking, wild parties, and escort services — that is, what most of us would call a "scandal."

However, that's not the right word, according to Boulder's leading football coach, Gary Barnett: "I'd like to officially not acknowledge that word 'scandal,'" he said last week. "I refuse to think of that as the proper word to describe it."

From what I read, he didn't offer a "proper word," and thus the word that comes to mind to describe Barnett's attitude is "denial." But he's hardly the only one who speaks Boulderese, a dialect that eliminates unpleasantness from English.

Go back a few years, and there was the official Boulder municipal spokesperson, Leslie Aaholm. She was handling a lot of inquiries about the still-unsolved murder of six-year-old JonBenét Ramsey on December 26, 1996.

Aaholm did her best to avoid using unpalatable but accurate terms like "murder." Instead, she kept calling it an "incident," which could mean anything from jaywalking to the September 11 attacks.

More recently, in the summer of 2000, Boulder became the first city in the United States to change the language of its municipal code so that a person no longer "owns" a "pet." Instead of being a pet owner, a Boulderite with a dog or cat or ferret is the "guardian" of a "companion animal."

The theory behind this was that it would make people more responsible by changing the way they think — which, upon further thought, sounds rather Orwellian. One job of the Ministry of Truth in George Orwell's novel "1984" was to purge the language of any words that could communicate rebellion, thus making it more or less impossible for people even to think about overthrowing Big Brother, who was always watching.

Orwell also wrote a brilliant essay in 1946, "Politics and the English Language," wherein he stated that "Defenseless villages are bombarded from the air, the inhabitants driven out into the countryside, the cattle machine-gunned, the huts set on fire with incendiary bullets: this is called pacification. … People are imprisoned for years without trial, or shot in the back of the neck or sent to die of scurvy in Arctic lumber camps: this is called 'elimination of undesirable elements.'"

Orwell saw this abuse of language as a major problem, since it corrupted public discourse. "All issues are political issues," he wrote, and, "Political language — and with variations this is true of all political parties, from Conservatives to Anarchists — is designed to make lies sound truthful and murder respectable, and to give appearances of solidity to pure wind."

And, it appears, to make Boulder sound like a place whose guardians of companion animals are troubled by neither murder nor scandal, merely an incident and a word to be announced later by the football coach.

Boulder won't be the only offender; there will be much more blather, since this is an election year. We'll hear about the "liberation of Iraq" when the civilian death toll there is about the same as it was when Saddam Hussein was in charge.

According to Human Rights Watch, about 250,000 Iraqis were "disappeared" during the twenty-five years of Ba'athist rule, or 10,000 per year. The best estimates of related civilian deaths since the 2003 invasion come to about 12,000, which works out to 9,000 per year.

We will hear about the "preservation of traditional values," and endure the advocacy of our own special "Colorado values," whatever they are. Indeed, if Orwell were around today, he'd doubtless add "values" to his list of political expressions that sound solid but are actually just "pure wind."

That might be the worst aspect of Boulderese — that it's not confined to Boulder. No matter what your political persuasion, there is always a need to gloss over disturbing facts and pretend that certain things didn't happen.

TO WRITE LIKE HUNTER S.
FEBRUARY 22, 2005

EVERY TIME I SIT DOWN TO WRITE, I want to create the perfect opening paragraph — that is, one that so grabs the reader that he drops everything and thinks, "I've got to read the rest of this, right now." And in nearly fifty years of reading, I've encountered only two such openers.

One began a short story, "An Imperfect Conflagration," written in the 1880s by Ambrose Bierce: "Early one June morning in 1872 I murdered my father — an act which made a deep impression on me at the time."

The other, by Hunter S. Thompson, appeared in 1971: "We were somewhere around Barstow on the edge of the desert when the drugs began to take hold. I remember saying something like 'I feel a bit lightheaded; maybe you should drive.' And suddenly there was a terrible roar all around us and the sky was full of what looked like huge bats, all swooping and screeching and diving around the car, which was going about a hundred miles an hour with the top down to Las Vegas."

In December 1913, Bierce rode a horse into Mexico, which was then suffering from a civil war. He had earlier written to a friend, "If you hear of my being stood up against a Mexican stone wall and shot to rags please know that I think that a pretty good way to depart this life. It beats old age, disease, or falling down the cellar stairs. To be a Gringo in Mexico — ah, that is euthanasia!"

And then he vanished, although his last adventures inspired a fine novel, *Gringo Viejo* by Carlos Fuentes, and a decent movie, *The Old Gringo*, based on the novel.

Thompson killed himself over the weekend. I have no idea why, and the one time I ever talked to him — he called me in the wee hours once to talk about the Lisl Auman case — I was rather tongue-tied and star-struck, for he might have been the most influential journalist of the late twentieth century.

Thompson's famous gonzo style didn't just hatch one morning. If you read the best collection of his work, *The Great Shark Hunt*, which came out in 1979, you'll find a lot of great more-or-less traditional journalism, much of it written from South America for mainstream publications, as with this from 1963:

"When the cold Andean dusk comes down on Cuzco, the waiters hurry to shut the venetian blinds in the lounge of the big hotel in the middle of town. They do it because the Indians come up on the stone porch and stare at the people inside. It tends to make tourists uncomfortable, so the blinds are pulled. The tall, oak-paneled room immediately seems more cheerful."

Then came his 1966 book *Hell's Angels*. He didn't just interview people and quote police authorities; he got into the story, so deeply that he ended up getting stomped. A friend in college was highly impressed by the book and urged me to read it, so I did, and when we encountered that memorable 1971 opening Barstow paragraph in Rolling Stone magazine, we checked to see if it was the same Hunter Thompson who had written the Hell's Angels book.

It was, and Thompson was at his prime then, writing not only what he saw but speculating about what might be happening, making himself a character who might be half-crazy, but that made him a lot saner than the full-bore lunatics who ran our country.

Thompson had some good effects on American journalism. He loosened it up with a vicious style that captured the situation in just a few words. In the 1972 Democratic primaries, Hubert Humphrey "campaigned like a rat in heat," and Edward Muskie sounded "like a farmer with terminal cancer trying to borrow money on next year's crop."

He had some bad effects on American journalists of my generation, many of whom seemed to think that creativity required trunkloads of uncontrollable substances, and that bragging about your consumption somehow improved your writing.

I yearned to be able to write like Thompson or Bierce. Bierce fought the good fight against the railroad barons that dominated California politics.

Thompson was more of an idealist than the cynical Bierce, as evidenced in 1973: "What a fantastic monument to the better instincts of the human race this country might have been, if we could have kept it out of the hands of greedy little hustlers like Richard Nixon."

The greedy little hustlers are still running this country, thirty-two years later. Good writing only goes so far, no matter how compelling the opening paragraph.

Fixing the bad news
July 23, 2006

Frequently I read complaints that the Biased Liberal Mainstream Media focus on bad news while ignoring positive developments throughout the world, and truth be told, there is some merit to those grievances. I follow the news closely, and very little of what I see, hear and read lately could be classified as "good."

But that's a problem that's easy to solve. Just think how much better you'd feel if you read stories like these instead of the usual negative stuff:

"Constance Fundament, president of Christian Mothers Against Presidential Blasphemy, Scatology and Profanity, yesterday praised President George W. Bush for going a whole week without accidentally uttering a common four-letter word for fecal matter into a live microphone that he thought was off.

Or we could try this from our own state:

"Fall colors will be more vibrant and distinctive in the mountains this September, according to Bob Booster, head of the Centennial State Marketing Commission.

"'In many previous years,' he said, 'the aspen dominated the views, and so people often missed the subtle autumn glories of the stream-side willows, riparian cottonwoods and hill-side scrub oaks. But now the flamboyant xanthous aspen are getting out of the way of the more expansive views that we're eagerly anticipating, and we're sure that visitors will be amazed by what they see this fall.'

"He also pointed out that aspen appear to be thriving on at least a million acres in Colorado, 'so people who go in for that sort of thing will still have that opportunity.'"

Elsewhere on the home front, we're not getting this good news:

"Testifying before a congressional oversight committee last week, Attorney General Alberto Gonzales said there were upwards of two billion telephone calls, e-mails and credit-card transactions that American security agencies did not examine in 2005.

"'For obvious reasons, I cannot provide an exact number,' Gonzales said, 'but we have a pretty good estimate. There are occasions when we respect the rights and privacy of American citizens.'"

And why dwell on the dismal when it comes to education?

"A nationwide survey earlier this year found that a majority of 2006 high-school graduates could read and write at a sixth-grade level. And nationwide tests disclosed that many other graduates could understand street signs, make change and send and receive short electronic text messages."

In foreign news, we could accentuate the positive:

"Secretary of State Condoleezza Rice yesterday pointed out that there are at least four Middle Eastern nations not current warring with other Middle Eastern nations.

"Citing Qatar and Dubai, 'as well as other countries that I will not mention for security reasons,' she said their current pacific status 'should demonstrate to the world that peace dominates in the region.'

"When a reporter asked about how many Americans would be evacuated from the region on account of an alleged conflict between Israel and Hezbollah forces in Lebanon, she took issue with the word 'evacuate,' and said the State Department had found 'a good deal for passage on a Mediterranean cruise ship, and we wanted to share this bargain with American citizens who happened to be in that area. This is a great time of year to visit Cyprus.'"

Tired of bad news from Iraq? Then look at the bright side:

"At a press briefing in Baghdad yesterday, Major General Wallace Pangloss announced that 144,871 American military personnel in Iraq had remained healthy on the preceding day. "They were not killed or injured by insurgent forces in direct conflict. Nor were they harmed in any way by improvised roadside explosives or suicide bombers, he added. Further, there were also 26,074,548 Iraqis who made it through the day without injury, and 'I think that pretty well negates anything you might have heard about a mosque being bombed with heavy civilian casualties.'"

When you think about how pleasant the news could be if it were just presented properly, you have to wonder why there's so much bad news. It's just a matter of emphasis, after all.

THE TRADEMARK TANGLE
AUGUST 20, 2006

LAST WEEK I LEARNED A NEW WORD, "genericide," when I read about some letters that Google attorneys have been sending to the media.

The Internet search company is trying to protect its trademark and keep it from becoming a generic term for Internet searching. So the company advises that this is an appropriate use: "I ran a Google search to check out that guy from the party." And this is inappropriate: "I googled that hottie."

Over the years, American courts have held that companies have to make this effort, lest their proprietary proper noun become a public-domain common noun.

The companies can be quite zealous, which is understandable given the millions of dollars that are spent on "building brand identity." When I edited the local daily twenty-five years ago, which was a very small newspaper whose circulation area was quite limited, I was astonished to get a letter from the attorneys for the Binney & Smith Company.

A local columnist had described a sunset as offering "more colors than you could find in a crayola box." Somehow that reached the corporate world, and the lawyers advised Crayola was a brand name, not another word for "crayon," and would I in the future please revise such expressions to "crayon box" or "Crayola crayon box."

No problem there. But sometimes it's more difficult. For example, Dumpster is a trademarked brand name of Dempster Brothers, Inc., which invented the "Dempster Dumpster." But there's no other convenient term for "box-shaped trash receptacle that can be tipped and emptied with hydraulic-powered prongs on the garbage truck." And so there's no other way to express something like "Aspiring free-lance writers should learn dumpster-diving."

Some inventors try to get around that by inventing a generic term to go with their trademarked term. Chester Carlson invented the Xerox machine in 1937. He also coined a generic word for the process: "xerography" from the Greek word "xeros," which means dry, and "graph," which derives from the Greek for "to write." It was "dry writing" because no messy photographic liquids were involved.

Even so, Americans were fond of saying "Please xerox that for me" rather that "Please make a xerographic copy." And that kept the company and its attorneys busy trying to protect the trademark. A related term, "Xeriscape," is often used generically to describe a yard designed to minimize water consumption. But it is actually a trademark of Denver Water, which coined it in 1981. It has inspired another term, "zeroscape," for those hideous yards of cobbles and concrete.

If companies don't try to protect their trademarks, they can become common words. That happened to aspirin, once owned by Bayer, the German pharmaceutical company that first formulated acetylsalicyclic acid. Another

Bayer drug trademark, heroin (diacetylmorphine), also fell into the public domain.

Such usages seem to go in and out of style. If you read a novel from the 1930s, you might find someone "hoovering a room," or "kodaking a scene," because back then, Hoover was nearly synonymous with vacuum cleaner and Kodak for photography. They somehow saved their trademarks, even though cellophane, escalator, linoleum, zipper and thermos all lost their brand-name properties.

The problem, whether you're writing for public consumption or compiling a dictionary, is "How people actually express themselves" versus "How people should express themselves." Or as we English majors were told, descriptive vs. prescriptive.

In other words, I've never asked Martha "Do you want to play the Scrabble-brand crossword game tonight?" That's just not how people talk, and if you quote people accurately, you'll get "That picture from Lebanon looks like it's been photoshopped" rather than "The image appears to have been digitally manipulated."

It's hard to predict whether Google can maintain its trademark and avoid genericide. But at least the company ought to be pleased that it has a positive connotation. After all, the process could produce conversations like this:

"Bad day. My computer microsofted three times and I had to reboot, then I found out my investments had qwested."

JOURNAL SLID BEFORE MURDOCH
AUGUST 19, 2007

WE'VE HAD A PRIEST JOGGING NAKED in Frederick. In Denver, Edward Nottingham's off-duty activities have gone a long way toward explaining why no one uses the phrase "sober as a judge" anymore.

Clearly the silly season is upon us, to the degree that it was difficult to believe that "Rove leaving White House" was a real story, and not the result of alleged UFO activity, except that the place where we learn of such things, the *Weekly World News* in the supermarket checkout line, is planning to suspend its print edition.

The combination of aliens and newsprint brings us to the purchase of *The Wall Street Journal* by Rupert Murdoch, the Australian native who once paid one of our previous local cable monopolies $10 a head to drop a PBS channel and The Weather Channel so it had room for Fox News.

Murdoch's purchase of the Journal has caused a lot of anguished hand-wringing about how one of America's great national newspapers might slide into mediocrity, but the *Journal* actually began to slip years ago.

I used to subscribe. My liberal friends would see me toting it from the post office, and stare pointedly. I would reply that it's important to know your enemy; the military calls it "intelligence."

A decade ago, the *Journal* presented a sober appearance and first-class writing. Almost daily, a whimsical front-page feature sparkled and made me wish I could observe and write that well. The first symptom of decay came when barbarisms like "alright" and "would of" appeared with increasing frequency. Reporters, like all other writers, will make mistakes, especially under daily deadlines. Copy editors are supposed to catch them.

If you're going to pinch on the news side of a publication, that's an easy place. You can still have as many reporters in the field, filing as much copy as before. The results of this cutback are not immediately obvious. But copy editors are the "quality control" of the news side of a newspaper, and eventually readers start to think, "If these morons don't know to use 'could have' rather than the idiotic 'could of,' why should we trust them to know how the GATT works?"

The *Journal* started running more "reader service" features, especially in its new Saturday edition. Granted, the *Journal* caters to an affluent audience, but I'm not especially interested in comparative yacht shopping or diamond-adorned wristwatches.

The *Journal* started running photographs and color. Those have their place, of course, but I had hoped their place would not be *The Wall Street Journal*. It started selling merchandise with *Journal* branding, like flashlights, tote bags and ponchos. This may "extend the brand" in modern marketing parlance, but I'd have preferred some "brand building" from solid reporting and editing.

Dismayed by the *Journal's* course, I let my subscription lapse. I thought I should get some national publication, so I tried *The Economist*. It had the merit of philosophical consistency — for example, *The Economist* sensibly believed the war on drugs was evil, whereas the *Journal* somehow acted as though a rational person could believe in both "free men and free markets" and the "war on drugs." But *The Economist's* fine print was too fine for my bifocals, so I tried the Sunday *New York Times* for a year. Sure, there was some good writing — but the *Times* also published too much plutography to suit me. I didn't renew.

There's the Internet, except that every time I build a faster computer or get a faster connection, the genius of American commerce soon finds a way to slow things down. Pages take longer and longer to load, pieces are chopped up so that you spend more time staring at their ads while you wait for the next few paragraphs, gaudy graphics add no information, etcetera.

Unlike many modern media barons, Murdoch does seem to believe in print. And given the course the Journal took all on its own, it's hard to see how he could make it worse than it would have been anyway.

FINDING A NAME FOR A/H1N1
MAY 5, 2009

THE TWENTY-FOUR-HOUR CABLE NEWS STATIONS love nothing more than a growing crisis, so that we'll feel compelled to check frequently for developments. That improves their ratings, thereby allowing them to raise ad rates and do their part for an economic recovery.

So it's in their interest to make the latest influenza outbreak sound like one of the Four Horsemen of the Apocalypse: As of press time, it's spread into thirty-six states and there are 340 confirmed cases in the U.S. Hundreds of schools have closed. The vice president says to stay off airplanes. Mexican fatalities are up to twenty-six. Wear masks and stock up on food and water.

In this frenzy to be sure that we're scared and desperately searching for more information, they omit some context. According to the U.S. Centers for Disease Control, in an average year, 36,300 Americans die from the flu or flu-related complications.

The CDC noted that the fatality count varies considerably — from 17,000 to 52,000 — "because flu seasons often fluctuate in length and severity."

But on an average day, 100 Americans die from regular old flu without attracting the attention of the cable outlets, whereas we're getting a round-the-clock bombardment after one American death from the exotic flu-du-jour whose proper name, we are told, is H1N1 after it started out as swine flu.

Christening a flu is a tricky business. Few people are alive today who remember the great 1918 outbreak, the deadliest epidemic known to history. Estimates range from 20 million to 100 million fatalities around the world.

It may have originated at Fort Riley, Kansas, in the heart of America, but it was generally called "Spanish Flu." That's because Spain was neutral during World War I. Thus, there were no military censors leaning on its press to ignore disease-outbreak stories because they could depress morale and discourage enlistment. So the first accounts were published in Spain, which made people think that the disease originated in Spain.

When I was reading old Salida newspapers in pursuit of something else a while ago, I learned the local theory of that day: the Spanish Influenza was spread by Italian immigrants, who should be kept out of town by any means necessary.

The outbreak here augmented the legend of Laura Evans, madam of a bordello in "the Front Street Resort District." Business was way down during the epidemic, so she sent her working girls out to serve as nurses in the respectable parts of town.

Elsewhere in the mountains, flu-fighting took different forms. Gunnison closed its schools and other public places, and put barricades on the roads into town. Railroad passengers stepping off the narrow-gauge were quarantined for at least two days. The result: no flu cases in town during the first outbreak, and only two in the county.

Contrast that to Silverton, where there were fifty-two deaths in just ten days. Silverton, then and now, is more isolated than Gunnison, but some accounts indicate that the flu was spread there at a public meeting called to address the "Spanish Influenza."

What to call the current outbreak? It appears to have originated in Mexico, but for obvious reasons, "Mexican flu" is a non-starter. It's still being called "swine flu," but America's pork producers want a different name, since sales are down even though you can't get the flu from pork chops. The virus has been linked to human flu and avian flu as well, but since it's a mix it's not fair to label it either one of those.

The authorities have been calling it A/H1N1, which is fast to type but awkward to utter. The cable folks do need to keep this revved up, so how about "Perchance Pandemic Disorder," "Ratings Enhancement Influenza" or "Sweeps Month Flu"

PLIGHT OF THE DOG CATCHER
AUGUST 22, 2010

LATELY I'VE SEEN STATEMENTS LIKE THESE about the Republican nominee for governor, Dan Maes: "The guy has no business being dog catcher," and "I wouldn't vote for him for dog catcher." I've used the term in this political context. In 1992, I referred to "anyone above the level of dog catcher," and a year earlier, to "every election from dog catcher to the White House."

Let's ponder the two political meanings of dog catcher: 1) The lowest elected office, and 2) A job so simple that only a total incompetent could fail at it.

As for the first, I'm familiar with small venues. I grew up in Evans, just south of Greeley, which had about 1,500 residents then. I lived in Pierce, north of Greeley, when it held 452 people. Kremmling, with about 1,000 residents, was the largest town in Grand County when I lived there thirty-five years ago. Now I'm in a relative metropolis of 5,500.

I remember elections for town trustees and mayors, for municipal clerks and treasurers, for school boards and sanitation boards, for offices that have since been abolished like county school superintendent and county surveyor, but never for "municipal dog warden" or "county superintendent of canine control."

I have pored through nineteenth century newspapers from our mining camps, where sometimes they elected constables (whose duties included rounding up stray drunks and donkeys), but never a dog catcher. As nearly as I can tell, dog catcher has never been an elective office in Colorado.

As to the job skills, when I worked in Breckenridge, I admired the labor-saving methods of the two dog catchers. One explained to me that they'd find a bitch in heat — either in the pound or running loose at the start of their patrol — and then troll the streets with her in the back of their truck. Unconfined male dogs came running and were easily picked up.

But obviously, the job isn't always that easy, as you can tell from the "Animal Cops" show on the Animal Planet channel. So how did "dog catcher" become a political insult? The *Oxford English Dictionary* provided no help. But a contributor to that work, New York lawyer and etymologist Barry Popik, has found that in some jurisdictions in the 19th century, dog catchers were elected, although "it was the lowest position on the ballot."

His earliest political reference is from the February 26, 1889, edition of the *Courier-Journal* of Louisville, Ky.: "An insolent Republican newspaper asserts that Mr. [lame-duck President Grover] Cleveland is so unpopular in Washington that he could not be elected dog-catcher for the district."

In 1891, a Chicago newspaper referred to "a man who could not be elected dog-catcher in Kansas." In another story a month later, that paper quoted someone saying "You could not be elected dog-catcher in your ward."

Dog catchers have remained part of our political discourse. In part, I suspect that's because they're rather unpopular with dog owners, a large and vocal group that includes me. Even so, I quit using the term, and here's why:

After I last used it in 1992, I got a letter from a woman in Adams County. Her husband, she wrote, was an animal control officer. It was hard work, occasionally dangerous, but he loved animals. His job made their community a safer and better place. So why was I demeaning dog catchers?

She was right. Dog catchers generally do improve our communities at some risk to themselves. So why insult them by comparing them to politicians?

Politics in the West

As for counties, here in Chaffee County we have an abundance of things that closed while Reagan was president and our unemployment rate was pushing 25 percent. While people elsewhere may have thought he was saying "Morning in America" in 1984, it sounded like "Mourning in America" here, where stores were closing and half the town was for sale with no takers.

MAKE SURE THAT YOUR VEHICULAR STATEMENTS ARE CONSISTENT
JANUARY 7, 2001

EVERY SO OFTEN, I suffer from a temptation to apply for "pioneer license plates," which indicate that you had ancestors in Colorado a century ago.

However, it looks like a lot of work to delve into musty old repossession records, foreclosure proceedings and bankruptcy filings to establish my Colorado lineage, and so I have manfully resisted the pioneer-plate temptation.

Further, if one needs to display Colorado roots while nervously scanning for patches of black ice on the road, the vehicle itself is a better mechanism than a license plate or bumper sticker.

For sixteen years, I owned a wonderful old pickup, a 1967 Chevy. It was a three-quarter ton with a narrow box, a four-speed manual transmission with compound low and a stump-puller 292 six-cylinder engine. It did not have power steering, power brakes, power windows or power anything except the rear wheels.

It was painted road-department orange, and when I bought it used from Jameson Chevrolet in Kremmling in 1977, it still had "Routt County. District 1 A-3" painted on the doors.

I was somewhat leery on that account, but the salesman assured me that it had been the pickup assigned to the foreman in the Oak Creek district, "so you know it got good care and never got worked real hard. Now, if it had been a crew member's truck, you'd be right to be worried."

The truck did not age gracefully in my hands. Its windshield cracked, it acquired dents and it began to burn some oil.

And when I saw a sticker I liked, I put it on what was left of the rear bumper (it lost some pieces during a towing effort along Halfmoon Creek west of Leadville during a failed effort to ascend Mount Elbert, which had followed some serious pre-climb training at the bar of the Golden Burro the night before).

One sticker said "Ch*ng* el ingles oficial," which perfectly expressed my attitude about Colorado's official English law, and which certainly could not be deemed legally obscene, since the obscenity was in an unofficial language (the sticker had vowels rather than asterisks).

The other was a "Native" sticker. Martha said it was superfluous. "That pickup obviously wouldn't make it to the state line," she explained, "so what's the point of the sticker? Nobody except someone bred and born in Colorado would think you could get away with driving that thing on a public road."

The state patrol apparently agreed with her. Every time I drove the truck out of town with the "ingles oficial" sticker, I got pulled over. Never for the sticker, at least officially — it was always something like a possible intermittent brake light.

One night in the Victoria Tavern here, I spotted a friend who had been a state trooper for about a decade before going into business for himself. I asked why I always got pulled over but never ticketed.

"We're trained to look for things that don't quite fit together. You've got this classic good-ol'-boy redneck pickup, complete with gun rack. As far as the typical trooper is concerned, it should have an "NRA Life Member' or "Get US out of the UN' sticker, and it would all add up and you wouldn't get pulled over all the time.

"But you've also got a bumper sticker that could be construed as some radical left-wing Chicano protest statement, which would be okay if you were driving a low-rider '64 Chevy Impala, but you aren't. This odd combination is going to make any trooper curious, and he's going to want to pull you over and check things out."

That was about a decade ago, and I sold the pickup in 1993. But I suspect that our state troopers are still trained to look for unlikely combinations, and so I offer a suggestion to those who get pioneer plates.

First note that most Colorado pioneers came here with one primary idea — to get rich quickly and then move back to civilization. Thus, those who stayed and had families here were failures, since they didn't make enough money to leave. And so pioneer plates would fit perfectly on a vehicle with bald tires and a cracked windshield that hasn't been washed since the first Reagan administration.

But if you put pioneer plates on a new car, especially something ostentatious like a Lexus or Mercedes spewt — well, don't blame me if you get pulled over frequently for strange reasons. After all, you've now been warned about the danger of taking an anomaly out on the public roads. Be consistent, or be prepared to spend a lot of time talking to troopers.

OUR STEREOTYPE DOESN'T FIT
FEBRUARY 4, 2001

AS GOOD AMERICANS, we not only endure a presidential election, but we also tolerate the analysis that emerges afterward.

This time around, the right-thinking pundits couldn't accept the simple fact that the 2000 presidential election was one of the closest in history. Instead, they looked for a mandate for the winner, and found one in acreage.

As Mark Steyn explained in the December 4, 2000 *National Review*, "677 counties voted for Gore, 2,434 for Bush," and "the Gore counties cover 580,134 square miles, the Bush counties, 2,427,039 square miles."

He seems to think that the federal Constitution starts with "We, the townships and sections of the United States," rather than "We, the people."

Steyn saw a geographic pattern. Gore carried states in the Northeast, around the Great Lakes and along the Pacific Coast. The interior where we live is part of "a big Republican "L' running down the Rockies and sweeping through the South."

This was also noted by another conservative publication, *The Wall Street Journal*, which on January 19 published an article by staff writer John Harwood.

He wrote that our L-shaped Republican zone is part of a nation "split not by economics or politics so much as by culture. On one side is the America Mr. Bush already identifies with: mainly rural, religiously observant and devoted to traditional notions of marriage and morality. On the other is the group he is reaching out to: largely urban, secular and tolerant of feminism and gay rights."

While this reads well, and fits nicely with common stereotypes about how traditional virtues thrive in the hinterlands, it has one big problem with the Mountain West. It doesn't fit.

Start with the "rural" part of the Bush political domain. According to the Census Bureau, 79.9 percent of all Americans live in one of the country's 256 standard metropolitan statistical areas. But in many of our states, the urban percentage is even higher: 87.6 percent in Arizona, 85.7 percent in Nevada and 84.0 percent in Colorado. At 77.1 percent, Utah comes close to the national average.

And besides, if rural means "Republican," why does America's most rural state, Vermont (only 27.7 percent urban) keep electing socialists and independents? So we're not especially rural. How wholesome are we in other respects?

The most recent available statistics for church membership are from 1990. Back then, 52.7 percent of Americans belonged to a Christian church or attended one regularly.

The only Western states that exceeded the national average for church membership and attendance were New Mexico (58.3) and Utah (79.6) — both founded by religious colonists. As for the rest of us, it's a wonder that we don't see more missionaries on our doorsteps, because we're about as heathen as Americans get. Only 50.4 percent of Idahoans and only 47.6 percent of Wyomingites belonged or attended regularly. In Montana, it was 42.7 percent; in Arizona, 41.1 percent; in Colorado, 37.8 percent; in Nevada, 29.6 percent.

Nor is the Mountain West a zone of stable marriages. The American average in 1997 was 3.3 divorces per 1,000 population. For the eight states in the Mountain West, it was 5.8. None of our states is below that average, not even Utah, which had 4.4 divorces — 33 percent higher than the national average — per 1,000 residents. Our other states range from 4.6 in Montana to 10.4 in Nevada.

We're not especially wholesome in other respects, either. Nationally, 32.4 percent of all births are to unwed mothers. It's 37.7 percent in Arizona and 43.5 percent in New Mexico.

The national rate of reported crime in 1997 was 4,923 per 100,000 population; in the Mountain West, it was 5,822. The West leads the nation in drug-arrest rates, and the federal Drug Enforcement Administration recently announced that Colorado leads the nation in marijuana use.

Colorado voters did pass the anti-gay Amendment 2 in 1992, but history says the Mountain West is "tolerant of feminism," in that American women first voted in Wyoming Territory in 1869, and the next states to adopt female suffrage were Colorado, Utah and Idaho.

The Mountain West did vote Republican in the most recent national elections. There's no argument about that. But those East Coast pundits need to find another explanation for our voting patterns inside the vertical part of the Republican "L." We are not more rural, more religious or more "devoted to traditional notions of marriage and morality" than the rest of America. It's time for them to find another stereotype.

DOING OUR DUTY TO NAME SOMETHING AFTER RONALD REAGAN
MARCH 27, 2001

AMERICA'S RIGHT-THINKERS apparently have too much time on their hands these days.

You'd think that they still had plenty of their regular work to do. After all, opponents of school prayer still dare to venture out on our streets, in broad daylight at that. Some women have been able to reach medical clinics without being harassed or prosecuted for murder. Millions of unrepentant pot-smokers remain at large, and in many locales, the government schools continue to operate while misguided citizens persist in using the government postal service.

But the right-thinkers have added a new goal. It comes from the Ronald Reagan Legacy Project, whose director, Grover Norquist, recently told Congress that his goal is for every state in the nation, and indeed every county in each state, to have something named after Ronald Reagan, our fortieth president.

A former executive director of the project, Michael Kamburowski, explained, "We want to create a tangible legacy so that thirty or forty years from now, someone who may never have heard of Reagan will be forced to ask himself, "Who was this man to have so many things named after him?"'

One problem with naming things after people is that it may not bring to mind the proper eponym.

For instance, I'd wager that if you took a survey, at least 95 percent of the residents of Adams County would tell you that it was named for John Adams, second president of the United States. It makes sense, since we have a Washington County for the first president, and a Jefferson County for the third. But it was actually named for Alva Adams, governor of Colorado from 1897 to 1899, and for part of one day in 1905.

Much the same holds for Wilson Peak and Mount Wilson, two 14ers in the San Juans. They were named for A.D. Wilson, a topographer with the Hayden survey of 1874, although most people would assume they were named for Thomas Woodrow Wilson, our twenty-eighth president.

So there's no guarantee that if we name something after Ronald Reagan, his accomplishments will leap to future minds.

But as a good citizen, I figure it is my obligation to offer some suggestions as to how Colorado and various counties might participate.

At first thought, naming one of our mountains (perhaps one of the two Wilsons, since Wilson was Reagan's middle name) after Reagan seems appropriate — after all, when people think of Colorado, they think of mountains.

Naming a mountain is a lengthy process, as I've learned in working with the project to put a formal name on Headwaters Hill in Saguache County. Further, most of our mountains are on federal land, and since Reagan ran with the support of the "Sagebrush Rebels" who wanted to eliminate public land, this doesn't seem to fit very well.

Perhaps Cheyenne Mountain near Colorado Springs would work. Its hollowed interior held a major air-defense command center during the Cold War, which peaked under Reagan, and there's talk now of making it a national monument. Put Reagan's name on it, and Colorado will have done its duty by the Legacy Project.

As for counties, here in Chaffee County we have an abundance of things that closed while Reagan was president and our unemployment rate was pushing 25 percent. While people elsewhere may have thought he was saying "Morning in America" in 1984, it sounded like "Mourning in America" here, where stores were closing and half the town was for sale with no takers. At any rate, I certainly have no objection if the Monarch Quarry becomes the Reagan Pit.

Lake County got hit even worse then — its population fell by a third during the Reagan regime. Certainly a tailings pile from an abandoned mine could become the Reagan Dump.

Over the Divide, in Eagle County, there's a major development that started during the Reagan years. It's seriously upscale, a glittering display of the conspicuous consumption that was popular in the 1980s. So it seems appropriate if Beaver Creek becomes Reagan Creek. Residents of other counties can doubtless think of appropriate items. Then there remains our largest city — since it's the capital of all of Colorado, it's only fair that we outlanders get to make suggestions.

Thus, what in Qwestville (it is my understanding that this is the current name for the city formerly known as Denver, and perhaps to be known as Boeingberg in the near future) should be named for Reagan, so that we don't forget those years.

My nomination is the skyscraper that used to bear the word "Silverado," as in the sleazy savings and loan operation that went bust during the Reagan years and cost U.S. taxpayers millions of dollars. And, since Neil Bush, brother of the current president, was a director, this would demonstrate historical continuity.

After all, there really are some things from the Reagan days that we should strive to remember.

A REFRESHING TWIST IN THE MASCOT WARS
MARCH 17, 2002

DURING MY SCHOOLBOY DAYS in the greater Greeley area, our Evans Rams sometimes played the Eaton Reds. We usually got trounced, since Eaton was a bigger school. And that's as much attention as I ever paid to the Eaton mascot until last week. But the color is only part of it. Eaton teams are the "Fightin' Reds," symbolized by a caricature of an Indian with a big nose, a loincloth and an eagle feather.

This annoyed some Native American students at the University of Northern Colorado in Greeley, who wanted to talk to the Eaton school administration — but the desire was not mutual. The college students had an intra-mural basketball team, formally known as "Native Pride." Last week they decided to be the "Fightin' Whities."

They turned the tables. If a bunch of mostly white players are "Fightin' Reds" with an emblem that Native Americans see as demeaning, then why not a bunch of mostly Native American players as the "Fightin' Whities," with an unflattering emblem of a middle-aged white guy?

If the plan was to make us white folks rethink our ways, it didn't work. The answer to "How would you feel if someone used your ethnic group and a crude stereotype as the emblem of a team?" has been, "Where can I get one of those T-shirts?"

That shouldn't have come as any great surprise, because hardly anybody takes this mascot stuff seriously. For instance, go a few miles south of Greeley, and you're in the farming town of Gilcrest, home of the Valley High School Vikings: the tall, blond, blue-eyed vicious warriors who plundered and pillaged from the Mediterranean to North America and terrorized early England.

Some recent scholarship suggests that the Vikings weren't nearly as warlike as their reputation, that many may have been farmers, rather than raiders. So this school-mascot Viking could be as inaccurate a stereotype as the tomahawk-wielding Native American. But have you ever heard any complaints from anyone of Scandinavian ancestry?

To be sure, others besides Native Americans also find offense in school mascots. Every few years, we endure another mascot battle in Chaffee County. The Buena Vista High School teams are the Demons. Various Christian groups quietly build up steam for a while, then start agitating for a change. The upholders of community traditions successfully resist. The issue goes away for a while, then returns.

The anti-Demons imply that this mascot signifies approval of Satanism and thus some impressionable children might go down the wrong path on that account.

If this did happen, it would be the first time — how many graduates of Alameda or Cotopaxi High School have gone on to careers of piracy? My own career as an Evans Ram ended in 1965 when they closed the school and bused us away to be Greeley West Spartans. The Spartans of antiquity were soldiers in a police state. My class had its share of draft-dodgers. Spartans were renowned for a simple life, so free of luxury that they didn't even use pillows when they slept. Despite three years of Spartan indoctrination, I still like my pillows and other luxuries, and as far as I know, so do my classmates.

Of course, the team name could be sending other messages. In this sensitive age, I am somewhat surprised that I haven't read of any complaints by the abstinence lobby against the Trojans of Longmont, Antonito and elsewhere. Nor have I read of any complaints about the Windsor Wizards, even though it sounds occult and has unsavory Ku Klux Klan connotations.

Most Colorado high school teams have rather generic names that could go anywhere: Wildcats, Eagles, Mustangs, etcetera. But there were some pleasant exceptions on the Colorado High School Activity Association website.

For instance, there are teams that reflect the local economy, either present or past: Aspen Skiers, Brush Beetdiggers, Creede Miners, Idaho Springs Golddiggers.

Others use animal names, but not the usual ones. Limon's Badgers honor a tough critter. South Park High School in Fairplay has Burros, and it fits, since Fairplay has our only monument to a burro and it's the birthplace of pack-burro racing. There are the Lobos of Rocky Mountain High in Fort Collins and the Scorpions of Sand Creek in Colorado Springs. And though it isn't in Colorado, I must mention the name of a team one brother-in-law used to coach, the Gregory Gorillas in South Dakota.

But some names just make you wonder. The Roman Coliseum was known for contests between Christians and lions — so how do we get Christian Lions, from Alpine Christian in Basalt? Our nation is at war with terror

— so will the Palmer High School Terrors in Colorado Springs change their name? What does the ACLU have to say about the Denver East Angels?

Thus there appears to be plenty of fodder for future mascot controversies. Meanwhile, I want one of those Fightin' Whities T-shirts so I can honor my own warrior heritage — remember those brutal savages with blue-painted faces in *Braveheart*?

ALL ABOUT STUPID ZONES
MAY 26, 2002

JUDGING BY SOME RECENT INQUIRIES and current events, it must be time for another explanation of the Stupid Zone, a term I may have invented a few years ago.

The Stupid Zone was proposed as a compromise. On one hand, there is private property with the associated rights to use your land. On the other, people want low taxes.

These two forces collide when rural land is subdivided and people start building houses on five-or 10-acre lots. They bought the land, and they want to exercise their property rights by building houses and moving in.

When they do this, they cause a need for governmental services: road construction and maintenance, school bus routes, law-enforcement investigations and patrols, that sort of thing.

Do they pay their own way? Apparently not. Custer County, in the Wet Mountain Valley of Colorado, was one of the fastest-growing counties in the United States during the 1990s, and most of that growth came in the form of rural residences on multi-acre lots.

So there was a study to determine whether county taxpayers were better or worse off for all this conversion of agricultural land into residential land.

It turned out that for every dollar that local governments (essentially, the county and the school district) received in taxes from agricultural land, they spent only 54 cents on services. But for every tax dollar that came in from these exurban developments, they were spending $1.16 on governmental services.

Thus the working families who live in trailer parks in town are subsidizing the folks who build 3,000-square-foot houses on wooded twenty-acre estates.

But in modern America, that's not an issue that resonates with a public that keeps building sports stadiums to subsidize billionaire team owners and millionaire athletes. Phrasing a question as "why are we taxing the poor to benefit the rich?" just brings accusations that you're trying to start a class war, and we already have other wars in process.

Some of these rural subdivisions are in sensible places, but many are not. Most notably in recent years, some sit in tinderbox forests where devastating fires are merely a question of time.

If a county tried to protect its taxpayers by zoning against such subdivisions, it would impinge on property rights. But if it allows such developments, then it's forcing its taxpayers to subsidize them.

The Stupid Zone is a way to resolve that dilemma, and it would work like this: A county planning office would consult with every sort of expert to determine where it would be stupid to build houses, and people within those zones would be on their own.

Mining historians would map old shafts, stopes and tunnels. Hydrologists would specify flood plains. Foresters would identify wildfire potential. Geologists would be busy with rockslide and mudslide routes, major fault systems and swelling or unstable soils. Biologists would describe bear habitat, porcupine haunts and deer migration routes. It should be noted that most of this information is already available, and so assembling the requisite data shouldn't cost much.

Once it was assembled, the county government would use it to draw Stupid Zones. People would be free to build whatever they wanted in the Stupid Zones, but local government would provide no services other than the absolute minimum.

That is, the sheriff would serve warrants in the Stupid Zone, but there would be no routine patrols or investigations of property crimes. Stupid Zone children could go to school in town, but the district would not concern itself with their transportation. Roads in the Stupid Zone might be maintained or plowed - but by the property owners in the zone, not by the county. Marauding bears or hungry mountain lions in the Stupid Zone would not be a matter of public concern or expense.

When wildfires broke out in the Stupid Zone, the local fire district would build its fire line at the Stupid Zone boundary - you should have the idea by now.

The Stupid Zone lets people do whatever they want with their own property. It also reduces, or perhaps even eliminates, local subsidies for development in Colorado's many Stupid Zones. The state could take it a step further and require insurers to take Stupid Zones into account when setting rates for homeowner policies - shared risk is one thing, but why should you and I pay more just become some people want shake-shingle roofs and wooden decks in a fire-prone forest?

And if the idea caught on, the federal government might adjust its fire fighting and disaster-relief policies - after all, just how many times should we all be expected to pay for rebuilding Florida after a hurricane?

Stupid Zones are a way to respect property rights and to reduce taxes — Republican political themes in a Republican state. So when is some county going to take this sensible step?

WHAT ELSE IS USEFUL FOR SECURITY?
MARCH 4, 2003

IT WAS A PLEASANT SURPRISE RECENTLY when I read that we civilians can assist with Homeland Security in case of an attack.

Not that I'd been real worried about an attack. During World War II, Salida was a significant railroad junction, where trains were dispatched to important defense production facilities like the Monarch Quarry (limestone for the steel mills in Pueblo), Crested Butte (coal for the steel mills in Pueblo) and Climax Molybdenum (molybdenum hardens steel for better armor and cannon barrels). On that account, I have been told, soldiers patrolled constantly to guard against potential sabotage in this area.

But that was sixty years ago, and this time around, Salida is not an important place. It does not have a population concentration, famous people do not cavort here and nothing nearby is of symbolic value (the closest national monument, soon to be a national park, is the Great Sand Dunes, and the dunes are so expendable that they were a leading candidate for the test site for the first atomic bomb in 1945).

Even so, it never hurts to be prepared, and some of us felt rather prescient when the Homeland Security Administration announced that people should keep plastic sheeting and duct tape on hand, so that windows could be sealed if terrorists released anthrax or the like.

This is a familiar drill if you're an economically challenged rural resident. We went through it every fall, along about Halloween, at our first house in Salida (the current house has decent storm windows, except on the back porch, where plastic remains in use).

Granted, we were trying to keep out cold air, rather than anthrax spores, but the principle is the same, and I wish they'd consulted me so I could pass on my experience with what were then known as "Reaganomics Storm Windows."

Initially, I tried the suggested Homeland Security method: plastic on the interior, held by duct tape. It doesn't work well because duct tape is made to be wrapped around ducts; the adhesive doesn't hold well when the tape is run along the flat seam between plastic and wall (or window frame).

Thus, to get everything to stay up, you need a heavy-duty staple gun, and the resulting staple holes, along with the gouge marks that result when you remove staples with fencing pliers, make a mess of the window frame, which means filler and paint when you could be drinking beer with your friends and discussing how safe you feel now that there's a Department of Homeland Security.

Interior plastic is also subject to attack by cats, projectile toys and curious toddlers.

To be sure, some people live in apartments far above ground level, and they'll need to apply plastic on the interior. But for the rest of us, exterior plastic works better. Don't mess with duct tape, except for patching when the wind blows sharp twigs that tear the plastic.

Instead, staple the plastic in place, then frame the plastic with narrow wood slats. If you can afford it, flat-screen molding from the lumberyard works well; if you're scrounging, a cabinet shop's scrap pile is a good place to start.

This will make almost any drafty old house somewhat secure, but it raises a question I haven't seen in the security information. If you make the place so tight that spores can't enter, won't you eventually run out of oxygen and die of suffocation? And if you're getting fresh air from some exterior source, aren't you still in danger?

Better not to wonder about such matters, I suppose. Instead, I pondered whether any of our other small- town ways might, like window plastic, be of some use for homeland security.

There are many woodpiles, for instance. Most are neatly stacked, but there are a quite a few like mine.

Having cordwood on hand does make you feel more secure about getting through a utility disruption that could result from terrorism. But I can't imagine this administration promoting wood heat for homeland security, since good Americans should rely on multinational oil companies.

Some of my fellow Salidans store old tires in their yards. I had thought it was just because they didn't care to spend the $3 tire-disposal fee, but then again, if the terrorists launch a mosquito attack, the tires could be ignited to produce smudge to repel the insects.

Many local yards also have junkpiles, usually near the alley. And for all I know, there might come a time when our homeland security will require half a bedframe, a rusted tractor seat, a cream separator, a wheelbarrow that has no wheel or a gas barbecue with a dead burner. Not that I know how these items might improve Homeland Security, but until recently, I didn't know that plastic on our windows could have anything to do with national defense, either.

SILLY LAWS KEEP COMING
FEBRUARY 13, 2005

WHEN DEMOCRATS TOOK OVER our legislature, I had hopes that our General Assembly would focus on significant matters like higher education and transportation, rather than protecting children from displays of racy DVD covers or requiring libraries to filter Internet access.

But the first spate of proposed laws has not supported those hopes. One bill, introduced after two college students in Colorado died of alcohol overdoses last fall, would require the registration of beer kegs.

If you bought a keg, you'd have to show identification. The store would record your personal data, along with the keg's registration number and related information. If that keg were later found at a party where minors had been drinking, then presumably you'd be in trouble. But if the idea is to reduce the number of deaths from alcohol overdose, keg registration will be counterproductive. That's because it's so difficult to kill yourself just by drinking too much beer.

People vary greatly in their tolerance to alcohol, but on average a blood-alcohol concentration of 0.4 percent is lethal (by state law, you're too drunk to drive if it exceeds 0.08 percent).

To reach that deadly level, a 150-pound person would have to drink twenty-five 12-ounce servings of mass-market beer in four hours. That's about 2.3 gallons, nearly ten times the capacity of the average human stomach, which is about one quart.

To be sure, all that beer doesn't stay in the stomach during the binge, but enough does so that by about the fifth beer during the first hour, you're going to have trouble getting it down, and consumption gets even more difficult after that. Thus, it's hard to die of alcohol poisoning with beer. (You can, of course, kill yourself or others by driving under the influence, but that's a different matter.)

By contrast, a quart of eighty-proof whiskey has about the same amount of alcohol as those twenty-five servings of beer, and consuming that quart over four hours does not come anywhere close to stretching the stomach's capacity.

From what I've read, distilled spirits, not beer, were the major factors in the two alcohol-poisoning cases in Colorado last fall, and that fits with the facts of alcohol and human physiology.

Thus registering kegs is not going to prevent such tragedies, and it might even encourage them. The law will discourage keg purchases, which means people are more likely to buy distilled spirits. And it's the spirits, not the kegs, that have been lethal.

It would make more sense to register the sales of Everclear, orange vodka, peppermint schnapps, Jagermeister and similar concoctions that hardly anyone touches after turning twenty-one.

Another bad bill in the new legislative session would require employers to give unpaid time off to parents to attend their children's school functions. The sponsor called it "public policy that actually helps families."

Sure. I enjoy spending time with my own kids, but that pleasure seldom extends to other people's children, especially when they come in herds. And it's even worse at an amateurish production in an overcrowded school facility with uncomfortable chairs where you're sitting behind eight or ten folks who stand to capture every precious moment with their video cameras.

Often I was glad to have the excuse that "Daddy's got to work" when one of these torture sessions was scheduled, and I cannot believe that reasonable people would vote to take that away.

Time off to picnic with your kids, or fly kites, explore ghost towns, ride bikes, visit museums, just hang out, or do something as a family — that would help families, and thus might be worth the hassle of adding yet another law to the books.

But taking away an employed parent's right not to attend school functions? Not only is this cruel, but it will put sensible parents in terrible moods, and that cannot be good for families. It makes even less sense than registering beer kegs when it's the hard liquor that kills college students.

The War on a Plant
April 12, 2009

Historians of the future will doubtless marvel that a great and powerful republic, founded in part on "liberty and the pursuit of happiness" but now suffering from difficult economic times would waste billions of dollars every year in a futile war against a humble plant.

That plant, of course, is hemp — source of oil, fiber and a mild psychoactive drug. It's so mild that in all of history, no one has ever died from a marijuana overdose.

And those who used it in their youth, like the three most recent American presidents (Clinton claimed he "didn't inhale," Bush was "young and foolish" in his jejune days, and Obama confessed that "pot had helped" during his youth), somehow managed to go on to reasonably productive lives.

So why is the stuff still illegal?

For one thing, there's an immense federal bureaucracy, the Drug Enforcement Administration, which naturally seeks to stay in business. As long as pot is illegal, the DEA has plenty of work. And when the need arises for a headline to show that the DEA is on the ball, its agents can always drive to some home that uses too much electricity, shoot the dogs, kick in the door, and announce that American youth are protected because it just seized plants with an estimated street value of $4.2 gazillion.

For another, there's our pharmaceutical industry, a major source of campaign contributions. The pill-makers buy candidates so they can protect their revenue streams.

Now, it might be too much to expect the federal government to move sensibly here. There are, after all, two wars and a crumbling economy to contend with. But Colorado could help itself by legalizing the cultivation, sale and use of marijuana with a reasonable excise tax of $25 an ounce. It would save money in several ways, like lower law-enforcement costs, as well as a reduction in the prison population. Further, the corruption and violence associated with black markets should diminish.

More money would circulate in our state, as Colorado hemp farmers received money now going to Mexican drug cartels. Profitable farms mean that open space gets preserved through market mechanisms, rather than taxes and zoning. Further, it might enhance tourism, at least until other states catch on.

One possible snag is the federal government. No matter how sensible we make our state laws, there would still be draconian and moronic federal laws enforced by federal agents.

So initially, the marijuana excise tax proceeds should go to our state attorney general's office, with instructions that the money be used to defend all Coloradans charged with marijuana violations that are crimes under federal law but not under our enlightened state law.

In other words, every "probable cause" for a search warrant would be vigorously contested. The chain of evidence would come under intense scrutiny. The credibility of informants and agents would be subject to brutal cross-examination.

Every such trial — our tenacious defense teams would never plea-bargain — would be a grinding ordeal for the U.S. Attorney's office. The federal Department of Justice would soon move its prosecutorial resources away from pot and toward real crimes that people care about.

The downside? Maybe a few more lazy potheads munching junk food. But in today's economy, there aren't jobs for them anyway, so where's the harm to society?

Contrast that with the benefits of reduced spending on cops and prisons, a boost to Colorado agriculture, and increased revenue for our hard-pressed state government, if we'd just give up on this silly war against a plant.

WHO YOU CALLING ELITE?
JANUARY 29, 2012

UNDERSTANDING CURRENT EVENTS can be difficult. For instance, our statehouse Republicans, like their colleagues throughout the country, clearly want to preserve my freedom to die of some chronic disease. Thus they want to see the Affordable Care Act repealed before it goes into full effect.

But Republicans in our House of Representatives couldn't content themselves with a resolution in favor of more death and suffering among the economically challenged. No, they had to pass a resolution calling for a national convention to propose a constitutional amendment to repeal the Affordable Care Act.

One GOP argument against the law is that it's unconstitutional. Since courts will act on that, why would Republicans think an amendment was necessary? To make it double-dog super-duper unconstitutional? Who knows?

But the sponsor of the resolution, Representative David Balmer of Centennial, said it was about saving jobs that Colorado would lose under the 2010 federal Affordable Care Act. Good to see somebody cares about keeping Colorado's embalmers and gravediggers at work. Or maybe they just want the federal constitution to be as cluttered and incomprehensible as our state constitution.

Even as it is, though, the federal constitution must be difficult to understand because Representative Michele Bachmann, back when she was in the running, promised that, if elected, "I will repeal Obamacare."

Under our federal constitution with its separation of powers, presidents don't get to repeal or enact laws. That's a legislative function performed by Congress. You'd think Bachmann might have read up about the job before she decided to apply for it.

And then there's another applicant, Newt Gingrich, who recently threw some raw meat to the mob with a few snarls at "the elite media." I'll grant that there are some elite media in this country. For instance, in 2005 *The Wall Street Journal* bragged to potential advertisers that its readers "have an average household income of $234,000 and average nearly $2.1 million in net worth."

In other words, these "affluent individual consumers" are part of the American elite, yet I never hear Republicans criticizing *The Wall Street Journal* as part of the "elite media."

Instead, Gingrich used the term for CNN, whose reporter asked the question, or ABC, which aired the interview with a former Mrs. Gingrich. Or maybe it was both. But how the networks of Larry King and "Desperate Housewives" can be "elitist" is beyond me. Both want high ratings and that means aiming at the lowest common denominator. Networks that vie to bring us the latest in celebrity rehab are not elite media.

And of course, all these elite media cover up scandals involving Democrats. So it must be mental telepathy that told me about Anthony Weiner, John Edwards, William Jefferson and Elliot Spitzer.

Of course, if you forsake the elites and aim at the great general public, as most broadcasters and newspapers do, then you can run afoul of another Republican, Sarah Palin, who'll bad-mouth you for being part of the "Lame Stream Media," a take-off on "mainstream media." Now it would seem to me that "mainstream" is by definition something for most Americans, not just the elite.

Now I have to confess that I long aspired to join "the media elite" and enjoy the money and influence of a George Will or Rush Limbaugh. But like many youthful ambitions, it never happened and probably won't. But I have a request: The next time somebody wants to call me part of the elite, please send enough money to make it true.

Pets, Small-Town Living, and Extreme Weather

For the past decade or so, many of us around here have joked that we really needed a good old-fashioned hard winter. Heavy snows would improve Colorado's erratic water supply, of course, but our motives were not so generous. We figured that a few months of arctic misery would drive out the lightweights who migrated here in recent years. There would be many mornings when their cars would not start. And even if the car did start, there would be nowhere to go, on account of closed roads. ... Have that happen about once a month from November to April, and these pantywaist newcomers would be gone by Memorial Day. Meanwhile, we veteran Coloradans, a tough and hardy bunch, would be sitting comfortably with our woodpiles and canned-food stores, enjoying quiet evenings of cribbage by lantern light.

FINALLY, A WAY TO PROFIT FROM AN ANNOYING CAT
FEBRUARY 25, 2002

SCIENTISTS IN TEXAS have cloned a common house cat, and they see great commercial potential in the process.

After all, America teems with people who have more money than good sense, and these folks might pay handsomely for a genetic copy of Puff (although these critters will more likely have names like Reginald Oglethorpe van Schuyler XIV) as the beloved family pet enters its dotage.

We have two cats. One is only six or seven years old. She's fluffy and gray and resembles a dust bunny more than anything feline. Her name was Princess Joan when some friends gave her to us. I insisted we change it, because I'd feel stupid standing on the porch calling out, "Here, Princess," in the requisite falsetto.

Granted, a name is as irrelevant to a cat as the Bill of Rights is to John Ashcroft. Cats operate in blissful ignorance of anything you say, so the name is only for your own convenience. For several days, we struggled to rechristen this companion animal until Martha had a stroke of genius: The Cat Formerly Known As Princess.

It's a mouthful, but it works, since we seldom need to employ it because she turned out to be an indoor cat. Since she's perfectly useless, I can't imagine why anyone would want to clone her. But it's different with our other cat, Hector. If they want to clone him, I want a piece of the action, because he's got some valuable DNA.

For one thing, he resembles a celebrity. He's mostly black with white paws and some white around his lower jaw and throat, which makes him almost a dead ringer for Socks, who was once the First Cat of the United States.

Socks hasn't been in the news much lately since the Clintons gave him away when they left the White House, but suppose Hillary runs for president in 2004? Republican propagandists will hasten to portray her as a witch. Witches always appear with cats, and what better cat for the attack commercials than one who looks like Socks, who you could get from our Hector's DNA?

Or maybe not. Cat coloration, from what I read, is affected by factors other than genetics.

But there are other valuable genes in Hector. He's now seventeen years old. That's nowhere close to the longevity record, but consider this: He's an outdoor cat, and I just read that indoor cats live four times longer than outdoor cats. By this logic, a Hector clone, if you kept him inside, would live to be at least sixty-eight-years old — pretty much a lifetime cat.

Hector's double helix contains another valuable genetic component, one that could restore Enron to financial health: The colder it is outside, the longer he stands in the open doorway, trying to decide whether he really wants to go out. You can guess the effect on the utility bill.

An ailing natural-gas supplier merely needs to generate several million Hector clones, then plant the cute little kittens in alleys behind homes with soft-hearted children and soft-headed parents who eventually say, "OK, you can keep him," after the thousandth heart-rending plea.

No matter how well those people insulate their houses and practice conservation, their gas bills will quintuple due to the indecisive pet standing in the open door on subzero days and nights.

I'd almost bet this was the topic of those meetings between Enron and Vice President Dick Cheney that the White House is refusing to talk about.

I've tried to get around this financial drain by firing up the airtight wood-burner in the living room. However, I spend most of the day toiling in a back room, so I'm not devout about tending the front-room fire.

Or I wouldn't be, except that Hector functions as an ambulatory thermostat. If he wakes from a two-hour nap near the stove and is the least bit chilly, he comes back and gently bites my ankles until I've restored the fire to a level that will sustain another two-hour feline siesta. Millions of other wood-burners would doubtless purchase Hector clones to maintain their home-heat levels.

And if some of his DNA could be transferred to humans, the stuff should sell better than Viagra. We got Hector castrated at the proper age. The veterinarian assured us he would henceforth be fat and lie around the house.

Instead, he's sleek and adventurous. In the years since his neutering, he's lost an eye, the tips of both ears and the end of his tail, and on several occasions has needed stitches for gouges on his scalp. His post-midnight caterwauling with neighborhood females has awakened us on many summer nights. Some men would pay plenty for this.

For years, I've thought of Hector as a nuisance, a marginal improvement on the mice we might have if we didn't have him (as opposed to mice, cats don't defecate in your cereal, but that's about the only way they're an improvement).

But after pondering the implications of a cat-cloning industry, I now see that Hector is a valuable collection of useful genetic traits, and I'm looking forward to a lucrative future of collecting royalties.

RESPONSIBILITY FOR THE DROUGHT
MAY 5, 2002

THE TROUBLE WITH DROUGHTS is that they're a chronic condition, rather than an acute injury, and so they're hard to talk about in the same way that we talk about other dire events that happen at a specific time.

For instance, anybody who was in Salida a year ago will remember the Great Dump of '01 — five feet of snow at the start of May. That's a specific event.

Likewise the Great Blizzard of 1949 that struck the Great Plains of Colorado and Wyoming. I wasn't born when it hit, but my parents and their friends and relatives all had stories about it, like how my Uncle Jim went to check on a neighbor and disappeared incommunicado for a fortnight or so, and when he finally called home, he was running a road grader somewhere in western Nebraska, 200 miles away.

Floods are also specific events; my Fort Morgan relatives often spoke of the Flood of 1965, which also struck Denver. It started as a thunderstorm on the Palmer Divide, which swelled Plum Creek to Nile proportions, and consequently the South Platte roared through Denver.

But that storm also poured water into Bijou and Kiowa creeks, which headwater in the same area but join the South Platte just above Fort Morgan, so the river was several miles wide there. For many years thereafter, a visit to Fort Morgan involved a tour of flood scars, as well as much local bragging about the old concrete-arch Rainbow Bridge, which survived the flood that took out its newer neighbor.

Fires, tornadoes, blizzards, floods — they come in fury and depart quickly, and leave indelible memories. But droughts just sneak in and persist, so you there's no single event to remember.

Perhaps that's because it's hard to notice the onset of a drought. As in 1977 and 1981, this year's drought began last fall with reports from the ski industry that some resorts might have to postpone their openings.

But the ski industry is always complaining about something — if it isn't a lack of snow, it's that the state doesn't plow the snow off the highways quickly enough, or that storms delay air traffic, or that the depressed Canadian dollar is attracting skiers to British Columbia, or that Utah got all the publicity this year, that visitors are spending their money in lodging and retail establishments not owned by the resort corporation, etcetera.

So, it's a lot of work to find something that might matter to the rest of us in all that whining, and thus it's no wonder that we don't notice the onset of a drought in the same way that we observe the arrival of a flood or blizzard.

The next signal that a drought is upon us comes from the Water Buffaloes. They will announce that we need more storage because Two Forks and Narrows dams weren't built as once proposed, and so water that should belong to Colorado unfortunately obeys the law of gravity instead of sensibly following the Love Doctrine (named for the late Governor John A. Love, who once observed that "in Colorado, water flows uphill toward money"). However, the Water Buffaloes are always telling us we need new reservoirs — if not for storage during dry years, then for flood-protection during wet years, and for irrigation and recreation in the middling years. Indeed, it's impossible to imagine a situation that would not inspire them to call for new reservoirs, so the ordinary citizen can be forgiven for not noticing the arrival of a drought.

How to respond to a drought? We'll be asked to conserve water in our homes. But since agriculture uses about 85 percent of the water in Colorado, a few bricks in our toilet tanks aren't going to make much difference.

In ancient times, people had a perfectly sensible response to drought — they moved from the dry place to a wetter one, as with the Anasazi, who apparently abandoned Mesa Verde and Chaco Canyon for pueblos along the Rio Grande.

However, that practical response would just depress the real estate market. So we can take another tack and look for something to blame — global warming, ozone depletion, deforestation, etcetera. That will take a while, though, and innocent people could get hurt in the process. So as a public service, I will step forward and accept responsibility.

Here's how I did it. Our house was built in two parts. The one-story back part, with a normal pitched roof, was erected in 1885. The two-story front part, circa 1908, has a flat roof. It leaked, as did the back roof near the joint with the front.

We'd get it patched frequently by Greg Truitt, a local contractor who has a journalism degree but fortunately found a career of much greater benefit to society. He enjoyed the steady income from our dripping roof, but last fall he said that it was reaching a point past patching.

Since one reason to have a house is to stay out of the weather, and the other reason is to keep vast sectors of the American economy in operation, we borrowed money and got a new membrane roof over the afflicted portions of the house.

And of course, not one drop of water has fallen from the sky since then. It's my fault, I know, but what can I do about it now?

EVERY DOG HAS HER DAY
NOVEMBER 12, 2002

I'M THE FAMILY DOG, a female coal-black chow-husky mix. Today is Ed's birthday (he's almost seven and a half in dog years), and so he's taking some time off and asked me to fill in for him.

My name is Ted or Teddy, or maybe something else. To honor my chow heritage, I pay no attention to what they call me. If I can hear my leash jingle, which means it's time for a walk, or if I smell some food at hand, then I respond. Otherwise, why bother? It could be a bath or a trip to the vet, or maybe being imprisoned in the side yard because they're expecting company.

They yell a lot when the weather's nice and they're sitting on the porch swing and somebody walks or drives by with a fellow canine. I run up and down along the fence and bark loudly. They holler at me.

But I think they're yelling for the benefit of other people, not really to tell me anything. The way I interpret their barking, they're trying to say "We don't really approve of our dog doing this, and we hope you don't hold this against us." Whatever. It seems to make them feel better.

Their daughter Abby named me Teddy because she thought I looked like a Teddy Bear when I was a puppy. People still tell me I look a lot like a bear. Ed says that's a good thing because I'm his entire home-security system, and maybe my fearsome ursine appearance will scare away bill collectors, missionaries, polltakers, siding salesmen and other nuisances. That's what he calls them — most of them pet me and tell me how cute I am, so I think they are pretty good people.

He keeps talking about training me to go for their throats whenever they get past the gate, but I know that's just talk. I'm an old dog, born in 1989, and I'm too old to learn new tricks, even if I could learn tricks.

They tried to educate me. At first it was worse than annoying, somebody holding a piece of food up and saying things I didn't understand, like "sit," "lie down," "shake hands" and "roll over."

But I finally figured out how to respond. If the food is up there in their forepaws and they're telling me to do something, I sit. Then I lie down, and roll over, and keep doing silly things until they give me the food. I've got them so well trained now that they usually drop the food to me as soon as I sit, and I don't have to go through the whole moronic drill.

Another thing I've figured out: Don't fight with cats; work with them. I like cat food a lot better than dog food. So Hector and I work together. He meows till his bowl is filled. He eats a bite or two, then goes back to sleeping by the stove. I eat the rest. We do this eight or ten times a day, and we're both happy.

But there are a lot of other things about humans that I just don't understand. Both Ed and Martha have these really boring jobs, mostly sitting around staring at screens and wiggling their paws trying to change what's on the screen. And even though they're bipeds, they could have good jobs.

Every Friday morning, right around sunrise, there are these guys that come down the alley and tip over every garbage can. They toss all this great stuff into a big truck, and I'm sure they go where they can play with it and roll in it. Now there's a good job. They do take me for a walk just about every day. But they haven't got a clue about what's going on. They'll stop and look at some shop window, or at somebody's garden — real boring stuff.

But when they're around something interesting, like a fresh territorial marking that says, "I am Mighty Wotan, supreme stud of the 300 Block of Park Avenue, and if you want a really good time, come down to the second coal shed and scratch twice at the fence," they don't even notice.

If we meet people they know, often they'll stop and talk. But if we meet somebody I know, and we just want to sniff each other and catch up on neighborhood gossip — they'll try to drag me away.

It really isn't fair. I indulge them in their social interests when we're out, but they keep me on a tight leash. Maybe I'll show them someday, though. I've heard that, back when I was a puppy, a book by some pooch named "Millie the White House Dog" outsold anything they ever wrote. So my day might come. Then again, I get to eat and sleep and play about as much as I want to, and when you get right down to it, what else matters?

Stress and the City
October 28, 2003

Many of my friends in Salida look upon a trip to Denver as something worse than a root canal, an IRS audit or an announcement that their in-laws are coming for a two-week visit. They worry about the traffic and the noise, the air quality, the panhandlers, the parking hassles, the metropolitan crime rate — there are reasons, after all, that some of us are country mice and other folks are city mice.

So if they could vote in the city, they'd probably support an initiative on the current Denver ballot, the "Initiative for Safety through Peace."

It's the product of Jeff Peckman, along with various activists and members of the Natural Law Party. They needed 2,458 signatures to get it on the ballot last summer, and they just made it, with 2,462 signatures.

Even though the Denver City Council didn't really want to put it on the ballot — perhaps out of fear that the city would become a national laughingstock — the city's election law left no choice.

So Denver voters will get to decide whether the city government should "ensure public safety by increasing peacefulness — that is, by defusing political, religious and ethnic tension both locally and globally — through the identification and implementation of any systematic, stress-reducing techniques or programs."

If this should pass, it shouldn't hurt the city's important branding-and-marketing project. After all, Boulder — where pets are officially "companion animals" and owners are "guardians" — is well known nationally without any expensive marketing program.

The same holds for other cities. Aspen is at least four kinds of strange, and everybody knows about it. San Francisco is seriously weird, and Los Angeles enjoys forms of dementia we haven't even imagined. An eccentric reputation shouldn't hurt Denver — indeed, it could help — in its efforts to attract tourists, residents and business.

However, I have to question the need for the stress-reduction initiative. If you make certain personal adjustments, then a visit to Denver need not be all that stressful, even when you're coming from the backwaters of Colorado.

Traffic? It is stressful indeed when I'm driving my old Blazer, with its standard transmission and minimal configuration. But we've also got a little car with air conditioning, an automatic transmission and a good stereo. Thus it's easy to relax; after all, you're not going anywhere because you're in gridlock. Plus, it's tiny and sits so low that we can't see over or around all the spewts. The less we can see, the less we have to worry about.

Noise? Sirens are so rare here that we usually run outdoors to see what's going on when we hear one. So Denver's abundance of sirens generated stress until I remembered that Denver drivers pay no attention to sirens, so why should I?

Parking? This used to make me nervous, because I was never sure where we could or couldn't park, especially when our younger daughter Abby attended the University of Denver. The parking stress got even more intense when she moved to Capitol Hill. But there are ways to adjust. Now I just figure I'm going to get a parking ticket on every trip to the city. That assumption reduces the stress. And if I don't get one? Then there's a pleasant surprise.

Police? There was a time when I worried about Denver's trigger-happy police department, fearing that I might match some profile, or back up at the wrong time in the wrong parking lot, or be visiting a friend when the drug squad got the wrong address. However, District Attorney Bill Ritter assures us that the police acted properly in every killing. After I learned that, I felt much better.

To be sure, Denver's municipal government could work to reduce stress. But reducing stress is not what governments do. The more stressful things there are, the more government we think we need. More government means more confusing laws, tickets and sirens. It can never mean less stress.

Peckman and his colleagues may mean well, but their goals can never be shared by the city. Besides, you don't need to take up transcendental meditation to reduce your personal stress levels. You just have to learn to see the parking ticket as a personalized souvenir from your peaceful journey to the enlightened city.

Salida Outed by Outside
July 18, 2004

Salida has been "discovered" again, this time by *Outside* magazine, whose August edition proclaimed Salida to be one of "The New Best Places to Live and Play." There are twenty of these "Dream Towns + Adventure Hideouts & Sweet Land Deals" that are "underpopulated and undiscovered slices of paradise" which offer "a lifetime of wild fun."

Perhaps they were undiscovered last month. But we were already among "The 100 Best Small Art Towns in America," and we have also been discovered by various publications devoted to mountain biking and kayaking.

The *Outside* piece was reasonably accurate, as opposed to some of the other recent discovery accounts; one put us in the San Juan Mountains, which are at least 100 miles away, and another gave highway directions that involved unpaved back roads through the subdivisions on the south edge of South Park.

To gauge local reactions to this *Outside* piece, earlier this month I attended a meeting whose very nature indicates how much Salida has changed in recent years: a single-malt scotch tasting. It's not that I have any special affection for scotch whisky, be it single or multiple malt. My tastes in hard liquor run to an occasional shot of rye, whatever rotgut Kirby Perschbacher has in his pocket flask when we run into each other at various events and, from Thanksgiving to Christmas, cheap rum with eggnog. While other tasters were murmuring comments like "good sooty aftertaste" or "clean fruity aroma," I was thinking, "I sure hope I'll be able to walk the five blocks home after we're done here."

I had expected the gathering to be rather snobbish, but as *Outside* noted, Salida is "sweetly unpretentious," and after a few comments on the contents of the two bottles, the topic moved to Salida's discovery by *Outside*. My fellow tasters generally agreed that this was a good thing because it meant we might be able to sell our real estate here for a lot more than we paid for it years ago, and that's about the only way to make money around here.

As *Outside* noted, this is a great place "to Live and Play," not to live and work. There aren't many jobs here, and most of them don't offer much in the way of pay or benefits. Many people who work here can't afford to live here. Property prices are driven, not by the local market, but by *Outside* factors — the growing attractiveness of this area to a leisure class. (Please note that I do not want to disparage the leisure class; I've been sick of working since I first punched a time clock when I was thirteen years old, and I have long aspired to join the leisure class.)

A decade ago, I would have worried about the effects of *Outside* publicity. But the things I would have worried about then have already happened, and this remains a pretty good place to live. Except I couldn't afford to live here if I hadn't bought in a long time ago, and like many of my friends, I wonder how much longer I will be able to afford to live here.

It all seems so strange. Fifteen years ago, we bought a bigger house. We put our old one on the market for $28,500 for nearly three years. We never got a single offer.

In those days, a lot of us felt we were marooned in Salida because we couldn't sell our houses, and so we worked to make our situation more tolerable.

Some of us agitated for improved parks and trails, others labored to expand the library, and bring in public radio, and convert an old generating plant into a theater, and dozens of other efforts which, we thought, would give us a better town to live in.

Apparently, we did a pretty good job with this ramshackle old railroad town. Trouble is, most of us are working too much these days to enjoy it.

WHEN A TRAP WORKS
OCTOBER 5, 2004

OUR ALLEY CAT (her name is "Ferrill," pronounced "feral") produced three kittens in April. Ever since she quit lactating, we've been trying to catch her so we can take her to the vet for spaying. She's fast and nimble, so we seldom even get a hand on her. A couple of times, we've grasped her, but she twists and claws so fiercely that we haven't been able to hold her for long enough to shove her into a transport cage.

We were out of ideas, so I called the Arkansas Valley Humane Society. They suggested a live trap, and they would rent us one for only $1 a day.

AVHS is a fine organization, but it's twenty-five miles away in Buena Vista, and I didn't want to drive up there if I could avoid it. Gasoline is expensive, and some of the money may well go to a nation that harbors terrorists, or even to Bush campaign contributors, and the Republicans must be getting through to me on the importance of values and respecting them in daily life.

So I called around town, looking for a live trap to rent. The vet's office didn't have any, but said the Salida Police might. It took several days to learn that the Salida Police didn't. That made me feel better. Any police department that needs the better part of a week to determine whether it has some live traps in inventory is unlikely to be a threat to our rights and liberties.

At AVHS, all the small traps had been rented, so we got a big one — a galvanized mesh cage about a foot square and four feet long. As recommended, we baited it with peanut butter on the trip bar and canned cat food at the back.

The first night, we put it atop the picnic table, one of Ferrill's favorite haunts. The trap was empty the next morning. I put it on the patio Tuesday night.

I rose before dawn Wednesday, and looked out the kitchen window as soon as there was enough light. The good news was that the trap had caught something. The bad news was that it was bigger than our cat, sported white stripes on shiny black fur, and lifted its bushy tail to demonstrate its annoyance, something my nose noticed about ten seconds later.

What to do with a trapped skunk? It was too early to call friends or the Division of Wildlife, so I poked around the Internet.

The most common advice: Get an old tarp or rug. Hold it before you, so that it's what gets sprayed. Throw it over the trap. The resulting darkness will settle the skunk. After a few minutes, put the tarp-wrapped cage in the bed of a pickup, drive about ten miles out of town, and release the beast.

I don't have a pickup, and this didn't sound like good cargo for the inside of my Blazer. I planned to call a friend with a pickup once the hour got more civilized, but in the interim, I found more skunk data on the Web.

The Colorado State University Extension Service advised that in our state, there are only two things you can legally do with a trapped skunk: kill it, or release it where you caught it. Pickup rides to the boondocks are illegal.

Aside from the illegality of discharging a firearm inside the city limits, I'm not a good shot. Besides, skunks have tiny heads, although this one's was big enough for a mouth with many sharp teeth. It reared and hissed every time I stepped onto the patio, and I hastened back inside when it started to turn around.

Finally I grabbed an old rug from the shed, held it like a body shield during my approach, and covered the trap. After making sure that our stupid dog (after her third skunking, you'd think she would have learned about certain small mammals) could not get near the spot, I opened the trap door and ran back inside the house. Half an hour later, I gingerly lifted the rug to see that the skunk had departed.

Several days thereafter, my contractor friend Kirby Perschbacher came by with a load of firewood. I told him how I'd almost called him to borrow a pickup, before I learned that the excursion would have been illegal.

"Too bad you read that," he said. "Because there must be plenty of good skunk habitat up in those new gated developments a few miles out of town. It would have been an honor to help you relocate that critter."

We wondered if that's why Colorado now forbids the transport of captured skunks, and shifted our conversation to more pleasant topics. George Bush was slipping in the polls, the apple tree had produced a bumper crop, and there was sufficient rye whiskey on hand for me to forget, however briefly, that Ferrill must still be caught. Somehow.

HOW WE REMEMBER THE YEARS
DECEMBER 28, 2004

TO JUDGE BY MOST SEASONAL COMMENTARY, people remember years by momentous global and national events, but I don't think that's true. For instance, I can remember that some American official said that we were seeing the light at the end of the tunnel in Vietnam, but I cannot remember whether he said it in 1964, 1965, 1966, 1967, 1968, 1969, 1970, 1971 or 1972.

Similarly, I suspect, most Americans in decades hence will remember that some politician stood under a "Mission Accomplished" sign while proclaiming that major combat operations were over in Iraq, but will not remember whether he said it in 2003, 2004, 2005, 2006, etcetera.

In our own lives, we remember years differently — births and deaths, moves, job changes, droughts, blizzards. In our house, this will likely be remembered as the year we lost our old dog. She went by "Ted," which was short for "Teddy," because she looked like a teddy bear when we got her from the "please take one of these adorable puppies that somebody left here" pen at the veterinarian's office in May of 1989.

They said she was a collie mix, but as matters developed, this caused me to lose some respect for the staff at the vet's office. As our Teddy Bear grew, no dog ever looked less like a collie. She looked like, well, a bear. She also had a black tongue, and when we feared that this indicated some expensive disease, we made inquiries and learned that this meant that Ted was a chow, or at least a chow mix.

The small-town gossip mill soon satisfied our curiosity. Some people on the west edge of Salida had a purebred husky female who loved to run figure eights in the street, just like our dog when she got out. Their neighbors had a purebred chow-chow male. The resulting half-breed litter was an affront to the husky owner, who deposited them at the vet's office.

Huskies I knew about, but a chow was a novelty. I've had dogs that were bred to retrieve or to herd, and I've known dogs bred to hunt, point, pull and the like. But our chow mix had no useful skills. Throw a stick, and she might go get it or she might not. And if she got it, she might come back or might not. Call her, and she might come. Walk with her in the country, and she might stay with you.

But she had a stout, well-muscled body, which led me to believe that long ago in China, chows were bred for just that — chow. Her eating habits supported the theory that they were bred to be fattened. She voraciously consumed anything she thought was food. Once when I was loading charcoal into a grill, she sat there and begged. I tossed her a briquette; she ran off and ate it, and came back for more.

She had thick, black fur that was like Velcro, in that everything stuck to it. We joked that we never had to rake the yard in the fall, because all the leaves came in on Ted, and we could just sweep the hall. She hated to be combed or washed — her first act, after every bath, was to run out into the yard and roll around until she got comfortably filthy. It surprised me greatly to learn that Martha Stewart kept chows, but then again, she could probably afford to hire a full-time groomer for each dog, and that's what it would take to maintain a chow to her standards.

Our chow was scruffy, but she was good-natured and loved to be petted — and she got plenty of that from neighborhood children, bouncing on all-fours to greet them as though she had springs on her feet.

As Ted aged, she bounced less, and we saw it was harder and harder for her to get up. We feared the day she couldn't stand, and dreaded the decision we'd have to make then. But it never came to that. On December 7, we could tell she was ailing, for her breath came hard and she moaned a lot.

We thought about taking her to the vet, but she hated riding in cars. She was walking around that afternoon until sundown, when she curled up in front of the house, went to sleep, and never woke up.

So I'll remember 2004 as the year we lost the old dog. And I also hope I can remember her loyalty, affection and general enthusiasm for life, virtues which should not be confined to canines.

BE CAREFUL WHAT YOU WISH FOR
JANUARY 9, 2005

FOR THE PAST DECADE OR SO, many of us around here have joked that we really needed a good old-fashioned hard winter. Heavy snows would improve Colorado's erratic water supply, of course, but our motives were not so generous.

We figured that a few months of arctic misery would drive out the light-weights who migrated here in recent years. There would be many mornings when their cars would not start. And even if the car did start, there would be nowhere to go, on account of closed roads. If the roads were plowed, they would still be as slick as greased glass, so that the borrow ditches exerted an irresistible attractive force.

Staying home would be the sensible option, except that the propane tank was almost empty, as was the larder. There is no running water because the pipes are frozen. The electricity, despite the valiant efforts of the local co-op, would arrive sporadically, and attempts to call the county dispatcher and demand immediate emergency plowing would be met with sarcastic laughter, if the call even went through.

Have that happen about once a month from November to April, and these pantywaist newcomers would be gone by Memorial Day. Meanwhile, we veteran Coloradans, a tough and hardy bunch, would be sitting comfortably with our woodpiles and canned-food stores, enjoying quiet evenings of crib-bage by lantern light.

We do appear to be getting such a winter now, with storm after storm, and many sub-zero nights, but the rest of this montane reverie is mere fantasy.

For one thing, winter hits much harder on the plains than in the mountains. Most of last week, there were frequent announcements on radio and TV of schools delayed or closed on account of the storms. They were out on the plains; in 125 years of operation, Leadville's public schools have never closed on account of snow.

Leadville is the highest city in the U.S. (Alma, about fifteen miles away on the other side of Mosquito Pass, is the highest town), and note that a Fourth of July baseball game there was once canceled on account of snow. Miners there used to joke that "I sure hope summer comes on a weekend this year, because I had to work through it last year."

But if there's any part of Colorado with a climate designed to discourage the faint-hearted, it's the high plains, not the mountains. They're hotter in the summer and there's nothing to stop the wind in the winter. The high plains were the last part of Colorado to be settled, and they may be the first part to be abandoned — Baca, Kiowa, Otero, Sedgwick and Washington counties all have fewer people now than they did in 1980.

Back to the mountains, where even if you think you're prepared, you're not. I had a good supply of firewood to feed the air-tight stove in our living room, a device with only one flaw: Productivity suffers greatly because I'm tempted to relax next to the warm fire after pushing one of the cats out of her customary place, and sometimes hours pass before I return to work.

The woodpile is back by the alley. Just about every afternoon, I go there with a wheelbarrow that I fill with wood, splitting it then as necessary. Then I wheel the load to the front porch, convenient to the stove. This route takes me on the shady north side of the house, where the wheelbarrow has packed the snow into a foot-high ice ridge that probably won't melt until March. Footing is perilous, and even if I can keep myself from tipping, the wheelbarrow often does.

Thoughts of tropical beaches appear. Then I think of the tragic tsunami pictures and realize they have their problems, too.

This winter it has dawned on me. The people who live in cities and brave daily commutes, long drives to ski resorts, ice-covered freeways, constant highway construction, frequent changes in jobs and residence — they're the tough ones. Up here, we don't adapt well to change and surprise, like this miserably cold and wet winter.

THE DOG DAYS OF SUMMER
JULY 19, 2005

THESE ARE THE "DOG DAYS" OF SUMMER, so named because the sun rises in the constellation Canis Major (Big Dog). Sirius is its brightest star, as well as the brightest star in the sky, and Sirius was the name of the dog of the mythical Orion the Hunter. Supposedly, the Dog Days are the hottest time of the year, and I sure hope that's true — the bank thermometer hit ninety-six here a couple of days last week, and that's not why anyone lives in the mountains.

The Dog Days are also a timely excuse for writing about my difficulties in finding what I want when we're shopping for the dog, Bodie, a neutered shepherd-collie mix who's about ten months old.

I'm old enough to remember when household dogs ate table scraps, stray rabbits, sundry rodents and whatever they could find in the garbage cans they tipped over. But that's not acceptable anymore. You're supposed to buy dog food.

And not just any old dog food. Every place that sells the stuff offers special "high-performance diet" concoctions, in canned or dry form. The propaganda on the label promises that your pooch will be a dynamo after a week or two of the enhanced-protein vitamin-enriched mineral-supplemented flavor-rich victuals developed by experienced teams of canine-nutrition specialists.

But why would I want that? Bodie likes to get me up at six in the morning for a two-mile walk (my two miles; he gets more like five or ten, chasing birds along the river). Then he wants an afternoon outing, and an evening excursion. Between those, he's bedeviling the cats or chasing cars along our side of the front fence, except when he jumps the fence and I have to go find him before a municipal employee does.

What I need, and can't find, is a special "low-performance diet," formulated so that he'll lie about most of the day, minding his own business, and be content with a daily stroll to the post office and back.

It would be even better if this low-performance dog chow had a weight-enhancing supplement you could add as necessary, until the beast was too fat to leap the fence, crawl under the gate or even climb on your lap when you want to watch TV.

I have nothing against canine health, but there can be too much of a good thing. This could also apply in dental matters.

The pet-care aisle offers special doggie toothbrushes and even toothpaste, along with brochures that explain the importance of their regular use.

But why fight canine cavities? I speak from experience here: When you've got bad teeth, you reach a point where you prefer sissy stuff like tofu to red-blooded he-man beefsteaks.

In other words, if your teeth are hurting, chewing is painful. And if the dog had a few excruciating cavities, he wouldn't be so interested in our shoes, hats, books, computer cables and remote-controls. As it is, I get hoarse from shouting "Leave it." If gnawing brought instant pain, he'd give up all on his own. We need some sugar-laden doggie treats, not special toothpaste.

As for remotes, it would be great if they sold them for dogs. Why bother with time-consuming training classes if you could just push "Play," "Pause" and "Mute"?

But then I realized that our technology still has a ways to go. Electron microscopes can display atomic structure, and perhaps even find the compassion in a "compassionate conservative," but that immense degree of magnification might not suffice to find the portion of a dog's brain that is not devoted to food, and thus it would be impossible to implant the control electrodes in the proper locations.

However, if an electronic ankle bracelet allows the authorities to keep tabs on Martha Stewart, then an electronic dog collar should function in much the same manner: It could send you an alarm every time the critter ventured outside the yard, and perhaps even provide detailed GPS coordinates for finding him when he's skulking down a distant alley.

Of course, if the dog was fat and lazy, he wouldn't be wandering around. Nutrition is the key here, and if the American fast-food industry can produce stuff that makes humans fat and lazy, then our pet-food purveyors certainly ought to be able to provide some useful, low-performance dog food. Otherwise I'll be getting way more exercise than I want, even after these torrid Dog Days fade into the delights of autumn.

TALE OF UNENDING GALES
MARCH 19, 2006

BY NOW I SHOULD KNOW BETTER, for I get fooled almost every year. I start to expect some pleasant time outdoors, and my hopes are dashed. This time around, it wasn't the annual two-foot snow dump that generally strikes on the first day that the local schools are out for spring break, but the incessant wind.

This has been the windiest winter I can remember. However, I've spent more exposed time this year than in previous winters. That's because dogs are incapable of listening to reason, as in "Be still and lie by the fire with the cats." Thus on most mornings, unless I can con Martha into the job, I'm out in the savage wind with our new dog Bodie for half an hour. He bounds with glee; I discover that no matter what direction I walk, I'm facing an arctic headwind that penetrates a down coat, a knit sweater and a flannel shirt.

The wind is not something you read about in the chamber-of-commerce brochures extolling the Colorado climate, although sometimes public officials are honest about it.

For instance, there's an unsettled question as to what the "Poncha" in "Poncha Springs" means. Some point out that on certain old maps, it was "Poncho Springs," and we all know what a poncho is.

Others say that "poncha" is a Spanish word for "gentle," describing 9,016-foot Poncha Pass above the town and its namesake hot springs. However, Juan Bautista de Anza crossed it in 1779; he called it "a very narrow canyon with almost unscalable walls," which casts doubt on the "gentle" theory.

There were early accounts of tobacco, in a form known as "punche," being traded in Taos, and the pass is one way to get there from the north, so the name might have come from that. Or it might not have.

One of my favorite troublemakers, Jeanne Englert of Lafayette, edited the Southern Ute Drum, the tribal newspaper, when she lived in Durango years ago. To settle the Poncha question for me, she contacted some Ute speakers who said it likely came from a Nuche locution for "foot-path," which seems logical. But others say that doesn't fit.

I once put the question to John Engelbrecht, who was then mayor of Poncha Springs. "Poncha? I always thought it was a Ute term for 'place where the wind rips the flesh from your bones.'"

One common theory has it that South Park gets only a foot of snow each year, but the constant wind holds those flakes in suspension all winter to form perpetual terrifying white-out ground blizzards. On one winter crossing, I stopped in Fairplay for gas and junk food and commented to the convenience-store clerk that this was a blessedly calm day without much wind.

She put her fingers to her lips, pointed to two kids at a video game, and said "You shouldn't say that in front of children. If you must comment, call it the 'w-word.'"

So to be politically correct about South Park this winter, let us note that on at least two occasions, the w-word blew semi-trucks off the highway.

My only visit to Alamosa this winter, to ride the excursion train on February 9, was a peach of a day, sunny and calm. So when I later chatted with a friend and colleague there, Marcia Darnell, I congratulated her on the easy winter.

"You hit the only nice day since Halloween," she said. "The wind has been horrible. It never stops. Old-timers say they're worried that the April winds started in January, and won't quit until June."

I tried to offer solace by pointing out that those gales and their loads of grit would surely elevate that area's leading tourist attraction, the Great Sand Dunes.

But I wanted some hard data about this year's wind. I called the National Weather Service office in Pueblo, which handles this part of the state. Certainly there would be wind data, current and historic, the meteorologist said. He referred me to a weather data website.

And there I discovered that I was expected to pay for information that was collected and collated at public expense. I know, the federal government is short on money these days. But if they can find more than a billion dollars a week for Iraq, shouldn't there be a better way for mere American citizens to find out whether this really has been the windiest winter on record?

THE TRADE-OFFS OF WINTER
FEBRUARY 6, 2007

AFTER YEARS OF TELLING US TO SAVE every precious drop of water, the Salida city government last week told us we had to waste water or face a $100 fine.

Naturally, this results from an effort to save water. In 1990, our General Assembly passed the Water Metering Act, which required meters for all domestic water providers with more than 600 customers.

Talk about an unfunded mandate. The city did provide some long-term payment plans for householders who couldn't quickly spring for the cost of digging the pits, placing the bottle-shaped fiberglass shells, installing the meters, then covering it up. But the water lines are only four feet deep. That seems to be below the frost line hereabouts, but the recent sustained cold spells have invaded some pits. The meter freezes, and city crews have to go out in wretched weather to thaw it.

Thus the recent order to prevent freezing by leaving some water running inside. If you don't, and the meter freezes, then you'll be charged $100 for thawing.

So, the meters that were supposed to save water now require us to waste water by just running it down the drain.

The real problem, of course, is that Salida, like many other communities in Colorado, was not designed to handle a long stretch of snow and cold. You figure that every winter will bring some snow every now and again; you push it aside, our brilliant sunshine arrives and the snow goes away before the next storm.

But with weekly storms and frequent incursions of arctic air, that hasn't happened yet in Salida, or in much of Colorado. I still read of city residents complaining about streets that have been covered with hard-packed ice since before Christmas.

Towns that generally get a lot of winter know how to handle it. I survived several winters in Kremmling, which might have been the warmest town in Middle Park. But that's not saying a lot; there were many thirty-below nights, and you seldom saw liquid water outdoors between Halloween and Easter.

Kremmling water lines were seven feet deep, so they didn't freeze. But household lines could, so we all kept a tap flowing. As for snow removal, Kremmling just didn't bother on the side streets — the town ran a grader to smooth the surface after every decent snowfall, and left it at that.

You got around town with a four-wheel-drive vehicle, sometimes chained. For a chance of having it start in the morning, you plugged in the tank heater every night.

Failing that, you could don cross-country skis, which worked fine unless you had to cross U.S. 40, which the state highway department kept too clear for skiing. Or you walked, and if you were going to the store, you pulled a sled so you'd have a way to carry your groceries home. (Sometimes there would be half a dozen sleds parked outside the market.)

Breckenridge had a different approach to snow in the late 1970s. It plowed with a vengeance after every snowfall, and there were strict parking laws to ensure that the plows could reach every square foot of street. If you left your car parked on the street overnight, it got towed and the plows went through. But streets remained slick; when I worked there, there were streets my car would slide backward down, and one time a snowplow slid and tipped over on Main Street.

Gunnison handles winter with extremely wide streets, so there's room for the plowed snow to be piled in the center until it can be hauled off. Meanwhile, the sun can get to what's left.

Salida's narrow streets make it more pleasant to walk around town, but the long shadows of winter keep some shaded narrow streets slick. That's one of the trade-offs in dealing with a hard winter.

Towns that usually get a lot of winter have been built for it, but there are costs. Most of us in small towns don't want to maintain extra-wide streets, and we prefer not to have to move our cars for street plowing. If the city proposed burying all water lines seven feet deep, we'd complain about how the municipal government was wasting money by preparing for unlikely scenarios — the same way I once complained when the Kremmling police chief wanted to organize a SWAT team.

Meanwhile, I'll enjoy wasting water, especially with official consent. Every drop wasted is a drop that won't go to a new subdivision.

FAREWELL TO AN OLD HOUSE
JANUARY 15, 2008

IF ALL GOES ACCORDING TO PLAN, Martha and I will get out of the landlord business today. We're supposed to close on the little house we bought when we moved to Salida nearly thirty years ago. We lived in it for eleven years before buying a bigger house in 1989.

Sitting just down the street from the post office, it has two peaked roofs with a valley in the middle. No one in his right mind would build a house that way from scratch. But the house shows up in the earliest pictures of Salida, taken in June 1880, sitting out on what was then the edge of town. Some major fires in the 1880s swept through most of town, but that little twin-roofed house on the outskirts survived.

It may well be the oldest building in Salida, although there are certainly older structures in the area, such as the 1878 Jackson Hotel in Poncha Springs and the 1872 Hutchinson Homestead between Salida and Poncha.

The two halves of the house resemble old railroad section houses. In 1878-80, the Royal Gorge War was underway between the Santa Fe and Rio Grande railroads. Both wanted to go up the Arkansas River from Cañon City to reach Leadville, but the gorge had room for only one line. Most of the battle was in the courts, but some shooting was involved as well.

For a time, it appeared the Santa Fe would win. That railroad's land company went to work promoting Cleora, a townsite near the junction of the Arkansas and South Arkansas rivers. When the Rio Grande won in March 1880, it laid out its own town, which became Salida, two miles upstream.

Most buildings that had been in Cleora were moved to Salida. Our theory is that two small Santa Fe structures, each about fifteen feet by thirty-five feet, were among them, and somebody patched them together after moving them to Salida. Local historian Donna Nevens found records that dated the house to May 1880, with Milford R. Moore as the builder.

When she told me that, it seemed like a cosmic coincidence. Moore and his partner, Henry C. Olney, founded Salida's newspaper, *The Mountain Mail*, which first appeared on June 5, 1880. And the reason I had moved to Salida was to become managing editor of *The Mountain Mail*. (Our current house was owned in the 1930s and '40s by the Marquardt family, who owned the *Salida Record*, which later merged into the Mail.)

Of course, we didn't know any of that when we bought the little house in the summer of 1978 for $23,500. Like all old houses, it demanded plenty of work, and I soon learned that "old house maintenance" should be classified as a branch of archaeology.

You never knew what you'd find: horsehair insulation behind the plaster and lath that was behind the new paneling, tube-and-knob wiring in the attic, or a hidden wall made of flattened coffee cans nailed over rough-cut lumber.

By the late 1980s, with the collapse of mining hereabouts, there were some good deals on Salida real estate, and we bought our current house in 1989. We planned to sell the little house, so we listed it at $30,000 for a year. No offers. We dropped the price for another eighteen months. Still no offers, not even an insulting offer.

But we had no trouble keeping it rented, so we took it off the market. There were good tenants and bad ones, and there seemed to be no reliable way of predicting how a renter would turn out.

That enterprise should end today, and somebody else can maintain the oldest house in Salida. In a few years, we might be kicking ourselves for selling it because real-estate prices had just kept climbing beyond all reason. Or we might feel fortunate that we got out while the getting was good.

But I do suspect that if Milford R. Moore were to return, he'd be pleasantly surprised that his newspaper was still in business and his cobbled-together house was still standing, nearly 128 years later.

The Committee that Really Runs America

Ziegler was in a good mood. "How are things out there in the big empty middle of one of those big square states?" he asked.

Not bad for a Bush administration, I said. Quite a few storefronts are still open, and at least 75 percent of the houses in town aren't listed for sale. Some people are getting by on only two part-time jobs.

THE REAL REASON THAT CLINTON STAYS IN THE NEWS
MARCH 18, 2001

SEVERAL MONTHS HAD PASSED since I last spoke with my best inside Washington source, Lieutenant Colonel Ananias Ziegler (retired), media relations director of the Committee That Really Runs America.

Part of the problem was that the Committee apparently had hired the same telecommunications consultant as the one who installed the system in the Park County government offices in Fairplay, and getting through to him required more patience than I had. But finally I had an afternoon free, so I could ask Ziegler about why I kept reading stuff about Bill Clinton when he's been out of office for nearly two months.

"For one thing, he was our first supermarket tabloid president," Ziegler explained. "Put him on the cover with an alien or a bimbo, and you sell a lot of papers. You think they're going to give up on something that profitable just because he's not in the White House any more?"

But surely the Committee could do something about that?

"We have a First Amendment in this country, remember? And besides, he's the best fund-raiser in Republican history."

I had known Clinton could rake in the bucks for his own party, but for the Republicans? This was taking bipartisanship past all common sense.

"Not directly," Ziegler said. "But if you want to raise funds for Republicans, all you need to do is say that you need money to fight off the effects of eight years of Clintonism, plus you need a war chest to defeat Hillary when she runs for president. They don't have commies to run against any more and even some elected Republicans are questioning the War on Drugs - so you take your enemies where you can find them when you're hustling money."

But why all the focus on Clinton's last-minute pardons?

"Because if the sheep in this country are busy looking at a possible relationship between contributions to the Clinton Library and the pardons he issued, then they won't notice the relationship between coal-industry contributions to President Bush's campaign and how he reversed his position on carbon-dioxide emissions last week."

Sort of like the misdirection that stage magicians use?

"You got it," Ziegler agreed. "The more attention that people pay to various Clintons, the less they notice about what's really going on."

Like the proposal to reduce taxes for our oppressed billionaires, even if there may not be enough federal surplus available?

"I don't know where you got the idea that there was anything wrong with a huge federal debt," Ziegler said, "unless you actually took one of Ronald Reagan's campaign speeches seriously twenty-odd years ago.

"The people who collect the interest are the holders of treasury bills and notes, people of means. The people who pay the interest are the people who get it deducted from their paychecks. The bigger the debt, the more that gets transferred from the undeserving to the deserving. The Committee is all for doubling or tripling the national debt, especially if it also involves a tax break for our supporters."

But aren't they hurt when the stock market goes into the tank?

"That looks like bad news at first," Ziegler said, "but it solves a lot of problems."

How could that be?

"A year ago, when the markets were soaring, you had all these irreverent twenty-something multi-millionaires with tattoos and nose rings, right? Do you know what that could have done to the social order in this country if it had continued, this trend of putting money into the hands of the wrong sort of people? It means that Americans might have lost their traditional deference to wealth."

It would be a different country if the rich didn't get their proper respect, I agreed.

"And the labor market was getting really tight last year," he continued. "It was leading to uppity workers - they wanted respect and some control over their lives, privileges that most people are really not entitled to. Our entire social order was in danger of being upset."

So the Committee is behind this economic slowdown?

"I'd say it's more a matter of spin," Ziegler said. "You see, if there's a recession right at the start of W.'s term, and if the former president is the news, then it's the Clinton-Gore Downturn."

But there will be a recovery? "Of course. And as soon as it starts, the Committee will issue orders to drop the pardon investigations. We'll want people to focus on the current president, so that it will be known as the Bush Recovery."

Ziegler sighed. "These things are so simple. I don't know why I have to explain them to you."

EVEN THE COMMITTEE CAN'T FIGURE OUT WHAT TO DO
OCTOBER 16, 2001

AMERICAN LIFE HAS BEEN SO DISRUPTED during the past five weeks that I thought I had permanently lost contact with my favorite inside source: Ananias Ziegler, media relations director for the Committee That Really Runs America.

But the call came. He wouldn't tell me where he was calling from, although I thought I heard Dick Cheney's voice in the background.

"I knew you'd be concerned," he said, "So I sent you an e-mail."

His e-mails always had return addresses like "aVnonX349LZ47@hotmail.com" and the address changed with every missive. Unable to tell his important messages from the useless or dangerous junk shooting through cyberspace, I had been deleting them unread, lest some Trojan horse, virus or worm infect my computer. I wasn't sure even that drastic step would prevent contamination, but on the other hand, it spared me the time I would have otherwise wasted opening offers for Viagra, hot teen sluts who wanted to chat with me and a variety of online off-shore casino games.

"Fair enough," Ziegler said. "Everybody's got to be careful these days. But what about the fax I sent you a few days ago? Did you get it?"

Our machine seems to work only for junk faxes that offer low-cost Caribbean cruises and discount office supplies. The others seem to lead to paper jams or the phone ringing constantly at three in the morning, because for some reason, the automatic switch can't tell it's a fax then even though it works fine during normal waking hours.

"OK, I understand that," he said, "but why don't you just get a dedicated fax line?"

Because I can't afford one.

"There's another service that could help you. It's called 'distinctive ringing,' and you should look into it."

I had, I told him, and even though I had a letter from Qwest that called me a "valued customer" and assured me that the company was "delighted to have the opportunity to serve you in the future" - the fact was, Qwest isn't offering any additional services I want, like distinctive ringing or DSL. It tried to sell our exchange, the deal didn't go through, and Qwest isn't going to spend a nickel adding features to rural exchanges.

"That's because they're patriotic," Ziegler said, "and they're following the president's request that Americans go about business as usual. And for Qwest, neglecting rural customers is business as usual - they need to put their investments in cities where there's competition, not in the boondocks where you've got to do business with them whether you like it or not. And besides, even in your backwater, there's competition of a sort — why can't I find your pager or cell phone number?"

Because I don't have a pager or cell phone, I told him, as I've told many others, who then insist that I really do have those things, and if I trusted them, I'd give them the numbers. But the truth is that when I'm away from the phone, I want to be away from the phone, not at the beck and call of anyone who can tap in some numbers.

"Quillen, I never took you for a Luddite," he fumed.

I have nothing against technology - in its place, and its place wasn't on a back road. Isn't there some kind of right not to be disturbed?

He moved on. "What about the regular first-class letter I sent?"

There wasn't any mysterious white powder, or at least none that I could notice. However, there was no external return address, and my security system — a twelve-year-old chow mix who faithfully guards our doors when she feels like it — sneezed when I wafted that letter under her sensitive nose. And by holding the envelope up to the light, I could tell it didn't have a check inside, so it wasn't worth the potential risk of opening it. The unopened envelope went straight to the firebox of the wood-burner in the living room.

"Maybe you're taking that a little too far," Ziegler cautioned. "After all, if you give in to fear, then the terrorists will have won."

But us media types seem to be the target this time around, I responded, and caution seems to be in order. On the other hand, as good Americans, we're supposed to be going about business as usual, and how was I supposed to do that when I was also supposed to be concerned about viral e-mail, anthrax-infected postal mail, a quirky fax-line switch connected to a jam-prone fax machine, and even hidden or coded calls to action when that Osama bin Laden video appears on one of the news channels?

"You missed a few other possibilities," he noted. "What happens if there are so many calls about powdered pudding in a post office, or a piece of pipe on the street, that they can't respond properly to a real problem?"

Good question. And I presumed the Committee had the answer.

"No, we don't," Ziegler said. "But we're working on it, and we'll let you know.

WHATEVER HAPPENS, THE COMMITTEE IS READY
JUNE 2, 2002

CONFUSED BY CONFLICTING REPORTS about what might have been known before September 11, I called my favorite inside source: Ananias Ziegler, media relations director for the Committee That Really Runs America.

It wasn't easy — the Committee is more security-conscious these days, and to keep outsiders like me from penetrating, it has installed the latest Voice-Mail-From-Hell technology, apparently borrowed from Colorado's own Park County. But I persisted through the maze of "Press six to hear these options again" options until I finally got the human voice I wanted to hear.

"Quillen, good to hear from you. I was worried you'd all dried up and blown away out there in Flyover Country. I've got to tell you, though, that if you called because you want one of those $150 pictures of President Bush talking on the phone on September 11, you need to call the National Republican Senatorial Committee, not us. As you know, it is inappropriate to exploit a national tragedy for partisan advantage."

I pointed out that I hadn't been able to afford a night in the Lincoln Bedroom under the previous administration, so I wasn't about to buy a picture just to make sure Wayne Allard had enough cash to buy his re-election this year.

"So why did you call?"

Like many Americans, I said, I had been wondering how much the administration knew about the possibility of terrorist attacks before September 11.

"Haven't you been listening to the vice-president?" Ziegler asked. "Don't you know that you're giving aid and comfort to our enemies just by asking such questions? Rest assured, our $30 billion-a-year intelligence network knew that something was afoot, but didn't know enough to issue any specific warnings."

So why did Attorney General John Ashcroft quit flying on commercial airliners last summer, and instead travel on a leased jet that cost $1,600 an hour? Did he know something that we didn't about what was coming?

Ziegler sighed. "If you'd check into the truth, instead of listening to sensational rumors in the Biased Liberal Media, you'd know that Ashcroft was responding to a threat assessment performed by his FBI security detail, which then advised him not to fly commercially."

What was the threat then? Where did it come from?

"All I can do is repeat what Ashcroft said last summer," Ziegler replied, "and he said he didn't know, and that he didn't do threat assessments himself."

So he wasn't in the least bit curious about who might be after him, and it's none of our business how our money is being spent in response?

"Get off the high horse, Quillen. Look at it this way. Suppose you were part of his security detail. Wouldn't you find any possible excuse to fly on your own Gulfstream, rather than enduring a commercial fight? Does it have to be anything more than that?"

This wasn't going anywhere, so I moved on. What about the warnings from the Phoenix and Minneapolis FBI offices? What about the warning that the president received on August 6 that al-Qaeda might hijack American airliners?

"Hey, look, we had our priorities straight then. Our law-enforcement system managed to arrest about 750,000 pot smokers last year. And besides, what was the president supposed to do? Go on TV and tell Americans not to cooperate with hijackers, but instead to fight them?"

Wouldn't have been a bad idea, I muttered. Suppose a few votes in Florida had been different, and a President Al Gore had responded in precisely the same way.

"Oh, we'd be demanding his head on a platter for neglecting national security. Anything else you want to know?"

What's the future hold?

"As you know, we're taking great steps to improve airport and airline security."

Why don't you just give Amtrak some of that money so people won't have to fly?

"Were you born yesterday? Because a government-owned passenger railroad doesn't make campaign contributions. Back to improving Homeland Security - aren't you relieved on the blue days and wary on the orange days?"

I interrupted. So we're safer now than we were before September 11, and that sort of thing will never happen again?

"I wouldn't go that far. As the vice-president said, it's not a matter of if, but when."

Aren't you trying to have it both ways? You're saying you need to confiscate knitting needles and toenail clippers, all in the name of protecting us, but we can't assume we're being protected because another attack is almost a certainty?

"You got it," Ziegler said. "If there are no more attacks, it's because we took the right steps. If there are more, then they were inevitable and we said so. We come out ahead either way. Did you expect less from the Committee That Really Runs America?"

Of course not. Indeed, I was impressed by the Committee's skill in navigating a difficult course.

THE EVIL REGIME OF THE NORTH
JULY 13, 2003

THE RECEPTIONIST SEEMED HESITANT when she answered my call. This was odd, since I often contact my favorite inside source, Ananias Ziegler, media relations director for the Committee That Really Runs America. She knew my voice, as well as where I was calling from, the current balance on all my accounts, and what I had bought at the grocery store yesterday.

"I'm sorry, Mr. Quillen," she apologized. "Mr. Ziegler has just stepped away from his desk, and will be with you shortly."

While Mr. Ziegler was in the restroom, I asked her about the hesitation when she answered the phone.

"They're thinking about changing the committee's name," she explained. "We've been practicing with the new one in training sessions, although we're supposed to use the current name until the change is official. So it took me a second or two to remember which name to use."

And what would be the new name?

"I guess it's OK to tell you. They're thinking about going to the Committee That Really Runs America, Iraq, Canada and Any Place Else That Doesn't Toe the Party Line."

Before I could ask more, Ziegler came on. Iraq I could understand, but Canada? "They've been getting frisky up north, and we have to protect our traditional American values."

Just how were those values threatened by Canada?

"For a pundit, you sure don't keep up with the news, Quillen," he chided. "We can start with some proposal up there which might legalize gay marriage later this year in the whole country. They're already issuing licenses in Ontario, and British Columbia could be next."

And so what if Canada has a different definition of marriage than our states do? It brought to mind Thomas Jefferson's observation that "It does me no injury for my neighbor to say there are twenty gods, or no God. It neither picks my pocket nor breaks my leg."

Ziegler said I should care, though. "We're looking at our treaties with that evil neighbor of ours — they have socialized medicine — to see if we're obliged to honor their civil actions. Can you imagine what would happen if married Canadian homosexual couples began invading the United States? Would you want a gay couple in your neighborhood?"

Actually, we once lived across the street from a gay couple. The main problem was that they took such good care of their yard that ours looked rather shabby, and that produced social pressure on me to spend time unproductively on mowing, edging, trimming, fertilizing and the like. So I agreed that he had a point.

"That's not what I meant, Quillen, and you know that. The point is, we can't let the Canadians manage their own country if they're not going to do it properly. Besides, there's the marijuana issue."

I had heard that Canada might be wimping out on the all-important War on Plants, but I hadn't heard the committee spin.

"First they decriminalized possession of small amounts," he said. "And now the government is providing medical marijuana to doctors who prescribe it. What kind of message does that send to impressionable American youth? They could turn into slackers who don't make enough money to care about our tax cuts, and they could end up voting the wrong way in such numbers that even the U.S. Supreme Court couldn't adjust the outcome. Besides, how can we be allied with a government, or even maintain a peaceful relationship when it cares so little about such important matters?"

So what would happen? Would there be a carefully orchestrated campaign against Canada, like what happened when France led opposition to the invasion of Iraq?

"The manager of a bar near the Capitol will announce next week that he's no longer serving Canadian whiskey, and Molson's ale will be removed from the cooler. Then you'll see new houses with certificates that they are 100 percent free of Canadian wood. We'll go after you jackals in the press who print some of your historical revisionism on paper that came from Canada. Plus, don't forget that we have some military options, along with economic sanctions, lengthened customs inspections and procedures - but we hope we don't have to deploy those."

All this is coming just because Canada does things differently than we do? What ever happened to diversity?

"There's no such thing anymore, Quillen. As we all know, George W. Bush is the Leader of the Free World. What ever gave these other countries the idea that they had any right to manage their own affairs?"

Before I could ask more, Ziegler said he had a call from Karl Rove, and even if he enjoyed talking to me, he had his priorities at the committee.

CHECKING IN WITH THE COMMITTEE
SEPTEMBER 7, 2003

LIKE SOME COLORADANS, I had been sampling the delights of late summer in the Rockies, spending a lot of time outdoors. This year has been better than most, since the mountains aren't as crowded, likely because more people have been staying indoors on account of the West Nile virus.

I figure that you run a risk any time you go outdoors in Colorado - lightning, avalanche, plague, tick fever, mountain lions, giardia, hunters, cyanide, to name a few - so why worry about one more lethal threat?

But a couple of rainy days pushed me back inside to the "real world," where I realized I'd fallen out of touch with current events because I was spending all that time looking at rocks, flowers and trees. (It must be some sort of desperate unconscious urge to enjoy them before the Bush administration carries through on its plans for our public lands.)

At any rate, I needed to catch up, and the easiest way to do that was to call my favorite inside source: Ananias Ziegler, media relations director for the Committee That Really Runs America.

Ziegler was in a good mood. "How are things out there in the big empty middle of one of those big square states?" he asked.

Not bad for a Bush administration, I said. Quite a few storefronts are still open, and at least 75 percent of the houses in town aren't listed for sale. Some people are getting by on only two part-time jobs. But I was concerned about the recent announcement from Governor Owens' office.

"What are you talking about?" Ziegler asked. "Isn't he still America's Best Governor in all the right-thinking circles?"

I didn't know whether he still held that status, but I did know that he and his wife were separating. That might hurt his political career, since he's always been popular with the family-values crowd.

"No need to worry there, Quillen," Ziegler said. "There's something you obviously don't understand about the political use of family values."

And that would be?

"Family values are for other people. That is, it was perfectly proper for Newt Gingrich, no matter how many times he had extra-marital affairs, to attack Bill Clinton. If you work with the Committee, your own family values are not a factor - what matters is how well you can nail the other guy for not practicing and promoting traditional family values."

This had me confused, so Ziegler continued. "Look at your state's simple, common-sense Pledge of Allegiance law for schools, currently in abeyance on account of some liberal federal judge who has the mistaken notion that the government doesn't have the right to tell people what to say."

What about it?

"Do you really think the promoters of that law care about 'liberty and justice for all?' If you think so, why not call them the next time a teacher gets criticized for being gay or enjoying French cuisine on his own time. Right-thinking politics are the issue here, not liberty and justice. If you want to be free, then you've got to be right."

Now I understood, so I switched topics. I wanted to know how the committee was handling the gubernatorial recall election in California, especially since Arnold Schwarzenegger's old interview with *Oui* magazine had emerged, wherein he talked about how much he enjoyed illegal drugs and group sex.

"That does have us worried," Ziegler conceded, "because Arnold is pretty much ignoring it so that he can talk about state fiscal policies and other boring stuff. We're going to have a much harder time controlling elections if the campaign issues turn away from values. We told Arnold that he was free to use President Bush's line that 'When I was young and foolish, I was young and foolish,' but the big lunk hasn't been taking our advice."

I moved to the international forum. For nearly two years, the United States has been devoting considerable resources to the capture of Osama bin Laden, and for several months, similar efforts have been aimed toward Saddam Hussein, yet both are still at large. Was this just bad luck, or is there a reason?

"Of course there's a reason," Ziegler explained. "It's not in anybody's interest for them to be captured."

What?

"Think, Quillen. They certainly don't want to be captured. As for our side, as long as Osama and Saddam are on the loose, then our people can stay in power by protecting you from them. We couldn't do that if they were locked up somewhere. So it's not in the committee's interest to have them captured, at least not before the 2004 election."

That made perfect sense, so it was time to hang up and go face the mosquitoes.

TRUSTING THE GOVERNMENT
MAY 8, 2005

LIKE MANY AMERICANS, I find myself confused by the proposed changes in Social Security, and I'm reaching an age where it's prudent to start paying attention. At first I thought of attending one of President George W. Bush's sixty road-trip presentations, but it soon became evident that I'm not the proper sort of citizen for those events, since I might ask a real question or otherwise disrupt the smooth flow of propaganda.

So I called my favorite inside source, Ananias Ziegler, who handles media relations for the Committee That Really Runs America.

Before I could say much more than "Good morning," he launched into an explanation about the decay of the filibuster, or the threat thereof, in the U.S. Senate. In 1968 it had been deployed for a noble purpose by Republicans to thwart the nomination of Abe Fortas for chief justice of the United States.

But in these decadent times, it was being used by Democrats to delay action on some judicial nominations.

Finally, I had a chance to interrupt him, and explained that I had called about Social Security.

"What's so hard to understand?" he asked. "We're still working on the details, but basically, some of the money you now pay into Social Security would instead go to a personal account that you could pass on to your heirs. As it is, if you died when you were sixty-four, that money just disappears, as far as you or your family is concerned."

That sounded like a better deal than the current system, I agreed, but I wondered how I should invest my personal fund.

"You'll do fine in the private sector," he said. "With the current system, you're at the mercy of Congress and how it sets benefit levels. The private sector is more trustworthy."

Like those Merrill Lynch agents who touted stocks that they knew were turkeys because Merrill Lynch did investment banking for those companies? How could the federal government be less trustworthy?

"We're working on it," Ziegler muttered before realizing he'd said something he shouldn't.

Hmmm. Was the Committee trying to make Wall Street more honest? Or trying to make the government worse? I knew I wouldn't get an answer from him, so I moved on. What about all those retired people who thought they had solid pensions coming from United Airlines, and now the company is talking about eliminating all pensions? Just how is that more reliable than the federal government?

Ziegler put on some spin. "As our president has pointed out on many occasions, we all know that we can spend our own money more intelligently than the government can."

He was certainly right about that. I wouldn't spend a nickel, let alone borrow billions from my children and their descendants, to occupy Iraq.

"That's not what I meant," Ziegler said. "And let's get back to Social Security reform. A bleeding-heart like you should be impressed with the president's latest proposal, where future Social Security checks would increase more quickly for the lowest-income retirees than for everyone else."

That sounded compassionate, but then I thought about the politics of it. President Franklin D. Roosevelt set up Social Security to resemble insurance, so that it didn't just pay out to the poor.

He figured that if the rich were involved too, then it would enjoy broad political support. Start adjusting the benefits so that it's perceived as a system primarily for the poor, and that broad support narrows, then vanishes. Look at how quickly America surrendered in the War on Poverty.

Ziegler chuckled. "You catch on pretty fast, Quillen. By sounding compassionate now, we're laying the political groundwork for total elimination of the system a few years down the road. It won't be easy, but we've got to convey an important lesson."

And that is?

"You can't trust the government, especially when we're in charge." With that, he excused himself, for he had to take another call.

The elusive Bubba Factor
May 4, 2008

I was surprised when I got a call from Ananias Ziegler, media relations director for the Committee That Really Runs America; it was the first time he had ever called me out of the blue.

After the usual pleasantries, he asked, "Got time to answer a few questions for me today? Seems only fair, since I try to answer yours." I told him I would, but wondered why he was soliciting my views.

"Did you see the May 5 edition of *Newsweek*?" he asked. "It's about the Bubba Gap. Here at the Committee, we're working on the best ways to exploit it, and our database search produced you as a rural white guy. The other Committee staffers were scared to go out on the ground in flyover country to meet a Bubba in person, so I volunteered to call you, since we know each other."

I didn't know whether to be flattered or insulted, so I let it slide and told him to ask away.

"Have you ever lost a job on account of affirmative action?" he asked.

About thirty-five years ago, I applied at the Boulder Daily Camera. I was more than qualified to write obits. But the newspaper had just lost a sex-discrimination lawsuit, so I didn't get hired."

"Are you bitter about that?" he pursued.

"At the time, yeah. But I know now that my ideal workplace is where you can scratch yourself, belch, tell raunchy jokes and otherwise be comfortable while focusing on your work, instead of trying to control every little thing you might do or say. Newspaper offices aren't like that anymore, so I'm better off working from home," I explained.

Ziegler moved to the next question. "Do you prefer venison, elk or generic roadkill?"

"Never much cared for wild game," I said. "I'll sample it to be polite if someone's serving it, but give me beef any day."

"So I take it you prefer mass-market beer, like Bud or Coors," he proceeded.

"I like local microbrews," I said, "and have ever since I first tasted Anchor Steam in San Francisco."

"So you drive a Volvo and enjoy wine tastings?" he continued.

"Nope. I just bought a used Ford pickup, but usually I drive our old Prizm because it gets much better mileage. And I'm not much of a wine guy, since I usually can't tell the difference between a good vintage and the screw-top stuff that was aged in transit."

He jumped to another conclusion: "So I take it you enjoy NASCAR events and country music."

"I wouldn't walk across the street to see a stock-car race. As for music, Hank Williams was a genius, but country music has generally gone downhill since his day."

Ziegler sighed. "You're not helping me to define the Red, white and blue bloc."

"Red, white and blue?" I asked.

"Redneck, white trash and blue collar," he explained. "And why do you sound so peeved?"

"Because I'm sick of your ignorant stereotyping," I replied. "Most of my friends and neighbors are rural white folks. Some are vegetarians; some hunt and eat wild game. Some love classical music; others like down-and-dirty rock 'n' roll. Some are gearheads; others read a lot; some manage both. Some go to church every Sunday; some don't. Some quote Rush Limbaugh; others prefer Amy Goodman. About all we have in common - be we janitors, ranch hands, machinists or shopkeepers - is that we don't make a lot of money."

He cut me off. "I get the picture. But how's the Committee supposed to divide Americans into discrete demographic groups that can be manipulated by political campaigns if you guys don't cooperate by having a common culture?"

"That's not my problem," I said, and hung up on him.

A CARD-CARRYING, SIGN-TOTING CAUSE
AUGUST 16, 2009

After the dog and I returned from our daily trespass on Union Pacific Railroad property one afternoon last week, the answering machine had a call-back message from Ananias Ziegler, media relations director for the Committee That Really Runs America.

"Do you want to join our program of spontaneous authentic grass-roots activism to intimidate and shout down the evil fascist-communist-socialist death-panel supporters at the congressional town-hall meetings?" he asked after the usual pleasantries.

"I do have some experience at being obnoxious at public gatherings," I confessed. "But our congressman hasn't scheduled any such meetings yet. Plus, Representative Doug Lamborn is a hard-core Republican. If Obama walked on water, Lamborn would just say it's because he doesn't know how to swim. So I can't see much point in it."

Ziegler explained, "This isn't about changing congressional minds, at least not in your right-thinking district. It's about theater. We need to show that there are people who support the finest health care system in the world."

I objected. "If ours is so great, why don't other countries try to emulate it? Have you ever heard of any politician, in any other country, campaigning to install an American-style health-care system?"

Ziegler stayed his course. "If you'd like, we can provide a sign you can carry. It will look authentically hand-lettered, and will show up well on TV and YouTube."

"What would it say?" I asked.

"You have a choice, of course," he replied. "How about 'Don't let Nancy Pelosi kill my grandma'?"

"Too late," I said. "Both my grandmothers are long dead. Somebody might ask, and I wouldn't want to lie."

"No wonder you're so obscure," Ziegler said. "If you want to amount to anything, you've got to get past that. Joe the Plumber wasn't a plumber, Sarah Palin quits to show she's no quitter, and you know about Mark Sanford's family values. How about this sign: 'Stop liberal Dems from rationing my health care!'?"

"But health care is already rationed," I pointed out, "since there's not an infinite supply. Mostly it's rationed on the basis of money."

Ziegler growled. "OK, wise guy, come up with one of your own."

"Maybe you have some leftovers from 1994," I said. "I liked 'Keep the government out of my medicine cabinet.'"

"I know you did," Ziegler agreed, "but the problem is that you take that slogan seriously. What would result if we put thousands of Drug Enforcement Administration agents out of work?"

"A free country?" I answered. "Never mind. How about 'Save my right to go bankrupt because an uninsured texting motorist hit me while I was walking across the street'?"

"That's too long for a sign," Ziegler objected.

I tried a new tack. "Suppose you gave me some money that I could invest in health-insurance stocks."

Ziegler interrupted. "That's not how we work here."

I made my pitch. "But then I could carry a sign like 'Don't let a public option destroy my retirement.'"

"I don't get it," Ziegler confessed.

"It's simple," I explained. "When you get right down to it, a private health-insurance company makes money by denying claims. There's no profit in paying medical bills. A public option might change that, and then the private companies' profits would drop, and their dividends and stock prices would decline, and my hypothetical retirement fund would take a big hit."

"I see your point," Ziegler said. "But it's not something you can shout at a meeting. I'm afraid we're just going to have to leave you out of this one."

LOOKING FOR THE RIGHT SPIN ON TAXES
DECEMBER 5, 2010

THE PHONE CALL CAME while I was out splitting firewood and thereby performing the noble task of annoying Colorado's natural-gas lobbyists by contriving to burn less of their product. The answering machine held a "Please call me ASAP" from my favorite inside source, Ananias Ziegler, media relations director for the Committee That Really Runs America.

"We need some help on our spin," he explained when I called.

"Always glad to assist the rich and powerful," I said, "in the hope that someday I may be among them."

"That's the true American spirit," he said. "You know, that's why this country will never have a revolution. People with the talent and charisma to lead revolts become rich and powerful celebrities who quickly lose interest in changing the system that rewards them so handsomely."

I mulled over that. "Does this have to do with Sarah Palin?"

"Not really," Ziegler said. "But her reality show could lure tourists up north, and that's a tough competitive market. Have you thought about something similar for your flyover Colorado?"

"Exploring Colorado's back country?" I wondered aloud. "Pot growing, jacklighting some venison, fishing with dynamite, plus plane crashes and avalanches - could be quite a show."

"Likely wouldn't help your tourism," Ziegler pointed out. "And we're getting off track." He paused. "Our problem here is that we want to preserve the Bush tax cuts for the wealthy. And meanwhile we want to block any extension of unemployment benefits."

"I've been reading about that," I responded. "The national debt is immense, so no unemployment-benefit extension unless there's a way to pay for them now."

"Simple fiscal prudence," Ziegler said. "That's a popular stance these days."

"But there's no way to pay for extending those tax cuts, either," I pointed out. "And look where they got us. A decade ago the federal government was running a surplus and unemployment was at record lows. Enter those tax cuts, and look what happened."

"Now you see why we need some help to spin this," Ziegler said. "If it's right to borrow money to keep billionaires' taxes down, somebody's going to ask why it isn't also right to borrow money to keep the unemployed from freezing and starving. And I need an answer."

"We could spin it that good Americans believe in plutocracy," I proposed, "and question the morals and patriotism of any deviant who'd ask such a question."

"That only works up to a point," Ziegler responded. "There's got to be a better way."

An idea struck me. "Given the state of our educational system, might it be that no one will even think to ask that question? In which case, you've got nothing to worry about."

"Maybe that would work," Ziegler conceded. "The point is, it doesn't matter what's good for the economy or what's good for the country. If President Obama is for it, we're going to oppose it. I thought we'd been doing a pretty good job of framing him as an alien 'other,' rather than as the duly elected president of the United States."

"You have," I agreed, "but suppose Obama comes out in favor of motherhood."

"We'd have to oppose it," Ziegler countered, "which would make us pro-choice and alienate the base. And if he waved the flag, we'd have to say it's a collection of pagan pentacles. Quillen, you're no help at all." And with that, he hung up.

ETERNAL BIRTHERISM
MAY 1, 2011

NOW THAT PRESIDENT BARACK OBAMA has released a copy of his long-form birth certificate, I figure the birther movement will soon fade away. But it's hard to be sure about these matters, so I called my favorite inside source, Ananias Ziegler, media relations director of the Committee That Really Runs America.

After the usual pleasantries, he assured me that we can anticipate much more contention, even with the long-form certificate that the birthers have been demanding.

"How's that?" I asked. "Haven't they said that's what they wanted to see?"

"Sure," Ziegler said. "But it raises some questions that now need to be addressed."

"It looked pretty standard to me," I said. "So what questions could come up?"

"If you look at the certification," Ziegler explained, "the baby's name is listed as Barack Hussein Obama II. Yet he took the oath of office - a botched oath at that on the first try — as Barack Hussein Obama Jr. Now, which is it? Is he a Second or a Junior? If he's a Second, he wasn't sworn into office, and if he's really a Junior, then the released birth certificate could be spurious."

"That's an interesting point," I conceded, "Anything else?"

Ziegler sighed. "The long-form certificate can be attacked as a clever forgery that doesn't prove anything. It's just an image of a piece of paper, after all. So I'm sure you'll see some more attacks from birthers who won't give up trying to prove he wasn't born in Hawaii. After all, where's the video of his birth?"

"I don't think that was common in 1961," I pointed out. "They didn't even have home video cameras."

"But they did have eight-millimeter home-movie cameras. So why wasn't Obama's birth filmed? Or if it was, what happened to the film?"

"If there was an eight-millimeter home movie of Obama's birth at Kapiolani Maternity & Gynecological Hospital in Honolulu, couldn't they just say it was a fake, too?" I asked.

"Of course," Ziegler said. "You're finally getting the idea behind the whole birther deal. There will never be enough evidence to satisfy the birthers."

"But the whole thing is way too silly for your Committee to be taking part," I said. "What's in it for you?"

"You're right that birtherism may be a bunch of nonsense," Ziegler said. "But we get a lot out of it. It helps create the impression that Obama is an alien 'other,' and it adds to his distractions. Thus it leaves us more room to do the important stuff like eliminating Medicare, gutting Social Security, abolishing Medicaid, improving the tax climate for Big Oil and Big Money. The more time Obama's people spend countering the birther rumors, the less time they have to fight Paul Ryan's budget."

"I see," I said. "So no matter what happens, no matter what evidence is produced, birtherism won't go away."

"Of course not," Ziegler said. "There will also remain the question of Barry Soetoro's possible Indonesian citizenship. And some of your state legislators, who'd prefer that their constituents not pay attention to the condition of their schools and highways, can generate some publicity for themselves by introducing bills requiring candidates to prove citizenship. And Donald Trump will just find some other angle, like college transcripts and hidden messages in law-review articles."

I sighed. "In other words, this is never going away, no matter what documents are released."

Before he hung up, Ziegler agreed. "Too many people get too much mileage out of birtherism. So it won't disappear anytime soon."

Getting Schooled

There's the deeper question of whether the time spent in school really matters. Abraham Lincoln did pretty well for himself with less than a year of formal education, and Thomas Edison spent less than three months in school. Of course, Lincoln could then make time for his voracious reading habit, and Edison for his experimenting with chemistry and electricity. That sort of educational adventuring is what a lot of us used to do in the summer, when school was out, and it worries me that if they keep stretching the school year, kids won't have time to learn.

AFTER THEY ENACT THE MORALITY IN ELEMENTARY EDUCATION ACT
MAY 25, 1999

THE BELL RINGS and the squirming sixth-grade students adjust them-selves to their seats for the duration. The teacher calls the roll, leads the Pledge of Allegiance, collects lunch money and starts the lesson.

"Today, class, we're going to be doing something new, as required by the Morality in Elementary Education Act of 1999," she begins.

Immediately a hand goes up. It belongs to Jenny, a smart but mouthy little girl whose parents are rumored to be vegetarians or free-thinkers, per-haps even Democrats.

"Mrs. Hansen, wasn't this law passed by a Republican Congress, and don't Republicans say they are committed to local control of education? So why are they making laws in Washington to control what happens in our class-room here?"

The teacher sighs. "Jenny, in our civics lesson next week, you'll get to write to our congressman. So why don't you ask him about it then?"

Jenny doesn't shut up. "Mrs. Hansen, the last time I wrote our congress-man, to complain about the mushy Korean War surplus canned peas that the government provides to our school lunches, he just sent a form letter that of-fered to send our school a flag that had flown over the U.S. Capitol. I don't think he even reads our letters, unless we put money in them so that we're campaign contributors."

The teacher clears her throat and gets the class back on track. "Jenny, we can take that up at some other time. Now, class, did any of you notice anything new on the wall this morning?"

She calls on an observant boy. "Over where there used to be a copy of the Bill of Rights, there's a big framed copy of the Ten Commandments."

"Right, Jason. And as required by the new law, we're going to spend a minimum of eight classroom hours focusing on the commandments."

With her class back under control, Mrs. Hansen glances through the guidelines passed out by the principal. "All children with a Judeo-Christian domestic ethico-cultural heritage will stay in the room for this session — and I guess that includes you, too, Achmed, since Muslims also read the Old Testa-ment. Any others — Buddhists, Taoists, Animists, Native American, Wiccans, atheists and agnostics and other bad Americans — should go to the library for the next hour. Does anyone need to leave?" A few children fidget uncomfortably, but no one rises. Mrs. Hansen decides to start with one of the easier commandments. "Let's talk about 'Remember the sabbath day, to keep it holy.' What's that mean?"

Mollie answers. "Mrs. Hansen, it means you're supposed to take a day off each week, and go to church then."

"Right, Mollie." Alas, other hands are in the air. She avoids Jenny and calls on Rachel.

"Mrs. Hansen, isn't the sabbath supposed to be the seventh day of the week, which is Saturday, not Sunday? So why do we have school events on Saturdays when we're supposed to keep it holy?"

Before Mrs. Hansen can summon an answer, Achmed adds to the discussion. "Our day of rest is Friday, and we have to go to school anyway. How can you be telling us to honor the Sabbath when you won't let us honor our sabbath?" The teacher hurriedly scans the guidelines, and finds nothing about this development. She moves on. "Thou shalt not covet — what does it mean to covet?"

Thomas answers. "It means you're not supposed to want things that aren't yours."

Mollie has a question. "Does that mean you're not supposed to take them?"

A relieved teacher responds. "Mollie, I think that's covered by another commandment, "Thou shalt not steal.' Coveting is different from stealing. Remember what Thomas said, about how coveting is wanting things that aren't yours?"

Mrs. Hansen tries to keep the expression of dread off her face when she sees that Jenny's hand is the only one up. "Yes, Jenny."

"Mrs. Hansen, every time I watch TV, I see lots of ads to make me want things that aren't mine, like sneakers and "Star Wars' toys. And when I read the newspaper, I see the same thing — all these ads that try to make people covet new cars and big houses. Are they trying to make us break one of the sacred commandments? What would happen to America if everybody quit coveting? Would people just quit buying stuff?"

Mrs. Hansen glances at her wristwatch. Only a few minutes remain in today's required discussion of the Ten Commandments. She's a pro; she can spin and stall for those few minutes. And at the staff meeting this afternoon, she's going to tell the principal that federal law or not, she's not touching this stuff again until she gets some better guidelines.

COULD SCHOOL YEAR BE GETTING TOO LONG?

SEPTEMBER 4, 2001

BY TRADITION, TODAY — the day after Labor Day — should be the first day of school, and by the same tradition this term would end on May 24, 2002, the Friday before Memorial Day.

But such traditions are not much honored these days; some schools started more than a fortnight ago, during the torrid days of August, and some will not get out until June is well along.

This tradition — start after Labor Day, end before Memorial Day, hold 180 days of class in between — dates back more than a century to an agricultural America, when children were needed on the family farm in the summer.

That doesn't make much sense now, at least for the vast majority of school districts. In 1997, there were only 1.9 million farms in this country. Put a family of five people on each farm, and that's still only 3.4 percent of the population.

So there's one argument against the traditional school year. Another facet of that argument is that this school year was determined by "economic factors," rather than "the educational needs of the children."

That same argument is often employed here during discussions of the school calendar, although the economic factor is tourism rather than agriculture.

If kids are out of school in the summer, then they can function as a labor pool for seasonal tourist enterprises — they make beds, wait tables, fry burgers, wrangle horses, etcetera. And since they're living at home, they're less likely to demand a living wage. Further, the duration of our tourist season is often a result of other schools' calendars. The family trip to Colorado happens when the kids are out of school, and the shorter the summer vacation, the more congested the campgrounds and fishing holes, and the more likely people are to go somewhere else next time.

So it's in our economic interest for every school district in America to follow the traditional calendar with a long summer vacation. Again, though, the critics will correctly point out that this desire for a full three months of summer vacation is based on "economic factors," rather than "the educational needs of the children."

Assuming that a child's "educational needs" are the highest social priority and must come ahead of matters like "spending time with the family" or "earning some college money," then what school calendar would best meet these needs?

A frequent criticism of the traditional three-month summer break is that kids forget a lot of stuff during that time, and so the teacher has to spend the better part of September on review, which wastes time.

That sounds sensible, but think about it. How well did you learn anything in the first place if you forget it 100 days later? Assuming that you knew how to parse a sentence, solve a quadratic equation or recover from a Windows blue screen of death in May, don't you still know how to do that now? If you had the skill in the first place, you're not going to lose it in a few months.

So it would appear that this concern that children forget things during the summer is really a way to disguise the fear that they didn't learn the material in the first place — and perhaps that's where the attention should go, rather than to the school calendar.

By this theory, that retention is better without the long break, students in year-round schools should do better academically than students on the traditional calendar.

But that's not the case, according to a 1998 study by the North Carolina Department of Public Instruction. It compared students in year-round schools (still 180 days, but with short breaks scattered through the year) to those on a traditional calendar. The conclusion: "After controlling for possible effects due to district, grade level, gender, ethnicity, parental education level, prior achievement and average school-level achievement, there were no significant achievement differences between year-round and traditional calendar students in either reading or math."

So the long break really doesn't hinder learning. What about lengthening the calendar to 200 or more days, rather than the usual 180? Perhaps that's a good idea, but we might also consider that of the six hours at school, actual academic instruction typically occupies less than 40 percent of the time. There might be some room for increased efficiency in the existing days before we consider adding days.

There's the deeper question of whether the time spent in school really matters. Abraham Lincoln did pretty well for himself with less than a year of formal education, and Thomas Edison spent less than three months in school.

Of course, Lincoln could then make time for his voracious reading habit, and Edison for his experimenting with chemistry and electricity. That sort of educational adventuring is what a lot of us used to do in the summer, when school was out, and it worries me that if they keep stretching the school year, kids won't have time to learn.

HAVING IT BOTH WAYS AT THE FOOD COUNTER
FEBRUARY 16, 2003

LAST MONTH, A FEDERAL JUDGE in New York dismissed a lawsuit brought forth on behalf of two chubby teenagers. They claimed that McDonald's had made them fat — one of them weighs more than 400 pounds — and thus susceptible to maladies that ranged from diabetes to heart attacks.

Did McDonald's hold a gun to their heads, imprison them and force them to chow down on Big Macs with Supersize fries morning, noon and night? Of course not. Instead, the impressionable youngsters saw slogans like "McChicken Everyday" and "Big 'n' Tasty Everyday," and apparently concluded this was good advice, instead of commercial puffery. They also alleged that McDonald's products were addictive, leading to "foreseeable misuse," and thus the fast-food company acted irresponsibly.

Naturally, the critics of the litigation industry had much to say, all negative, about this frivolous lawsuit. After all, those kids had choices about where to spend their meal money, and they certainly could have known that most nutritionists do not recommend a constant diet of beef fat, sugar, salt, dimethylpolysiloxane and the like. If making that choice made them unhealthy, that's their problem.

That's more or less what Judge D.J. Sweet wrote: "If a person knows or should know that eating copious orders of supersized McDonald's products is unhealthy and may result in weight gain (and its concomitant problems) ... it is not the place of the law to protect them from their own excesses. Nobody is forced to eat at McDonald's. (Except, perhaps, parents of small children who desire McDonald's food, toy promotions or playgrounds and demand their parents' accompaniment.) Even more pertinent, nobody is forced to supersize their meal ... ."

Despite the judge's sensible ruling, this issue is unlikely to disappear. For one thing, there are millions of obese Americans (I'm one of them, a good twenty pounds over the chart). As good Americans, we would prefer to blame somebody else, rather than our own lack of willpower in the presence of tasty aromas, for our poundage and associated health risks.

For another, trial lawyers see a bonanza somewhere down the road. Just as they did with tobacco and asbestos, they'll persist until they find a court that will grant them a big settlement, some fraction of which their class-action clients may even see.

That said, my first thought after reading up on this litigation was that prospective clients might have a case — not against McDonald's, but against their schools.

After all, if there were things they should have known, but didn't, isn't that at least partly the fault of the school system that was supposed to teach them things like nutrition and propaganda analysis?

It's been thirty-five years since I was in high school, but I can still remember a health class that taught us about the evils of marijuana, the horrors of venereal diseases and the dangers of too much greasy food. Granted, my skeptical friends and I devoted considerable effort toward determining whether the teacher was really telling us the truth. But the point here is that we were informed by those whose duty was to educate us, and after that, it was up to us.

In another class, we learned to find the propaganda techniques in advertising, like the bandwagon ("everybody else has one") and the irrelevant celebrity endorsement.

Are schoolchildren today getting the same sort of knowledge? And if not, could that be because our schools are being taken over by the junk-food industry?

Pepsi and Coca-Cola pay millions to school districts to have exclusive distribution on campus, along with promotional signage — few schools, under these circumstances, are likely to be telling students, "This stuff has an addictive drug, caffeine. It rots your teeth and makes you fat, so go easy on it if you use it at all."

In 2000, a Centers for Disease Control and Prevention survey found that more than 20 percent of schools sell McDonald's hamburgers, Pizza Hut pizzas and other name-brand fast foods. Throw in promotions, like winning junk food if you read a certain number of books, and you've got pretty good penetration of our schools.

So it appears the fast-food industry wants it both ways. It argues that a case should be dismissed because people should know better, but also influences our educational system to keep people from knowing better.

We're not responsible for the fast-food industry, but we are responsible for our schools, and it could be time to be sure students indeed "know better," even if it means going without fast-food money.

THE PROTECTION RACKET?
NOVEMBER 18, 2003

FOR MANY YEARS, we have been told that conservatism was all about individual strength and courage, whereas it was those wimpy liberals who whined for protection from the government.

But now it appears that this perception was wrong, since a powerful state senator is stepping forward to protect the huddled and beleaguered conservatives on Colorado's college campuses.

That's not quite how state Senator John Andrews, a Republican from Centennial, puts it. Last week, he sent a letter to the presidents of Colorado's twenty-nine public institutions of higher education, inquiring as to how well they're protecting "academic freedom."

He said students and faculty have told him they fear for their grades or their careers "if they don't keep a lid on their patriotism or their faith," and there have been reports — unsubstantiated, of course — about a student getting some kind of criticism from a professor because the student, who was enrolled in ROTC, wore a military uniform to class.

Now, would you want to be commanded by some poltroon who couldn't handle a few words from a professor, let alone an enemy machine gun? Do you think our country could be well defended by such officers? Wouldn't we be better off if such lightweights were removed from the officers' training program long before they ever got near combat?

To put this another way, that's not anybody I'd ever want to share trench with. Andrews ought to thank whatever "hostile environment" there is for improving the quality of our officer corps. Similarly, you have to wonder about the commitment and faith of anyone who can't handle a skeptical environment. There were the early Christians, who faced lions in the coliseum of Rome rather than betray their faith. But the mousy modern believers in Colorado need protection?

Andrews seems to be confused about how colleges operate. One of his four questions asks, "What formal policies exist at your institution to guarantee that no student, faculty member or employee is subjected to discrimination, harassment or a hostile academic environment on account of his or her political or religious beliefs?"

That sounds noble, but now imagine there a student who believes that the earth came into being at 9 a.m. on October 23, 4004 B.C., as calculated by Archbishop James Ussher in the seventeenth century.

Now put that student in a college class — say, Petroleum Geology 201. And every time the professor starts to explain why crude oil might pool in 250-million-year-old Permian structures, this student objects. The professor tells the student that the class is not there to discuss his religious beliefs, but to learn how to find oil deposits, and the student should shut up and learn the material. Obviously, this student has been subjected to a "hostile academic environment," on account of his religious beliefs.

But what are the other students going to get out of the class if it turns into a discussion of creationism rather than an explanation of geology? And where are we going to find competent geologists in the future if our colleges are busy protecting the feelings of students, rather than educating them?

Another item in Andrews' inquisition asks, "What is your institution's process for handling complaints and determining remedies in the event someone experiences a violation of academic freedom?"

I wish Andrews would define "academic freedom." If it means freedom to pursue truth or freedom to interpret events in a way different from the Bush administration's line, then I'm all for it.

However, I recall only one encounter with it during my student days. I enrolled in a course called Twentieth Century American Literature.

On the first day, the instructor informed us that we were really going to study modern-American protest poetry because it was so much more relevant than Sinclair Lewis and H.L. Mencken. Since the regular campus classroom was "so sterile," we would meet at her apartment, which was on the other side of town and a major inconvenience to my schedule. And because she didn't like any bookstores in Greeley, the texts were available only at a little bookstore in Boulder, which just happened to be owned by a friend of hers.

This struck me as "breach of contract," but my only recourse was to drop the course, which I promptly did. In the process, I ran into the department chairman, explained why I was there, and asked if there was anything he could do about this.

Not really, he said, since it could be a matter of "academic freedom."

Oh well. It's sort of fun to speculate about how Andrews will defend that sort of thing.

A QUICK FIX FOR COLORADO COLLEGES
JANUARY 11, 2004

ONE OF THE BIG ISSUES before our legislature is higher education. Our colleges and universities point out that they're suffering from the state cutting funds in recent years. Meanwhile, students and potential students wonder where they're going to find the money for college.

Fortunately, the General Assembly could solve all of these problems with one simple amendment to our civil-rights laws. As it is, it's illegal for an employer to discriminate on the basis of race, religion, sex, age and the like. But it is quite legal to discriminate on the basis of education; just look through the classified ads and you'll see phrases like "BA required" and "minimum MBA."

It's true that many jobs require specialized knowledge and certain skills, and colleges often impart the knowledge and skills. But the skills and knowledge can be acquired in other ways — home study and apprenticeship come to mind — and employers could certainly test applicants, rather than rely on college credentials.

In my days as an editor who hired reporters, I never noticed that reporters with college degrees performed any better than reporters without college degrees. As an American citizen, I haven't noticed that any recent U.S. presidents, all with college degrees, have been much of an improvement on Harry Truman — who never went to college.

What of the licensed professions that now require college degrees? As it is, if you complain that a science teacher does not know that water boils at a lower temperature here than at sea level — and who won't even investigate the possibility — you'll hear that "She has a college degree and is certified by the state, so it's not our fault." Eliminate the educational requirement, so that the school board takes responsibility for the quality of people it hires. That would have to be a big improvement on the current system.

As for physicians, have the educational requirements protected us against malpractice, billing fraud and iatrogenic diseases? Aren't we free citizens in a market economy, perfectly capable of deciding ourselves whether to seek the services of a physician, a faith healer or the woman down the street who sells herbal remedies?

Law school? Clarence Darrow and Abraham Lincoln managed without it, and they served their clients well.

It might take a few years to adjust, but it's hard to see how society would suffer if we made it illegal to discriminate on the basis of education.

Further, discriminating on the basis of education (rather than knowledge or skills) is actually yet another way of oppressing the poor. In a recent *Newsweek* article, the president of the University of Michigan observed that less than 20 percent of her students came from households with annual incomes of less than $50,000. The median household income in Michigan is $46,000.

It's not hard to see what those numbers mean, and it isn't because poor kids are stupid. A study published about a year ago by the Century Fund reported that if you take two high-school graduates with the same grades and test scores, but one is from the top income quartile and the other from the bottom — the bottom is half as likely to go to college.

And even if the poor kid makes it through school, financial aid these days generally means a pile of debt at graduation.

The usual governmental solution to this problem is to increase financial aid, and thereby increase the debt burden.

But our state government could apply a different solution — by making it illegal to discriminate against people without college degrees while making it clear that employers are free to judge on real skills and knowledge. Then young people, rich and poor, could pursue careers without the "need" to attend college first.

Would this hurt our colleges?

No. Colleges today give equal degrees to students who have learned their lessons and to party animals who found the easiest classes and still barely passed.

Colleges would improve once they adapted to having students who wanted to broaden their knowledge, rather than grab a credential. In fact, all U.S. schools would improve if a diploma actually indicated that students had learned something, rather than that they had put in their time.

So, the legislature could fix several problems by just adding a few words to the state's anti-discrimination laws. It would improve our workforce and our schools, while easing the lot of the poor and assisting in upward mobility. It's so simple and easy that it's safe to predict it will never happen.

CONFESSIONS OF A POCKETKNIFE SURVIVOR
APRIL 18, 2004

SINCE MANY OF US are quick to criticize our courts when they make bizarre rulings, it seems only fair to commend both a Denver juvenile court and the state court of appeals for a sensible ruling.

It came earlier this month when the appeals court upheld the decision of Denver Juvenile Judge Dana Wakefield in the case of a boy found with a pocketknife at Henry Middle School in Denver. He had been charged with possessing a weapon at school.

The knife had a three-inch blade, and the relevant part of our state law defines a "dangerous weapon" as "A fixed blade knife with a blade that measures longer than three inches in length or a spring loaded knife or a pocket knife with a blade longer than three and one-half inches."

In other words, size matters. You don't need a long blade to clean your fingernails, sharpen a pencil, open something wrapped in tough plastic, slice an apple or scores of other mundane tasks which are part of the school day or any other day.

Thus the juvenile and appeals courts followed the law: A pocketknife with a short blade isn't a dangerous weapon, unless you wield it as a weapon, which wasn't the case here.

After all, if you're serious about causing harm with academic tools, you could stab with a pencil, pen or compass, or for that matter, club somebody with a book.

Denver District Attorney Bill Ritter, who brought the charges that were dismissed, said he will join other prosecutors in asking the legislature to change the law during the waning days of this session.

"Knives are sharp-edged weapons, and they really can be used for assaultive purposes," Ritter said. "All knives, because they are capable of producing death or serious bodily injury," he argued, should be prohibited from school grounds.

When I was in grade school, we survived even though we were encouraged to carry pocketknives to school. The encouragement came from the Cub Scouts.

At some point in the progression from Wolf to Bear to Lion, we were required to begin carrying pocketknife at all times (we aspired to be real Boy

Scouts, whose motto is "be prepared"), and we had to pass a test on safety, care and maintenance, which included keeping it sharp.

I barely passed that test, much to the shame of my family. My dad, my brothers, my uncles, my cousins — they're wizards of the whetstone. Give any of them an oilstone and an old spoon, and in a few minutes, you could be shaving with that spoon. Hand me a sharpening stone and a real knife, and the longer I work, the flatter the edge.

"This blade is so dull that you could ride to Europe on it," my father commented of one of my early sharpening efforts, and I haven't improved.

Even if my knife wasn't sharp, I still carried it to school, as did my fellow Cubs and most other boys. At recess, we played a game called "stretch," which involved facing each other and throwing your knife to your opponent's side. If the blade stuck in the ground, your opponent would have to stretch his free foot to the knife's sticking place. You won if you made a stick your opponent couldn't reach.

We weren't sure whether the game was legal at school, so we played clandestinely amid the trees on a remote corner of the grounds of Chappelow Elementary School in Evans, Colorado. One spring day the sixth-grade teacher, Mrs. Kaugh, had recess duty. She sneaked over and caught us in mid-toss.

We feared confiscation and a trip to the principal's office, where a huge paddle was rumored to be waiting for our rumps. Instead, she said she had played the same game in grade school, and she'd been pretty good at it. She pulled a pocketknife from her purse, and challenged the current winner. She won on the first toss, a clean stick at least eight feet away. After that, we regarded her with awe.

Bill Ritter must have gone to school when most boys carried pocketknives, so he should know that they're not inspirations to carnage. Many implements can be used as weapons; pocketknives are among the most useful of tools. The one I currently carry is a small Leatherman knockoff. It opens envelopes, tightens connections, removes bottle caps, files fingernails and cuts and strips wires. But Ritter thinks it is only a weapon, and that I should go to prison if I were to walk into a school with it in my pocket.

Fortunately, some people know better. They know that chairs, pencils, baseball bats, jump ropes, electrical cords and loads of other items can be turned into weapons. Useful tools that can be used as weapons aren't the problem — misbehavior is.

Let's hope the legislature retains the current law, the one that knows the difference between a tool and a weapon.

THE SOUND AND FURY
NOVEMBER 15, 2005

THE REVEREND PAT ROBERTSON fears for the people of Dover, Pennsylvania, because their school board will not follow his suggested curriculum. On Election Day last week, eight school-board members who had promoted "intelligent design" in biology classes were voted out of office.

Some folks would consider that good old American democracy at work, but not Robertson. "I'd like to say to the good citizens of Dover: If there is a disaster in your area, don't turn to God; you just rejected him from your city," Robertson said on his *700 Club* TV show. "Just remember, you voted God out of your city."

That's a bit of a stretch. Unless there is some sort of conspiracy by the mainstream media at work, God remains in Dover, as much as ever. I haven't read of any churches being shuttered in Dover. No mass round-ups of believers, no one arrested for possessing a Bible or a tract, no persecutions of the devout, no evidence at all that God is being removed from Dover.

Indeed, if Robertson is referring to the same God I learned about in Sunday School, removal would be impossible. We were taught that he was omniscient, omnipotent and omnipresent — that is, all-knowing and in all places, far beyond any human power to remove.

The Dover saga began before the election. The old school board tried to require a statement about intelligent design in biology classes. Some parents sued, saying that was an effort at religious indoctrination in public-school classrooms. The court has yet to announce a verdict.

It can be argued that there's nothing inherently religious about intelligent design — it's just another scientific theory which holds that the complexity of earthly life can best be explained by positing a designer, rather than time and chance. In itself, it says nothing about whether the designer was the God of Genesis or some cosmic archfiend whose perverse sense of humor shows in mass extinctions, lethal pandemics and frail human anatomy.

But Robertson doesn't provide any support for that argument, since he claims that removing a mention of intelligent design from the biology class is the same as ejecting God from the community.

On further analysis, though, this whole controversy is rather pointless. On one side we have some right-thinking devout people who fear that if only the theory of evolution is taught in biology classes, then children will absorb that and grow up to be not just followers of the scientific method, but Darwinists, maybe even social Darwinists who believe the strong should rule and the weak should have no rights — that is, modern Republicans.

On the other side, there are parents who fear that a few minutes' exposure to intelligent design theory will turn their children into slaves of ancient superstitions with no regard for reason or intellect — that is, crystal fondlers or necromancers or the like. But in reality, both fears are groundless. Consider that schools spend a lot of time teaching history. History is not without its controversies between revisionist and traditional or triumphalist camps.

But both sides agree, for instance, that the American Civil War occurred from 1861 to 1865, and that American schoolchildren ought to know that. Yet there are surveys which claim that 80 percent of high-school seniors can't tell you which decade the Civil War occurred in.

Schools spend a lot of time on math, too. In a 1998 survey, American high- school students ranked seventeenth in mathematical skills among eighteen nations.

Given that record of non-accomplishment, why would Pat Robertson or any other fundamentalist care what's taught in a biology class where the vast majority of students are not going to remember it anyway? If you need further confirmation, catch a "Jay Walking" segment on the *Tonight Show*.

Furthermore, the clever students will thwart their educations anyway. The great skeptic Voltaire was educated by Jesuits. Charles Darwin had a devout Anglican education. Robert Ingersoll, the famed American atheist of the 19th century, was raised and educated by a Congregationalist minister.

The real lesson in all this might be that if you don't want kids to learn about evolution, teach it every day in every classroom, K-12.

BIBLICAL FOUNDATION?
MARCH 4, 2007

ONE OF THOSE ODDITIES OF AMERICAN LIFE is that a reasonable proposal can be based on unreasonable premises. The case at hand comes from Moffat County, where the school board last week received a petition to add an elective course called The Bible in History and Literature.

As a writer, I'm all for more widespread biblical knowledge, for my work is simpler if I can refer to "the patience of Job" or "the wisdom of Solomon" when appropriate.

In that respect, I also support more widespread knowledge of all prominent ancient literature, such as the *Iliad* and the *Odyssey*, because there are times when "the wrath of Achilles" or "the virtue of Penelope" can be useful. The same holds for classical mythology, as with "the Midas touch" or "Echo and Narcissus."

When these tales are not common knowledge, as is the case after decades of enhanced spending on American education, then those references don't work, and my job gets harder. And without some biblical background, it's just about impossible to appreciate Abraham Lincoln's famous "House Divided" speech or the lyrics to Bob Dylan's "Highway 61 Revisited."

So there are good reasons that the Bible ought to be part of a good American education.

However, those are not the reasons presented to the school board in Craig, where local resident Deborah Powell explained that "The Bible was the foundation and blueprint for the Constitution, Declaration of Independence, educational system and our entire history until the last twenty to thirty years."

Let's start with the Declaration of Independence, which states, "All Men are created equal, that they are endowed by their Creator with certain unalienable Rights, that among these are Life, Liberty, and the Pursuit of Happiness."

Search as I might with Cruden's Concordance and the King James translation, I can find no mention of divinely endowed rights to life, liberty or anything else. The Bible could not have been the basis for the Declaration. The Declaration was a statement that Americans no longer desired to live under a king, as compared to, say, the demand of the elders of Israel to "Give us a king" so "that we also may be like all the nations."

Proceed to the federal constitution, which provides for a national government which is elected, either directly or indirectly. The word "vote" does not appear in the Bible, and "elect" appears only in the sense of "the chosen." The Bible mentions kingdoms and empires but is silent about the virtues or defects of the Athenian democracy or the Roman republic. Biblical decisions about public matters and public offices were often made by "casting lots" — that is, rolling dice or the like — rather than an election or referendum.

Put simply, our federal government does not have a biblical foundation, for it is nothing like any government mentioned in the Bible. Further, it has acted against practices sanctioned by the Bible, like slavery, polygamy and the subjugation of women.

This American departure from biblical ways is no recent development of the "last twenty to thirty years." The Emancipation Proclamation appeared in 1863. In the 1880s, federal soldiers were sent to Utah Territory to root out polygamists. Women got to vote in Wyoming Territory in 1869.

An understanding of the Bible greatly helps in understanding many elements of American history and literature, and that, along with some knowledge of other ancient classics, is something every American should have. But Deborah Powell's claim that the Bible provided "a foundation and blueprint" for a constitutional republic means that someone could use some more education.

FIXING SCHOOL FINANCE
APRIL 17, 2007

THE MINORITY REPUBLICANS in our General Assembly raised a good point recently. Majority Democrats have pushed a bill requiring local school districts to provide more than just "abstinence only" in their sex-education classes. Birth control and sexually transmitted diseases should also be addressed.

Meanwhile, there have been bills to require that high-school graduates attain certain levels of proficiency in science, math and English — and those bills have died.

Granted, sex education can be a matter of life and death these days, but just what are schools for if not to teach science, math and English?

It's not quite as simple as that, of course, since there are complications. One is the myth of "local control."

I used to believe in such a thing, until I went to local school board meetings for about a decade. Every time the feds offered grant money, no matter how moronic the purpose (put a cop in school, or test the chemical purity of teachers' blood) the school board would leap to comply.

And at most meetings, the superintendent would announce that "the state is now requiring ... ." Again, the local board would snap-to and salute. Once in a while, a board member would grumble, "What are they going to do to us if we don't? Put us in jail?" But that's as far as the dissent went.

So the argument that more state requirements would diminish local control is like an argument about whether Superman could fly under a purple sun. Superman is mythology, and so is "local control" of public schools.

The real issue is whether a Colorado high-school diploma means anything. That is, if you're an employer or a college admissions officer, and an applicant appears with diploma in hand, can you assume that the applicant possesses any specific set of skills and knowledge?

Granted, this hasn't mattered much in the past, and may not in the future, either. If you check, you'll see that Colorado ranks high in the percentage of college graduates in its population, and low in the percentage of high-school graduates that it sends to college. In other words, we import college graduates. Since education is difficult and expensive, this probably makes financial sense. Let other states spend the time and money, while we reap the benefits as their educated people make their careers in Colorado.

Assuming that anyone wants to change that sensible arrangement, then what should the graduate know? My list would start with proficiency in "commercial English" — writing business letters and the like. I'd also require fluency in one common English dialect, be it Ebonics or Blue-Collar English, and at least tourist proficiency ("Where is the bathroom?") in a foreign language.

Foreign-language instruction would start in kindergarten, since it's easier to learn languages then, and continue through twelfth grade. Aside from the cultural and commercial benefits, students would understand English better on account of learning another language.

In math, students need to know the commercial version, like calculating the net present value of an investment, as well as algebra, geometry and trigonometry. These skills are easy to test.

As for science, there are the basics of biology (including human reproduction), chemistry and physics, as well as some civics (Is it more effective to hire a lobbyist or donate to a campaign?), geography and local, national and world history. Most of this is pretty easy to test, too.

How would the state have school districts meet these requirements? The districts could figure it out themselves under my plan. As it is, the state provides money to school districts. For the purpose of argument, let's say it averages $5,000 per year, per student. That works out to $65,000 for the thirteen years of K-12.

So, just offer school districts $65,000 for every graduate they produce who meets the standards. Some might attain proficiency in ten years, some in fifteen, some never, but under this system, you can bet every school system would be efficient and innovative.

School districts would know what was expected of them, and Colorado taxpayers would know what they were getting for their money.

And it might turn out that it was worth the trouble to look after Colorado kids, instead of continuing to rely on imports.

WHO NEEDS J-SCHOOL?
APRIL 7, 2011

RECENTLY I READ that the journalism school at the University of Colorado may soon be shuttered. That's a welcome development because it's really hard to make the case for a special curriculum to produce journalists, especially when finances are tight.

America produced hundreds of accomplished journalists long before 1869, the year of the first college journalism class. It was offered at Washington College in Lexington, Virginia, and came at the behest of the college's president, former Confederate General Robert E. Lee.

Since Lee never wrote his memoirs, we don't know why he invented college-level journalism. To tone down the more lively aspects of Southern journalism of the day? (See Mark Twain's sketch about "Journalism in Tennessee.") Or to provide a teaching job for some impecunious relative now lost to history?

Back in my days as a newspaper employer, I didn't discriminate against journalism-school graduates. But I didn't favor them, either. They often babbled terms like "nut graf," and thought they knew all about the various ways that mass media influence society.

But to write a clear and coherent account of a city council meeting — some J-school graduates could do it, and some couldn't. They were just like any other group of people — J-school didn't make any difference.

Any reasonably curious and literate person can master the chief mysteries of journalism in a few months. Ideally, journalists have an abiding curiosity about everything from astronomy to zoology and a love of the language. Defining the difference between a pyramid lede and a summary lede is irrelevant classroom make-work. I did want job applicants to have taken at least Newswriting 101. That's because it might be the only college writing class that puts a premium on concision and clarity, as opposed to the bloat and obfuscation employed in most academic writing.

But beyond that, it didn't seem to matter how many other journalism classes the applicant had or hadn't taken. J-school classes like "Advanced Feature Writing" ranked with ed-school classes like "Methods of Using Audio-Visual Materials in the Secondary Classroom" as being essentially worthless.

As for CU's J-school specifically, I have a problem with it that goes back to 1980, when I was managing editor of the Mountain Mail here and we got sued for libel by a county commissioner.

The commissioner wanted a change of venue away from Salida on the grounds that the Mail had this immense 95-plus percent market penetration, and he brought in an expert witness from the CU J-school to testify to that.

But the best market penetration we could come up with was about 80 percent, so during a courtroom break I asked the CU teacher if we could use her numbers in marketing: "Hey advertisers, here's an expert who puts us at over 95 percent market penetration." She demurred.

I don't hold it against her for testifying for the plaintiff in a groundless libel suit that was quickly dismissed. But I did think it was ungracious of her not to let us use her numbers so we could brag about our awesome market penetration. You'd think that the state's leading J-school would gladly make its research available to the state's media — you know, the very enterprises that might employ J-school graduates.

But that's a side issue. The main issue is that good reporting is not the result of memorizing various journalistic terms. It is about knowing your subject and writing clearly. Robert E. Lee may have been good at a lot of things, but developing a college curriculum was not one of them.

The Centennial State

I have never paid much attention to those "Welcome to Colorful Colorado" signs at the borders. The signs do not convey a feeling of "It feels good to be back home." It's more like "Another two or three hours of twisting mountain road replete with black ice, rockslides, manic Gen-X extreme sports motorists, tortoise-paced land yachts towing Jeeps towing boats, over-loaded semis with bad brakes, suicidal deer and homicidal elk loitering on the blacktop, blinding glare from distant metal roofs, spewt drivers talking on their cellphones, wind gusts strong enough to knock over trains — then I'll be home to discover that the cats have shredded the couch and the hot water pipes are frozen."

HOW COLORADO CAN BEST MEET ITS OBLIGATIONS TO KANSAS
MARCH 20, 2001

THERE ARE TIMES when Colorado does not enjoy a good reputation with its neighbors, and one of those occasions was a family picnic I attended in the summer of 1983.

That was a wet year, and I figured one of my cousins, who farmed wheat in western Kansas, would be anticipating a bountiful and profitable harvest.

But instead, he was complaining. "Did you know that it was front-page news in Dodge City that there was water flowing in the Arkansas River?"

No, I hadn't. "And do you know how much damage that caused, to have water in the river, to all the farm machinery and other stuff parked in the river bed?"

I started to explain that anyone with more intelligence than a Kansas farmer might know better than to store valuable equipment in a river bed, but he interrupted me.

"We always thought that there was one thing we could absolutely rely on: That Colorado would never let a drop of water come into Kansas. You guys have half the water lawyers in the world to look after your interests. What went wrong this year?"

But not all Kansans share his attitude about the utility of a dry river bed. In 1985, Kansas sued Colorado for not living up to its obligations under a 1949 interstate compact that required a certain amount of water to reach the sunflower State via the Arkansas River.

Kansas won, and now the U.S. Supreme Court is trying to calculate how much we owe them. Colorado would prefer to send water, while Kansas wants cash — about $62 million, money that would be hard to find in our state budget.

But maybe we could make Kansas an offer that involves some state asset that we could spare.

For instance, we've got thousands of mountains. The highest point in Kansas — Mount Sunflower in Wallace County, hard by the Colorado line — is only 4,039 feet above sea level, and those who have seen it say that it's not much of an eminence.

Clearly, Kansas could use a better mountain. We could offer to tear down one of our obscure and unnamed peaks and ship it to Hamilton County for re-assembly as a tourist attraction.

And if Kansas took the offer, we could cheat just a little and solve some of our own problems. We've got thousands of cubic yards of mine dumps and mill tailings, and much of that is toxic or radioactive stuff that the EPA wants us to remove.

Stack the rocks and grit in Kansas. They get a handsome peak, and we solve some of our environmental problems while compensating our neighbors for the water we didn't send them. And in this era of adventure tourism, the opportunity to climb "Mount Toxic" or "Radium Glow Peak" should bring plenty of free-spending visitors to Syracuse and Coolidge.

Even better, if the pile were shaped like an Egyptian or Mayan pyramid, persons seeking cosmic enlightenment might visit Kendall or Lakin instead of various Colorado mountain towns. Trust me, we can spare a few thousand New Age pilgrims to Kansas. But Kansas has some sharp attorneys — it must to have beaten our water lawyers in court — so we'll probably need to offer something besides a mountain.

History offers a suggestion for further reparations. Before Colorado Territory was formed in 1861, the entire Western Slope was part of Utah Territory. On the east side, Nebraska extended down to the fortieth parallel (Baseline Road in Boulder). The San Luis Valley and eastward to the 103rd meridian (the west edge of the Oklahoma panhandle) was New Mexico. All the rest was part of Kansas Territory (and since Kansas gained statehood on January 29, 1861, shortly before Colorado Territory was organized on February 28, 1861, it was even part of the state for almost a month).

In that western Kansas panhandle was an El Paso County, pretty much where our El Paso County is today.

Why not give that back to Kansas?

It's certainly worth much more than $100 million, the most that Kansas has ever claimed as damage for not getting enough water.

We'd be losing a county with about 500,000 residents, almost all of them hard-core Republicans (I met an El Paso County Democrat once, and she said she'd introduce me to the other one the next time I visited Colorado Springs). Thus our statewide politics would be more competitive.

And as a substantial part of the Kansas electorate (about 20 percent of the population), El Paso County would ensure that there wouldn't be any more controversies about teaching evolution in the public schools — the elected state board of education would always have a solid creationist majority.

This offer provides substantial benefits on both sides. The only drawback would be that Colorado Springs residents would have to change their speech habits. I have some relatives in El Dorado, Kansas, and they pronounce it "El Do-RAY-do" and assure me that this barbarism is just as proper as "Our Kansas" River for the Arkansas River.

So it would be "Co-lo-RAY-do Springs" in "El PAY-so County." That's not a big deal. We could all learn to adjust, and save Colorado water and money in the process.

IMAGINING THE 1976 COLORADO WINTER GAMES
FEBRUARY 24, 2002

AS A HISTORY BUFF, of course I enjoy reading history books. But often I derive even more pleasure from a genre known as "alternative history."

Typically, these tales take an event and examine how it might have happened differently. For instance, "If America had lost the Revolutionary War" might have had a storm that kept the French fleet away from Chesapeake Bay in the fall of 1781, so that the British navy could reinforce Lord Cornwallis at Yorktown, Virginia. Eventually George Washington and Thomas Jefferson would be captured and hanged at a British drumhead court-martial, but they would deliver rousing messages for liberty as they stood on the gallows.

For the past fortnight, I've read about how the Salt Lake games show what we might have enjoyed in Colorado in 1976, if misguided citizens like me had not voted against the Games in 1972.

So, let's try an alternative. We'll go back to 1971. The International Olympic Committee has awarded the games to Denver, and most Coloradans are excited and enthusiastic.

There are some critics, like Dick Lamm, a young state legislator, who discovers that Colorado will have to spend at least $35 million to host the Games, even though the promoters have promised that the state will spend no more than $5 million.

He attracts a few followers who circulate petitions for a constitutional amendment against using tax money for "the $50 million snow job."

The Colorado Establishment of the time, led by Governor John Love, campaigns hard for the Olympics. The anti-Olympic amendment is overwhelmingly defeated in the 1972 election, and Colorado gets ready to host the Games.

Even though Winter Park is owned by the City of Denver, and it has a railroad station at its base, the organizers put the downhill events at Copper Mountain, saying it has better terrain.

That means Interstate 70 has to be completed in time for the games, so that spectators can get from Denver, where there are some hotel rooms, to the event venues, where there isn't much lodging.

The first bore of the Straight Creek Tunnel under Loveland Pass is completed on schedule in 1973, but in the rush to get the second bore done by late 1975, several dozen miners die in accidents caused by haste, and the contractors are accused of cutting corners.

But the work gets done, despite the cost overruns that threaten to bankrupt the state — an ice arena in Denver, nordic trails and jumps at Steamboat Springs, new lifts and runs at Copper, athletes' villages all over the place.

The world gets to see Colorado in February 1976 as Governor Bill Daniels presides over the welcoming ceremony.

Daniels had narrowly defeated Lieutenant Governor John Vanderhoof in the hard-fought 1974 Republican primary, charging that Vanderhoof was "too much a politician to get things done," and plenty had to be done to get Colorado ready for the Olympics. In the general election, he swept over Democrat Mark Hogan, a former lieutenant governor, after it turned out that Hogan, as a private attorney, had once represented environmentalists in a lawsuit against Rocky Flats.

"Let the games begin," Daniels proclaims. "Colorado is ready." Alas, even a successful entrepreneur like Bill Daniels can't control the weather.

It's been so dry that they had to truck in snow, and ominous cracks — the result of shoddy construction — have already appeared in the wall of the new Straight Creek bore, although the engineers' reports were hushed up.

The mother of all blizzards strikes two days later. Denver comes to a total standstill, and the airport is closed. Busloads of journalists, spectators and athletes are stranded in the mountains near the remote settlement of Toponas, and with the gale-force winds and 1ten-foot drifts, they can't be rescued for several days. Some lose their toes and fingers to frostbite, and there are many grim jokes about Alfred Packer — even on TV.

Shortly after the storm lifts and the state starts moving again, the second bore of the I-70 tunnel collapses, taking the first one with it, and the detouring German alpine team is swept away by one of the Seven Sisters on Loveland Pass. The sewage backs up and the roofs leak in the jerry-built athletes' villages.

Everyone involved is more than relieved when this miserable fiasco finally ends. Colorado is embarrassed before the world, and as state taxes rise to cover the costs, the state's population plummets; by 2002, it has only 1.2 million people.

They, however, find it a pleasant place to live, uncrowded and relatively pristine as grizzly bears wander along what had once been I-70, now abandoned to the elements and the occasional ghost-town buff looking for the site of Vail.

This alternative history ends with Dick Lamm confessing that he was wrong to oppose the Games, even though they were a financial disaster. "As it turned out," he concludes, "the 1976 Winter Games were the best thing that ever happened for Colorado's environment."

COLORADO'S SHOW TRIALS
APRIL 3, 2005

TO SOME EXTENT, JUSTICE WAS SERVED last week when the Colorado Supreme Court ruled that Lisl Auman should get a new trial. She had been serving a life sentence without possibility of parole after her 1998 conviction for the felony murder of Bruce VanderJagt, a Denver police officer. Auman was handcuffed in the back of a police car at the time of the murder. The person who actually shot and killed VanderJagt was a skinhead named Matthaeus Jaehnig, and he killed himself after killing VanderJagt.

Those killings on November 12, 1997, were an ugly event during an ugly time of skinhead violence in Denver. Had Auman been sentenced to a few supervised years for general bad judgment and misconduct in the way she went about retrieving her goods from an ex-boyfriend's apartment, the system would have seemed fair. After all, a woman riding with one Jerald D. Allen — who at about the same time fired forty-seven shots at pursuing police while he drove a stolen car (starting in Jefferson County and ending in Denver) — got two and a half years of probation, and that's about the size of Auman's real crime.

But the sad fact was that a police officer was down, so somebody had to pay. Jaehnig was dead and beyond the reach of Denver District Attorney Bill Ritter, and so his office turned to Auman for the demonstration.

They couldn't exactly try her for murder, but if they could show that she had instigated a felony, and the shootings were the outcome of that felony, then she was as guilty as the person who pulled the trigger.

Part of the logic behind the felony-murder law is sound. If you agree to be the driver while your gang robs a convenience store, and they kill the clerk, you're certainly a party to the crime even if you were sitting in the car when the trigger was pulled.

But prosecutors can stretch it far past that. I saw it myself about a decade ago when a local kid, Jeremy Denison, was convicted of the felony murder of Richard Johnson. Denison argued self-defense, and at worst it looked like a clear case of manslaughter — a fight got out of hand, and somebody died.

Johnson was a police informant, a soldier in the vile war on drugs. He'd gotten into trouble in Alamosa, where he cut a deal that would keep him out of prison if he'd find ways to get Salida kids into trouble. It's hard enough to raise kids without this kind of help from the local police department — bringing in a steroid dealer with a flashy car to impress teenagers. Especially a guy who could threaten a local merchant with a shotgun, which the local police ignored since he was, after all, their soldier.

So when Johnson ended up dead on a back road near an abandoned quarry about ten miles out of town, the DA couldn't just charge manslaughter. That wouldn't send the right message. But to get felony murder, the prosecutors had to prove that Denison killed Johnson in the course of another crime. So they said that Denison, as a passenger while Johnson was driving, persuaded him to go up a back road to smoke a joint, all the while intending to stab him to death and steal the flashy Trans Am.

However, Johnson's car had run out of gas the preceding night, and he'd dispatched Denison with a gas can to get it that morning. If Denison had auto theft on his mind, why didn't he just take it then?

To keep the jury from thinking about such matters, the prosecution kept alluding to a Metallica concert and a satanic cult that was supposedly ensnaring Salida kids, and then told the jurors that only they were in a position to stop this horror. I felt certain that the jurors would see through this hobgoblin crap, but I was wrong. The conviction came quickly and Denison has been in prison ever since.

Jeremy Denison did cause Richard Johnson's death, but all I ever saw was a case for manslaughter. Lisl Auman did do some stupid things, but she was not a murderer. The news reports, after the Supreme Court decision last week, had prosecutors rejoicing because the Supreme Court had, after all, upheld the felony-murder law. Perhaps they should celebrate, since they can continue to go after those front-page show-trial convictions where the punishment far exceeds the actual crime.

GREETINGS FROM OUR BORDERS
JANUARY 17, 2006

SINCE I LIVE NEAR THE CENTER OF OUR STATE (that is, at least 100 miles from any place that outsiders may have heard of, like Boulder or Aspen), and a trip to Leadville or Montrose is a major outing, I have never paid much attention to those "Welcome to Colorful Colorado" signs at the borders.

The signs do not convey a feeling of "It feels good to be back home." It's more like "Another two or three hours of twisting mountain road replete with black ice, rockslides, manic Gen-X extreme sports motorists, tortoise-paced land yachts towing Jeeps towing boats, over-loaded semis with bad brakes, suicidal deer and homicidal elk loitering on the blacktop, blinding glare from distant metal roofs, spewt drivers talking on their cellphones, wind gusts strong enough to knock over trains — then I'll be home to discover that the cats have shredded the couch and the hot water pipes are frozen."

But those signs have become controversial. They're wooden, so they need more maintenance than modern metal signs. They also have a retro fifties look, like a roadside stand offering rubber tomahawks.

So our state's Office of Economic Development proposed a new and improved border sign. It had a chaste off-white background, small red letters for "Welcome to" and a big blue "Colorado." The reaction was about what you'd expect if they had decided to replace the bighorn sheep with the skunk as the official state mammal.

Even if he isn't running for office this year, Governor Bill Owens still has excellent political skills. Catching the swell of public opinion, he promised that our current wooden "Welcome to Colorful Colorado" signs would stay if the legislature would provide more money for promoting tourism.

This deserves more consideration, though. There are two related factors. One is the design, the other the message. Our design problem is simple: Unlike many neighboring states, we don't have a convenient state symbol.

New Mexico, for instance, has the zia, a circle with four sets of four rays. Utah presents the beehive. Wyoming offers its trademarked Bucking Horse & Rider. Kansas displays its sunflower.

In this era of brand-building, Colorado must be suffering economically because we do not use a consistent image to brand our state. There are several candidates. The crossed hammer and pick on our state seal is simple and distinctive, but it has been decades since mining dominated Colorado's economy, and few modern tourists are likely to think "Let's go to Colorado to see some stopes and winzes."

Our state flower, the columbine, adorns the Scenic Byway signs inside our borders, but it presents several problems as a border emblem. Columbines grow in many states. The image is not a simple one that stays in the mind. And columbine means "dove-like," which could be interpreted by Republicans as an anti-war statement, thus discouraging tourists from other red states.

We do have a masterpiece in the montane silhouette on our license plates, though. It's clear and simple. We should use that design on the welcome signs.

But what should the signs say? Just about every state's border announces that "Mississippi welcomes you" or "Welcome to Maine" or "The People of Iowa welcome you." Do we have to be like everyone else? Especially when there are so many Coloradans with attitude problems in this regard? Do we really want to welcome undocumented aliens, jet-setting Euro-trash and ambitious real-estate speculators?

Probably not, so why bother with an insincere "welcome" message? Further, we live in litigious times, when people are apt to file lawsuits if they were welcomed, but not warned about hazards like avalanches, wildlife, flash floods, wildfires, gridlock and the like.

Some test marketing is clearly in order, and I know just the place. The Cumbres & Toltec Scenic Railroad crosses the state line eleven times in its sixty-four twisting miles between Antonito and Chama, New Mexico. The steam-powered narrow-gauge trains run at a leisurely pace, giving people ample time to view and judge the Colorado border signs being tested with messages like "Howdy," "Come on in," or "Stay till you've maxed out your credit cards."

And I would hope that my proposed border sign might win favor. Green and white, based on our traditional license plate, it would say "Colorado: Enter at your own risk."

ADVENTURES IN HYPSOMETRY
JANUARY 9, 2007

IN MOST STATES where I've driven, when you reach the municipal limits sign on the highway, you see a sign that says something like "Backwater Junction. Population 985," and you look anxiously for a speed-limit sign because you don't want to get caught by the radar-gun speed trap that supplies the bulk of the municipal revenue.

The Lone Star Republic is an exception. There, the signs advise that the public water supply has been approved by the Texas Department of Public Health; in the rest of the country, we take it for granted that you can safely imbibe the tap water.

Colorado is another exception. Here we proclaim the town's altitude above sea level. Elevation is also something towns brag on, and now it's starting to get nasty.

For a long time, it was pretty simple. Leadville, at 10,161 feet, is the highest city in Colorado and the United States. It also boasts many other hypsometric distinctions, like "highest church steeple," "highest golf course," "highest airport" and "highest auto parts store." It also has the "highest higher education" in the country, with the Timberline Campus of Colorado Mountain College. (Along the "high" line, an old joke in the central mountains goes like this: "How do you spot a CMC grad?" "He can roll a one-paper joint.")

CMC is a two-year school, though. The highest four-year institution in the nation, and perhaps the world, is Western State College in Gunnison, at 7,603 feet.

Back to Leadville. In Colorado, a municipality with more than 2,000 residents can be incorporated as a city, as is the case with Leadville. Those with fewer than 2,000 are officially towns.

Having sat through interminable meetings of the governing bodies of both cities and towns, I can attest that there's no practical difference. The main one is that statutory cities are run by city councils, and statutory towns have boards of trustees. (A "statutory" municipality runs under state regulations, as opposed to a "home-rule" municipality with a charter.)

With a population of only 179, Alma is a town. It sits across Mosquito Pass (13,179 feet and a strong contender for "Highest Pass in North America") from Leadville. Alma sits 10,361 feet above the tides, or 200 feet higher than Leadville. Alma is not the highest city, but it is the highest town and highest municipality.

(Neither has the highest post office. That distinction belongs to ZIP code 80429, Climax, which sits atop Fremont Pass at 11,358 feet. And if you want to win some bar bets, you can wager that Mile High Denver is not the highest state capital in the United States. Santa Fe, at 6,995, and Cheyenne, 6,089, are both higher.)

So for years, Alma and Leadville were comfortable in their distinctions. But last year, Winter Park, official elevation 9,052, annexed the ski area into its municipal boundaries. This was to simplify planning and zoning, so that the resort and the Forest Service could work with just the town government, rather than both the town and county governments.

However, this put the top of the ski lifts into the town limits, and that includes a 12,069-foot peak. So Winter Park, which wasn't even incorporated until 1979, plans to promote itself as the nation's highest municipality, even if the residential and commercial zones top out at under 10,000 feet.

Vince Turner, who serves on the Winter Park town board, said the altitude boasting was a marketing ploy to attract more skiers. "People in New York trying to book a vacation say, 'Let's go to the highest place. They're bound to have the best snow,'" he said.

Winter Park sits close by Fraser, which wanted to drop its "Icebox of the Nation" slogan. Apparently tourists do not say, "Let's go to the ski area by the coldest place. It's bound to have the best snow."

There's no real connection between snowfall and either cold or elevation. Gunnison is one of the most frigid inhabited spots in America, and it gets only 50.5 inches of snow in an average winter; Denver gets 59.4. Saguache is 1,500 feet higher than Denver, and averages only 25.9 inches. Buena Vista, half a mile higher than Denver, averages only 39.5 inches.

Since we're already nearing the average snowfall for this winter, I was hoping for a break. But there's another storm scheduled for later this week, and Winter Park is welcome to come and collect all the snow it wants from my sidewalk, street and woodpile. I can attest that it is snow of excellent quality that should impress New Yorkers.

And let little old Alma enjoy its distinction.

COLORADAN OR COLORADOAN?
MARCH 18, 2007

ONE PROBLEM WITH OUR STATE GOVERNMENT is that it has rules that are not enforced, specifically Article II, Section 30a, of our state constitution: "The English language is the official language of the State of Colorado."

Just what that means is rather vague. Since it says "English," rather than "American English," do our cars have bonnets, boots and windscreens instead of hoods, trunks and windshields? No court has ruled, so it falls on vigilantes like me to enforce Official English. One frequent question is what to call a resident: Are you a "Coloradoan" or a "Coloradan?"

The informal rule is explained in the 1945 book "Names on the Land" by George R. Stewart, which I do not have, so I cite it secondhand from "The American Language" by H.L. Mencken, updated in 1982 by Raven I. McDavid Jr., and David W. Maurer.

By and large, when a place name ends in "o," you add "an." The exception is if the place name is of Spanish origin; then you drop the "o" before adding "an."

This observed rule appears to work in practice. Idaho and Chicago derive from Native American languages, not Spanish, and their residents are Idahoans and Chicagoans.

San Francisco comes from Spanish, and thus San Franciscans reside there. Residents of other realms with Spanish names are Mexicans and Puerto Ricans. Since Colorado is a Spanish word for the color red, we are properly Coloradans, not Coloradoans.

As best I know, most Colorado newspapers follow this rule, but there have been exceptions. Most notable, perhaps, is the *Fort Collins Coloradoan*. It is owned by the Gannett chain, which until 1989 also owned the daily newspaper in the capital of the Land of Enchantment, the *Santa Fe New Mexican*.

Consistency would seem to require either a Fort Collins Coloradan or a Santa Fe New Mexicoan, at least when both newspapers were under the same ownership. At the Coloradoan, state residents used to be Coloradoans, but now we're Coloradans, according to Jason Melton, a copy editor at the paper. The change came a couple of years ago, and now the only Coloradoan published there is the paper's name.

The *Pueblo Chieftain* also used Coloradoan until a few years ago, when it switched to Coloradan, according to my friend Hal Walter, a part-time copy editor there. However, consistency does not rule. The residents of Pueblo (Spanish for town) should be Pueblans by the rule that gives us Coloradan, but in the *Chieftain*, they're Puebloans.

"Puebloan" also appears in the modern Politically Correct Southwestern Dialect, in reference to the people who built at Mesa Verde and Chaco Canyon a millennium ago. In recent years, I've been told that we should talk about "Ancestral Puebloans" rather than "Anasazi," since Anasazi derives from a Navajo term for "enemy ancestors" and is thus somehow insulting, or perhaps dismissive of modern Pueblo peoples because it ignores their ancestors' probable role in construction.

I continue to use "Anasazi." For one thing, it has no meaning in English other than "the people who built that old stuff around the Four Corners." For another, ever since the *Pueblo Chieftain* didn't hire me in 1983, I prefer not to spell "Pueblan" as "Puebloan."

At any rate, our legislature seems to enjoy passing resolutions this year, so could the General Assembly please settle this issue and officially resolve that residents of the Centennial State are Coloradans, lest some English-only fanatic try to make us Color-Reddians? A resolution would be one small but useful step toward our own Official English.

A COLORADO QUIZ FOR TOURIST SEASON
JUNE 3, 2010

NOW THAT SUMMER TOURIST SEASON has officially started, you likely want to travel around our fair state. Of course, the more you know about Colorado, the more you'll enjoy those trips. And to help you pursue that knowledge (none of which is likely to get you a promotion or a pay raise, alas), here's a little quiz.

1) Where would you go to find Zekes?

2) What river changes its name when it leaves Colorado?

3) Who is the best-paid writer in Colorado?

4) Where's the lowest point in Colorado?

5) Long before English became Colorado's "official language" in 1992, what languages were official in Colorado?

6) Which Colorado governor attempted to limit immigration by ordering the National Guard to turn back "aliens and indigent persons" at the state line?

7) What is the tallest Colorado mountain named for a woman?

ANSWERS

1) Zekes are found in Gilpin (sometimes locally pronounced "Gulpin"' County, whose seat is Central City. The term comes from the old "ZK" licenseplate prefix. The Zeke lifestyle is characterized by hard living and sporadic employment, and Zekes are a subgroup of an endangered species, Mountain Low Lifes, whose habitat is threatened by gentrification.

2) The Arkansas River is pronounced "Arkansaw" here. Immediately downstream, it's something like "Our Kanzus." Its proper pronunciation returns in Oklahoma and Arkansas.

3) Scott McInnis, a Republican candidate for governor. He received approximately $150,000 from the Hassan Family Foundation, for which, as he explained on a radio program, "I wrote a series of in-depth articles on water" that "could be used in a series for education on water in Colorado."

I follow water stuff fairly closely, and I never saw the work. Jason Salzman, former media critic for the *Rocky Mountain News*, talked to everybody who might have reasonably encountered this hydrologic epic, and came up empty; McInnis' office did not respond to his questions.

So $150,000 divided by zero disseminated words works out to something like infinity. Thus, Scooter must be the best-paid writer in our state. And if he doesn't get elected governor, I want to engage him as my literary agent, since he knows how to cut some sweet deals.

4) If you said "the Arkansas River at the Kansas line, about 3,350 feet," you haven't kept up on recent developments. A few years ago, it was discovered that the Arikaree River at the Kansas line in lower, at 3,317. However, Colorado still has the "highest lowest point" of any state.

5) The 1876 state constitution provided that the laws and ballots be published in German, Spanish and English until 1890.

6) Edwin C. "Big Ed" Johnson gave that order for Colorado's southern border with New Mexico and Oklahoma in 1936. One suspected indigent turned out to be carrying $5,000 in cash, and twenty of thirty-two suspected immigrants turned out to be U.S. citizens. The blockade was in effect for only eleven days before Johnson rescinded his proclamation of martial law.

7) One 14,249-foot peak was originally named Mount Rosalie, christened in honor of his mistress by nineteenth century landscape painter Albert

Bierstadt. But in 1895, the legislature changed it to Mount Evans to honor John Evans, railroad builder, university founder and territorial governor.

Mount Hope, 13,940 feet in Chaffee County, may be named for a woman; I haven't been able to discover its namesake. Mount Silverheels, 13,822 in Park County, is definitely named for a woman: a dance-hall girl (whose shoes had silver heels) in the mining camp of Buckskin Joe. She stayed to nurse stricken miners during an 1861 smallpox epidemic, then vanished from history.

WHY WE SHOULDN'T BE CELEBRATING COLORADO DAY
JULY 31, 2011

DURING OUR RECENT ROAD TRIP, we stayed in a chain motel in Dumas, Texas, which offered a breakfast buffet. I took some eggs and fruit juice; on account of my Type 2 diabetes, I ignored the waffle iron.

But our daughter Columbine used it. "Look at this waffle," she said as she buttered it before drenching it in syrup. "It's shaped just like Texas. Isn't that neat?"

Being a grumpy and chauvinistic resident of our Centennial State, I demurred. "Why's that so special? At home we can make waffles shaped just like Colorado."

Rectangular waffles might be as good as any way to celebrate Colorado Day on Monday. It's the 135th anniversary of Colorado becoming a state on August 1, 1876 — the centennial year of the Declaration of Independence, thereby providing a nickname which sounds classier than "One of those big square states out West."

Of the fifty states, only Colorado and Wyoming are rectangles, more or less. They're not perfect rectangles because rectangles are from plane geometry and state lines are drawn on an oblate spheroid. Thus their northern borders are about twenty miles shorter than their southern boundaries. Further, there are some minor jogs in the lines on account of surveying errors and mishaps over the years.

But Colorado is pretty close to rectangular, and delve as I might into our history, I've never learned how the pioneers determined its extent. The simple answer is that they borrowed the borders, to some degree, from the extra-legal

"Territory of Jefferson" which operated illegally from 1859 until Colorado Territory was created 150 years ago, in 1861.

However, Jefferson was bigger, including all of present Colorado plus some of Wyoming, Kansas, Nebraska and Utah. My best guess is that since the pioneers came for the "Pikes Peak Gold Rush," Colorado's organizers drew a big rectangle with Pikes Peak near its center.

Colorado almost attained statehood in 1864. The Civil War was not been going well for the Union that summer — William T. Sherman had apparently stalled in Georgia and Robert E. Lee was thwarting U.S. Grant in Virginia. President Abraham Lincoln despaired of re-election.

One way to get more Republican electoral votes for Lincoln was to admit more states likely to vote Republican. So Congress approved enabling acts for Nebraska, Nevada and Colorado to become states in time for the 1864 election. Nebraska elected delegates to a constitutional convention; they met and decided to postpone the expense and responsibility of statehood by not drafting a constitution. Nevadans produced and approved a constitution, thus gaining statehood on October 31, 1864, just in time to help re-elect Lincoln.

Coloradans produced a constitution in 1864, but a majority of territorial voters rejected it as a power grab by "the Denver crowd." Coloradans did pass a constitution in 1865, but the U.S. Senate turned it down at the urging of African-Americans, who were not guaranteed the right to vote in Colorado. Another statehood bill was vetoed by President Andrew Johnson in 1867.

Colorado did become a state in 1876, just in time to provide three electoral votes for Republican Rutherford B. Hayes, who won 185-184. If Colorado had not joined the Union, Samuel J. Tilden would have been elected president. The only other time Colorado made a difference in a national election was in 2000, when George W. Bush won 271-266 with the help of Colorado's eight electoral votes.

Given that without Colorado, Bush might well have stayed in Texas, it's hard to argue that our statehood is really worth celebrating. Maybe that's why Colorado Day is no longer an official holiday.

IN COLORADO, NORTH FORKS
ALL OVER THE MAP
APRIL 1, 2012

IF YOU CAN CATCH THINGS out of the corner of your eye, why not with the corner of an ear? That's how I heard something about "North Fork fire" from the TV set in another room.

I'd just been out walking the dog in a spot where I could see up the North Fork. The air was so clear I could almost count the rocks on 12,913-foot Sewanee Peak (a little-known "Collegiate Peak" christened in 1953 by Charles S. Robinson, a geologist who had attended Sewanee, the University of the South in Tennessee).

Obviously, there was no forest fire up the nearest North Fork. The next place that came to mind was the North Fork of the Gunnison, a pleasant valley of orchards and coal mines. I was concerned about friends there until I learned that the North Fork of the wildfire was in the Conifer area.

That's confusing. The U.S. Geological Survey lists 192 North Forks in Colorado. Not all of them are streams, as there's a North Fork Mine and a North Fork Dam and the like. But my own Chaffee County has ten North Forks, most of which were new to me, like the North Fork of Middle Cottonwood Creek.

The USGS lists seventy-three Cottonwood Creeks in Colorado. The famous Clear Creek rises west of Golden, but we've got one up here, too, and there are at least ten others. Cherry Creek? There's the one that ends in Denver, and there's one down the road from me in the Howard area. And about a dozen more. The most popular name may be Dry Creek, with 111 Colorado entries.

My mother grew up on a ranch in Wyoming and she once told me they hauled their household water from a Dry Creek. I was eight years old and "Dry Creek" sounded like a contradiction that couldn't have supplied water.

She explained that her Dry Creek, and maybe all the others, got its name because it always had water, even if it was dry everywhere else. That made sense, I suppose. But my Wyoming favorites were streams like Poison, Lightning or Crazy Woman Creek.

We have some fine creek names in Colorado, too, like Oh-Be-Joyful, Shoe-and-Stocking, Cinnamon and Troublesome. There ought to be a way to apply more colorful names to replace the banal and repetitive geographic nomenclature.

Colorado has one distinctive place name that pops up from time to time: Chivington. John M. Chivington commanded the soldiers who destroyed the Confederate supply train at Glorieta Pass on March 28, 1862. He was a staunch abolitionist who risked his life to fight slavery, so he's more complicated than just being the butcher of Sand Creek in 1864.

Chivington sits out on the plains near the site of the Sand Creek Massacre. It was named by the Missouri Pacific Railroad when it extended into Colorado in 1887. The railroad built a siding with a section house every six miles or so, and the spots were named alphabetically west from the Kansas line: Arden, Brandon, Chivington, Diston, Eads, Fergus, etcetera. So it wasn't as though the General Assembly passed a resolution saying, "Let's celebrate John M. Chivington by naming a town after him." An eastern corporation named the place. Blame Jay Gould if you have to blame somebody.

Chivington is not incorporated and no longer even has a post office. It's fading away and there's no need to push it along. Besides, John Milton Chivington was an important figure in our history, and we shouldn't forget him. Remembering isn't the same as honoring. Besides, it's a place name like no other.

'Tis the Season

The first Christmas celebration in Colorado happened 199 years ago today, a few miles north of Salida near the mouth of Brown's Canyon. Captain Zebulon Montgomery Pike and his fifteen soldiers had reason to celebrate. They were in the highest valley of the Rocky Mountains in the dead of winter, and their last food had been a turkey and a hare shot on December 22. But on Christmas Eve, Dr. John H. Robinson and interpreter Baroney Vasquez killed four bison, and another hunter, Private John Sparks, killed four more. They would enjoy a Christmas feast.

MORE SCARY COSTUMES
OCTOBER 31, 2000

ACCORDING TO THE PEOPLE who keep track of such things, Halloween now ranks second, just after Christmas, in the amount of holiday consumer spending that it inspires among Americans — something like $5 billion this year.

This must be a result of a role-reversal. When I was a kid, Halloween was something that kids observed and adults generally ignored, with two exceptions.

One is that mothers had us kids make some caramel apples for trick-or-treaters. The other adult involvement is that the men, like your father and uncles, would tell interesting stories about acts of vandalism they performed on Halloweens long ago — tipped-over privies, cherry bombs down the chimney, etcetera — with dire warnings as to how many times grandpa's old razor strop would be applied to your posterior if you even thought about emulating these heroic feats of yesteryear.

Meanwhile, we kids would assemble some pirate or ghost costumes on the cheap and wear them to school on Halloween. If the weather was nice, we'd parade through downtown Evans, Colorado, which then consisted of a park, post office and two small stores. (Our parade was not a major disruption of the academic process).

Now Halloween is an adult holiday with extravagant parties and costly costumes. Celebration by children in many schools has been forbidden, being as it could be an occult influence that would compel them to read astrology columns and flip coins during their adulthood, with dire consequences to the American way of life.

So, for you professional killjoys, the following costume suggestions are not for children. They're for adults who are looking for truly scary outfits to wear.

Prostitute. Costume shops say the most popular outfits this year are "pimps and hookers." But if you live in the metro area, save your money and just wear normal business clothes.

People might ask about this novel get-up. You can explain that a prostitute is someone who puts money ahead of honor or decency or public respect, and that your courtesan costume is that of a Metropolitan Football Stadium Board member who persists in trying to peddle the naming rights even though the vast majority of the people who are paying the bills want to keep "Mile High Stadium."

Multi-faced monster. Al Gore masks aren't selling well this year, so you should be able to get a break on the price, especially if you're buying in bulk.

And you'll need to, so that you can go out as the anti-abortion Al Gore and the pro-choice Al Gore, as the tobacco-farming Al Gore and the anti-smoking Al Gore, as the gun-rights Al Gore and the gun-control Al Gore. Just remember to walk stiffly and wear earth tones, just in case people have trouble figuring out who you're supposed to be.

Welfare recipient. No need to look through the rag bin for this one. A blue suit with a white shirt and a red tie should do the job. That's the normal costume for one fellow who in 1989 invested $600,000 in a sports franchise, then threatened to move it unless local voters bought a new stadium. With the new publicly financed stadium, the team was worth a lot more, so the fellow was able to sell out in 1998 and get $15 million for his share.

That's corporate welfare from the public till that comes to about $1.6 million a year — far more than Ronald Reagan's "Cadillac welfare queen" ever managed to hustle. Just in case the blue suit and red tie aren't enough for people to identify you as a welfare recipient, you can also put on a George W. Bush mask.

Amendment 24. This growth-management proposal could be the scariest of all, since the opposition propaganda says it's "too extreme for Colorado." That's extreme indeed, considering that Colorado's heritage includes Charlie Bent, Mother Jones and Big Bill Haywood. They were harassed, arrested and shot at — but nobody ever said they were "too extreme for Colorado."

For further evidence of Amendment 24's fright power, look at who's scared. All manner of normally confident organizations are rattled by the specter of Amendment 24: the Colorado Association of Realtors, the Colorado Bankers Association, the National Association of Industrial and Office Properties, just to name a few.

So it seems obvious that if you want to really frighten people this Halloween, Amendment 24 is the best costume. I'm not too sure what it would look like, though. A big stack of planning documents that people are supposed to read before an election? Or can you get a John Fielder mask somewhere?

Traditional Feast Hard to Swallow
November 25, 2001

ONE THING I'M VERY THANKFUL FOR is that Thanksgiving Day comes only once a year.

Not that I have anything against expressing gratitude; such a list could run for pages, and even then it would cover only a few of life's daily pleasures: "Simpsons" reruns, a cozy fire in the parlor stove, an old dog that still enjoys a daily walk, public radio, Linux and a small town with a high tolerance for eccentricity that sits far from scheduled air service or an interstate highway.

My problem with the fourth Thursday in November has nothing to do with gratitude. I have plenty to be thankful for, and I don't mind saying so. The problem is that I don't care for turkey. Everyone else in the family likes it, and this is their annual opportunity to enjoy it in copious amounts, so I go along.

I'm sure I'm not the only one who'd prefer ham or beef or even tofu to turkey. Yet while there are national toll-free hotlines to assist fowl cooks, I don't know of a single support group for people who would like to say "neither" when asked "light or dark?"

It makes one wish that the Founding Fathers had paid more attention to Benjamin Franklin, who argued the eagle was not a fitting mascot, and the turkey would be an improvement.

"For the truth," he wrote to his daughter in 1784, "the Turkey is in Comparison a much more respectable Bird, an withal a true original Native of America. He is besides, though a little vain and silly, a Bird of Courage, and would not hesitate to attack a Grenadier of the British Guards who should presume to invade his Farm Yard with a red Coat on."

If the turkey were the national emblem, then the bird would be protected, and we couldn't butcher and eat it, right?

By contrast, Franklin wrote that the bald eagle "is a Bird of bad moral Character. He does not get his Living honestly too lazy to fish for himself, he watches the Labour of the Fishing Hawk; and when that diligent Bird has at length taken a Fish, and is bearing it to his Nest for the Support of his Mate and young Ones, the Bald Eagle pursues him and takes it from him." Thus, Franklin concluded, the eagle is "like those among Men who live by Sharping & Robbing."

Which makes me think that perhaps the eagle really is a better symbol. No, never mind. Nosing around Franklin's work often brings up subversive material like "They that can give up essential liberty to obtain a little temporary safety deserve neither liberty nor safety."

Thoughts like that are inappropriate in these safety-conscious times, when the snoops have been empowered. Consider what happened recently in the city where Franklin conducted most of his career, Philadelphia. Neil Godfrey was attempting to board an airplane to Phoenix. He was detained and questioned for so long that he missed his flight, and even after he was searched, he was not permitted to board.

Why? Because he was carrying a book to read on the flight. The book was *Hayduke Lives!* by Edward Abbey. It has come to this in our "Land of the Free": You can't travel if your choice in reading displeases an airport security screener.

Somehow, I don't think this is what Benjamin Franklin had in mind when he helped establish this country.

But if you want to be on the safe side when you travel, I'm willing to help. Franklin, like Abbey, wrote some insurrectionary prose. There is a chance that you'll encounter a literate security screener who knows about those works. Thus you could get detained or worse if you happen to be carrying Franklin-related material.

So, before you go to the airport, examine your wallet. If you find any engraved portraits of Benjamin Franklin, just mail them to me at P.O. Box 548, Salida, CO 81201. I'll take care of the problem; it's the least I can do to help assure the safety of the traveling public.

And I will be thankful for this opportunity to assist my fellow citizens. I am also thankful that the Pilgrims landed in Massachusetts. Suppose they had made their way to the Great Lakes before settling down to farm in 1620.

Instead of encountering Squanto, Samoset and the Wampanoags, the Pilgrims might have settled among the Arapaho and Cheyenne, who lived beside the Great Lakes before migrating to the western edge of the Great Plains in about 1800.

A joint harvest feast could well have ensued, and naturally there would be indigenous cuisine. Our Thanksgiving tradition would not feature a roasted turkey, but instead a roasted dog. As far as I'm concerned, the only good turkey is a wild turkey — especially when it's on the label of a whiskey bottle.

But no matter how thankful I am when we run out of Thanksgiving leftovers and I can return to palatable food, I am even more thankful that the Pilgrims didn't land in Minnesota. The traditional turkey is hard enough to swallow.

MIXING OLD WEST WITH NEW
CAN BE RISKY
DECEMBER 22, 2002

IT'S THAT TIME OF THE YEAR AGAIN, and as usual, I'm running behind. For one thing, I was invited to several winter solstice celebrations this year, and as a bit of a social klutz, I don't know the etiquette for these gatherings.

I learned the hard way about the proper decorum for office Christmas parties when I worked at the local newspaper. It was 1980, the paper's centennial year. On that account, the party was held at the oldest business in Chaffee County, the 1878 Jackson Hotel in Poncha Springs. At that saloon, some months earlier, Allen Best and I had concocted a potation which, in our informed view, combined the Rugged Old West with the Enlightened New West: a double-shot of straight rye chased with Perrier. That seemed an appropriate libation for the December office party.

Little else do I remember directly. I do recall that A) I was probably the only one drinking rye, and B) the bartender opened more than one bottle of Old Overholt. I was later informed that I had orated at some length, telling certain co-workers exactly what I thought of them.

The following Monday, no one at work would speak to me. This continued well into the week, until I found a quotation attributed to Friedrich Nietzsche and posted it above my desk: "Man drinks to become a beast that he may forget the pain of being a man."

The more soft-hearted of my colleagues began seeing me as poor victim in need of support and sympathy, rather than as a tyrannical managing editor, and by February or so, harmony again reigned. Thereafter I made it a rule to drink nothing stronger than club soda at office parties, since a clear-headed observer can gather a great deal of information that can be useful later when it is necessary to practice office politics. In other words, it is better to amass ammunition than to provide it.

Granted, this is contrary to the spirit of the occasion, but at least I know the spirit of the occasion. When it comes to solstice celebrations, I'm not sure what we're celebrating. This year, I'm not even sure when to celebrate.

Our word "solstice" comes from the Latin word "solstitium," a compound of "sol," the sun, and "sistere," to stand still. Through the year, the place where the sun appears to rise and set moves north until June 22 or so, then south until December 22.

Although this day-to-day solar motion is usually apparent to one who watches these things, the sun appears to rise (or set) in the same place for a few days at either end. Thus the term "solstice," since the sun seems to be standing still. From parts of Salida, for instance, the sun sets behind Mount Ouray for a few days around the winter solstice, and behind Mount Shavano during the summer solstice.

According to the World Almanac, the sun reaches its southernmost point this year at 1:14 a.m., Coordinated Universal Time (the zone formerly known as Greenwich Mean Time), on December 23. Translate that to our unknown-to-the- TV-networks Mountain Time, and it's 6:14 p.m. on December 22.

That explains the December 22 solstice party, but not the solstice bonfire on the night of the 21st or the solstice potluck on the 20th.

The southern solstice is also "the first day of winter," just as the vernal equinox is the "first day of spring," etcetera, but whoever came up with those seasonal dates for the temperate zone of the northern hemisphere was not from Colorado. We don't have a "spring" ("tick season" and "mud season" are as close as we get). Some years, winter starts in September and continues into May, while in other years it barely comes at all.

Another reputed distinction for the southern solstice is that it is the shortest day of our year. That's basically true, at least for this December 22. The numbers at hand are for the intersection of the 105th meridian and the 40th parallel, a point about five miles east of Lafayette. Today, the sun rises at 7:19 a.m. and sets at 4:38 p.m., for only nine hours and nineteen minutes of sunlight. December 23 will be a minute longer, but we'll be back to 9:19 on Christmas Eve before the lengthening really starts. So it's a tie between December 22 and December 24 for "fewest hours of sunlight."

The solstice is the shortest day, but it's not the day of the latest sunrise or earliest sunset. The sun won't rise until 7:22 a.m. on December 31, and dawn won't come any earlier until January 11. We've already endured the earliest sunset, at 4:35 p.m. on December 1.

None of this knowledge, of course, provides any guidance for behavior at a solstice party — appropriate greetings, what to bring, what to wear and so forth. But I suspect it's a good idea to lay off the rye, no matter how appealing the notion of combining Old West with New.

TIME TO GIVE UP ON LABOR DAY?
AUGUST 31, 2003

PERHAPS IT'S TIME TO CHANGE the name of the state and federal holiday celebrated on the first Monday in September. For more than a century, it has been known as Labor Day, and it was created to honor "the contributions workers have made to the strength, prosperity and well-being of our country."

It was once celebrated with parades of union workers, but so far, I haven't found any mention of a Labor Day parade in Colorado this year. Denver is busy this weekend with a Broncos preseason game, the annual tear-gassing of the crowds at the CU-CSU game, three days of downtown auto racing and A Taste of Colorado — but no Labor Day Parade.

Up here in the mountains, there are scores of festivals designed to garner a few more tourist dollars before the cold sets in, but the only one that mentioned a parade was in Ridgway, and it's a "cowboy parade," not an exhibition of the solidarity of the working class.

Just to be sure I hadn't missed something in my search for a traditional Labor Day celebration, I called the Colorado office of the AFL-CIO. I got a recorded message that the office was moving and would not be open again until September 8.

According to the U.S. Department of Labor, Labor Day was first celebrated in 1882 in New York City, and by 1885 it had spread to most American industrial centers. With its mines, railroads and smelters, Colorado was more industrial than pastoral in the 1880s. Oregon was the first state to make Labor Day a state holiday, on February 21, 1887, but Colorado was second, enacting the official holiday on March 25, 1887. The first official celebration came that September in Denver with a parade and all-day picnic at Argo Park at 47th and Logan.

There were several reasons unions pushed for the holiday. One was to get a day off with pay. That day off could be used to build solidarity at a picnic. And the parade to the picnic grounds could demonstrate labor's strength so that politicians would support the labor agenda.

Colorado's labor leaders wanted the state to outlaw child labor, which persisted until the 1910s. They advocated a law that would force companies to pay in cash, rather than in scrip that was good only at the company store. They agitated for the eight-hour day, which came only after a long and bloody struggle — and a meaningless one, since it's nearly impossible now to support a family on one eight-hour-a-day job.

We have a rich and violent labor history in Colorado, complete with terrorist bombings, concentration camps, kangaroo courts and massacres. It has an engaging cast with agitators Mother Jones and Big Bill Haywood, capitalists John D. Rockefeller Jr. and Jay Gould, along with mad-bomber Harry Orchard and enlightened coal-mine owner Josephine Roche, to name a few. We had spineless governors like Elias Ammons and brave ones like Davis H. Waite, and we had socialists holding state office.

· Despite all this, it is a history that is generally ignored. Martha and I make a habit of visiting small-town museums. They're full of lore about the first gold strike, cattle ranch, railroad arrival or irrigation ditch. But in only one have we found more than passing mention of the major union in Colorado's history: the Western Federation of Miners. Appropriately, that museum is in Victor — the working-class neighbor of glittering Cripple Creek, six miles away. A century ago, Victor was a stronghold of the WFM, which had organized local gold mines to keep a $3 wage for an eight-hour day.

On that account, Victor was also a target of our state militia — no matter what the state or federal constitution says about "freedom of the press," its newspaper was shut down by the militia during the strike of 1903-04. Or, as militia Major Thomas McClelland put it, "To hell with the constitution! We are not following the constitution."

The WFM protested those outrages by issuing a poster, which asked, "Is Colorado in America?" Below that was a U.S. flag with some commentary in the stripes, such as "Free speech denied in Colorado!" and "Corporations corrupt and control administration in Colorado!"

Colorado's leaders did not respond by investigating these allegations and then correcting any problems. Instead, two officers of the WFM — Haywood and Charles Moyer — were arrested for "desecrating the American flag."

That's a very small part of a long and lively story, one worthy of contemplation if Labor Day lived up to its name in Colorado. As it is, we ought to be honest and change it to the End of Summer Tourist Season Festival, since that's what we actually celebrate.

Bones and Bonita
December 23, 2003

If you ever hear someone tell you that he was sitting in the lobby of a motel in Longmont on Christmas Eve three decades ago, and some people in robes showed up leading donkeys, one bearing a woman who appeared to be pregnant — you're hearing a true story.

In 1968, my parents moved from Greeley to Longmont just after I graduated from high school. Their Longmont house had a huge lot, which inspired my brother Kurt to buy a pet suited for a big yard. It was a jackass he named Bones. Bones ate all the bark off an apple tree, forced some fence improvements, and greeted every sunrise with a stentorian bray. The neighbors did not complain, since there were chickens in one adjacent yard and sheep on the other. (Longmont was still much a farm town in those days.)

I was in college in Greeley then, where I met Martha. In 1973, we had moved to Longmont, living a few blocks from my parents, and it struck us that Bones could use a companion. Plus, we had this dream of making a long summer pack trip in the mountains, and one donkey wouldn't be enough to tote all the gear we'd need while we walked from the Front Range to the San Juans.

We saw an ad in the paper; someone near Hygiene had a jenny for sale for $15. We drove over there in my old Ford van. My dad, who knew something about livestock, inspected the jenny's teeth, eyes and hooves, and pronounced her well worth the price. He also figured out how to load her into an Econoline van with two ropes, a blindfold and a chunk of two-by-four applied behind one knee while I poked her rump with a sharp stick.

We put her in the backyard with Bones, who was quite interested in her after years of celibacy. We had christened her Bonita, since that name fit with Bones, and we anticipated offspring. Bonita, however, kicked up a cloud of sharp hooves whenever Bones came near her with romance on his mind, and he soon settled for a platonic relationship.

This brings us to Christmas Eve in 1973. Martha and I had moved back to Greeley for another try at college, but we had gone to Longmont for Christmas. In the backyard were Bones and Bonita. After dinner, we thought about board games, when someone had another idea for entertainment.

Why not take the donkeys for a walk in Longmont? While we were at it, why not put Martha in robes, along with a pillow to mimic pregnancy? She could ride Bonita. I'd also dress in robes and lead, and Kurt would also don robes and lead Bones. We could visit any motels on Main Street that were open, and ask if there was room in the inn.

It sounded like fun, and so off we went, Martha padded out and aboard the old McClellan saddle that my dad had rescued years ago from the town dump in Douglas, Wyoming.

The only equine complication came at a motel that had one of those near-life-size plastic horse statues in front. The spectacle aroused Bones to carnal urges, and Kurt had a minute or two of hard work keeping him in place.

But otherwise, the journey went well. The few motorists we saw — including a cop or two — all smiled and waved.

At the motels, reactions were varied, but all were quite friendly. Most joked that they hated to ruin the story, but there was room in the inn — if we could figure out a place to stake out the donkeys for the night.

One manager said he really did have a stable we could stay in if necessary. He insisted on taking us around back to show it to us: a barnboard remnant from the nineteenth century, complete with two stalls and a manger.

At another, the couple in the lobby was reading the second chapter of Luke to their grandchildren when we showed up. They thought our arrival was just this side of miraculous, and the children were thrilled to pet the donkeys and feed them apples before riding Bonita while I led her around the parking lot. Today, of course, I'd never let little kids that close to a donkey I was leading. Donkeys can bite and kick. Litigation would doubtless ensue, and I can't imagine how I'd stand in a courtroom and explain why I was leading a jenny around on Christmas Eve.

I still don't know why we did it, but it brightened our Christmas and that of many others. May something just as strange brighten your Christmas in 2003.

BIRTH OF COLUMBUS DAY
OCTOBER 12, 2004

IT'S TURNING INTO A TRADITION. On the Saturday before the official federal Monday holiday, there's a Columbus Day parade in Denver. And there's a protest against the parade. This year, the protesters blocked the route for about an hour, and more than 200 people were arrested.

It's easy to understand the reason for the parade — it's a sort of "Italian-American celebration of ethnic pride." It's also easy to understand the protests — the intercourse that began on October 12, 1492, was devastating to American Indians.

But it's not quite so easy to understand why this happens in land-locked Colorado, rather than some maritime venue with a better connection to Columbus.

According to the protesters at the Transform Columbus Day Alliance, "There is no better place ... to begin than in Colorado, the birthplace of the Columbus Day holiday."

That's true. In 1907, Colorado was the first state to make Columbus Day a state holiday, followed by New York in 1909. How did it come about that Colorado was ahead of New York with something?

The answer lies with Casimiro Barela. Although he is one of only sixteen people honored with a stained-glass portrait in the rotunda of our state Capitol, he is not nearly as well-known as most of the others, like John Dyer, Kit Carson and Chief Ouray.

Barela was born in New Mexico in 1847, and moved to Las Animas County, Colorado, in 1867. He was involved in many enterprises, from freighting to newspaper publishing, but his major business was a profitable ranch that sat twenty miles east of Trinidad.

His political career started in 1869 when he was elected justice of the peace. He climbed the ladder quickly: county assessor and territorial representative in 1870, county sheriff in 1871, delegate to the Colorado constitutional convention in 1875, state senator for many years thereafter — a seat he kept even after switching from Democrat to Republican in 1904.

In the Territorial Assembly, Barela fought the "English only" lobby of the era, and got the laws published in Spanish as well. As a delegate to the constitutional convention, he argued that "If Colorado is made a state, its progress will be undeniable. This is good, so be it, but it needs the residents of southern Colorado to succeed. These inhabitants need the publication of the laws in Spanish ... ." Colorado thus began statehood with three official languages: English, German and Spanish.

A biographer observed that Barela "secured the vote for his people, a right of which they would undoubtedly have been disenfranchised, only God knows how early."

Barela also fought the prejudice of that era by ceaselessly advocating statehood for New Mexico, which remained a territory until 1912. It would be difficult to argue that Barela was a bigot, and yet he was the main mover behind Colorado's Columbus Day holiday. He introduced the bill in 1905, his first session as a Republican, but it was tabled.

Even so, a statue of Columbus was erected in Pueblo, and the governor proclaimed October 12, 1905, a holiday to be celebrated with a parade. Barela spoke there at some length, honoring Columbus as a man of humble origins who had "presented so many services of such note to civilization and human progress," with the "discovery of a new world where today so many free and independent nations enjoy peace and joy."

He noted that the Italians, Portuguese, and Spanish all claimed Columbus, but he "is not the property of a single nation. He is the property of all the Latin race."

Barela was likely working some practical politics, since that was a decade of heavy immigration from Italy. In 1900, his Las Animas County had thirteen residents of Italian birth; by 1910, it had 3,362. Pueblo County went from ninety-eight to 1,957; Huerfano from thirty-three to 710; the entire state from 517 to 14,375.

Barela had new constituents to serve, and promoting Columbus Day was a way to unify them, no matter where they came from. In 1907, his Columbus Day bill became law in Colorado; the federal government didn't adopt it until 1971.

So that's one of the ironies of history here in the state where Columbus Day was born. Columbus Day is now denounced as a celebration of racism and genocide, and yet it was the product of a Colorado pioneer who devoted his political career to fighting discrimination and bigotry.

COLORADO'S FIRST CHRISTMAS
DECEMBER 25, 2005

THE FIRST CHRISTMAS CELEBRATION in Colorado happened 199 years ago today, a few miles north of Salida near the mouth of Brown's Canyon. Captain Zebulon Montgomery Pike and his fifteen soldiers had reason to celebrate.

They were in the highest valley of the Rocky Mountains in the dead of winter, and their last food had been a turkey and a hare shot on December 22. But on Christmas Eve, Dr. John H. Robinson and interpreter Baroney Vasquez killed four bison, and another hunter, Private John Sparks, killed four more. They would enjoy a Christmas feast. We know what they were doing on this expedition that began near Saint Louis on July 15, 1806, and eventually reached Chihuahua, Mexico, on April 2, 1807. But to this day, historians are not sure why they were out here.

The Pike expedition was not an isolated frontier venture. It was intimately connected to Washington, Paris and Madrid. Globalization is nothing new in the West.

America had acquired the Louisiana Purchase from France in 1803, but the border between U.S. territory and the Spanish provinces of Texas and New Mexico was vague. Spanish claims extended well into Mississippi drainage. President Thomas Jefferson argued that Louisiana extended clear to the Rio Grande.

The last major stream to flow into the Mississippi from the west is the Red River — the crooked part of the boundary between Texas and Oklahoma. No one in Washington or Paris then knew that the Red began in the panhandle of Texas; the assumption was that its headwaters were in the Rocky Mountains, as are the origins of the Missouri, Yellowstone, Platte, Arkansas and Rio Grande.

It made sense to find out exactly where those rivers began and how they coursed before they reached civilization. And the more Americans who visited those regions, the better America's claim to them.

So Jefferson ordered the famous Lewis and Clark expedition. It is tempting to think that Pike's venture was a southern counterpart to Lewis and Clark, but it wasn't. The true southern version — so obscure that it has yet to inspire even one roadside historical marker — was led by Thomas Freeman, an astronomer and engineer, and Peter Custis, a naturalist. They got part way up the Red in 1806 before being turned back by Spanish soldiers in what is now Texas.

Pike's orders were different — he was supposed to ascend the Arkansas and descend the Red. And his orders did not come from Jefferson, but from one of the great scoundrels of American history: General James Wilkinson.

In 1803, Wilkinson was the highest-ranking soldier in the U.S. Army, which he commanded from St. Louis. He was also on the payroll of America's most likely enemy, the Spanish empire. And he colluded, off and on, with Aaron Burr, the former vice president who was later tried for treason. They were plotting to raise an army and set up their own country in the West.

Pike was a protégé of Wilkinson's. Why did Wilkinson order Pike up the Arkansas in 1806? If Wilkinson had his own designs on the West, then what

Pike learned about the route would be of great value. And if Pike could learn about the fortifications and military strength of the Spanish territorial capital at Santa Fe, so much the better for Wilkinson's invasion.

Tensions ran high between the United States and Spain then. War was expected imminently. Wilkinson had legitimate reasons, consistent with his military duty, to learn what he could of Spanish defenses. Pike did get to Santa Fe. After his Christmas camp on the Arkansas, which he supposed to be the Red, he went downstream, worked around the Royal Gorge, and found his old camp. He realized he had been on the Arkansas all along. He headed southwest into the San Luis Valley, where he built a stockade before his capture by Spanish soldiers on February 26, 1807. They took him and his men to Santa Fe, then Chihuahua. He made it back to Louisiana in July.

Why was Pike in such a hurry when he came to Colorado? He and his men were in their summer uniforms, and their lack of proper gear caused two privates to lose their feet to frostbite. Soldiers toted seventy-pound loads through waist-deep snow in sub-zero temperatures. Lewis and Clark holed up for the winter; we wonder why Pike didn't build cabins at what is now Pueblo or Cañon City and wait for better weather.

We may never know why Pike took the course he did; it's been a source of argument for nearly two centuries. But we do know what he had to say about the first Christmas in Colorado:

"Dec. 25th. It being stormy weather and having meat to dry, I concluded to lie by this day. Here I must take the liberty of observing that, in this situation, the hardships and privations we underwent were on this day brought more fully to our mind, having been accustomed to some degree of relaxation, and extra enjoyments. But here, 800 miles from the frontiers of our country, in the most inclement season of the year — not one person clothed for the winter — many without blankets, having been obliged to cut them up for socks, etc., and now lying down at night on the snow or wet ground, one side burning whilst the other was pierced with the cold wind — such was in part the situation of the party, whilst some were endeavoring to make a miserable substitute of raw buffalo hide for shoes, etc. ... We spent the day as agreeably as could be expected from men in our situation."

May we all spend the day as agreeably as can be expected in our situations.

CELEBRATE REPEAL DAY
DECEMBER 3, 2009

MY BARTENDER DAUGHTER COLUMBINE has advised me that this Saturday, December 5, should be celebrated. It's Repeal Day because on December 5, 1933, Utah became the thirty-sixth state to approve the 21st Amendment to the U.S. Constitution, thereby ending Prohibition.

The Twenty-first Amendment repealed the Eighteenth Amendment, which stated that "the manufacture, sale, or transportation of intoxicating liquors within, the importation thereof into, or the exportation thereof from the United States and all territory subject to the jurisdiction thereof for beverage purposes is hereby prohibited."

National prohibition took effect on January 17, 1920, a year after ratification. It didn't forbid possession or consumption. This allowed wealthy men like Colorado's Spencer Penrose, who owned the Broadmoor, to stock up (he bought the entire inventory of the Brown Palace) and legally slake his thirst during Prohibition.

When it came to Prohibition, Colorado was an "early adopter."

In 1893, Colorado became the second state where women could vote, and the cause of female suffrage was closely allied with the temperance crusade. Both were upper-class reform efforts, generally opposed by lower-class men who grumbled that women wanted the vote so they could close the saloons.

Ethnic bigotry was also a factor early in the twentieth century. Thousands of Italian immigrants came to Colorado, not always to a warm welcome, and they drank wine. By 1914, there was a war on in Europe, and the Huns drank beer, just like their possibly seditious relatives in America.

On November 3, 1914, Colorado voters approved an anti-alcohol amendment to the state constitution. It took effect on January 1, 1916, making this one of the first states to "go dry."

Some cities were already arid by then. Boulder had outlawed saloons in 1907. Greeley, founded by teetotal idealists as Union Colony in 1870, was dry from day one, and stayed that way for a century.

Wicked old Leadville took the reforms in stride. There was an exception for "medicinal alcohol," and Lake County led the state in such permits on a per-capita basis, with 1,025 for about 7,000 people. Local historian Ned Blair wrote that bootlegging was "the second largest business in Leadville, other than mining and smelting," and the mountain stills "not only supplied Leadville, but much of the state as well."

A major Colorado supporter of Prohibition in the 1920s was the Ku Klux Klan; its program of "100 percent Americanism" was aimed at immigrants, the Italians and Germans who continued to drink despite the Eighteenth Amendment.

Prohibition led to organized crime and violence. Denver Judge Benjamin Lindsey, an early supporter, turned against Prohibition because the rich openly violated the law without penalty, while the poor went to prison for minor violations.

Colorado repealed the state's prohibition law, effective July 1, 1933. Congress proposed the Twenty-first Amendment on February 20, 1933, and Colorado ratified it on September 26, 1933.

On December 5, 1933, Pennsylvania, Ohio and Utah all ratified the Twenty-first Amendment, thereby providing the thirty-six state ratifications — the necessary three-fourths of the forty-eight states then.

Thus, December 5 is National Repeal Day, and in Colorado, we could also celebrate on July 1, Colorado Repeal Day, and September 26, Colorado Ratification Day.

As for how to celebrate, my daughter plans to promote drinks that were popular before Prohibition. They're hard to make now because many of them used Boker's Bitters, a company put out of business during Prohibition. So Columbine made her own replica of Boker's Bitters.

I suspect that every publican will be glad to help you celebrate Repeal Day, one of those rare American political triumphs of common sense over straitjacket moral idealism.

A THEORY FOR PRESIDENTS DAY
FEBRUARY 19, 2012

BY FEDERAL LAW, Monday is a holiday known as Washington's Birthday. By Colorado state law, it's Washington-Lincoln Day. Doubtless many people in their ignorance of these laws will call it Presidents Day.

We seem to have at least three types of holidays. There are the Real Holidays like Christmas and Thanksgiving, when just about everything is closed, Monday is one of those Government Holidays when just about everything except city hall, the county courthouse and the post office is open. Martin Luther King Day is another such day, and in Colorado's tourist zones, much must remain open on Memorial Day, Independence Day and Labor Day.

Finally there are the Cultural Holidays that are pretty much normal workdays all the way around, but are still widely celebrated — Valentine's Day, St. Patrick's Day and Halloween. Or maybe we should call them Commercial Celebrations on account of the spending they inspire.

Back to Monday's holiday.

While Abraham Lincoln certainly had some admirable traits, recall that his main goal was to hold the Union together. Now, ponder what a fine country we'd have if Lincoln had just let the South go in peace.

Before the Civil War, Southerners in Congress blocked progressive legislation like the Homestead Act, the Pacific Railroad Act and the Morrill Act for land-grant colleges. They haven't been much better since they got back into the Union, although back then they were Democrats and now they're Republicans.

Without the South, we'd probably enjoy decent passenger rail service, improved public education and single-payer health insurance. Our federal taxes would be lower, as many of the old Confederate states enjoy substantial subsidies. Mississippi, for instance, collects $2.02 from the federal government for every dollar it pays in federal taxes. It's $1.78 for Louisiana, $1.65 for Alabama and $1.51 for Virginia.

Meanwhile New Jersey residents get but 61 cents back for every dollar they pay to the feds. It's 68 cents in Connecticut. 71 cents in New Hampshire and 82 cents in Colorado.

Granted, American popular music would be worse than dreadful without Southern contributions. And even if it could have seceded peacefully, the South might have gone to war anyway when the perfidious Yankees refused to return escaped slaves.

So Lincoln may not have done posterity any favors by preserving the Union, keeping the civilized portion of America yoked with the other part.

As for George Washington, he may have been a fine president for the eighteenth century, but he could never get elected today.

There was his ownership of slaves, along with his wealth — he was likely the richest man in North America. On his plantation, he grew tobacco and hemp, so he doubtless would have been attacked as a corrupter of youth.

The records show that he preferred fox hunting to church attendance. Although he sat through sermons on occasion, he did not take communion and there are no accounts of any "born again" conversion. He raised taxes, and when distillers in western Pennsylvania organized a tax protest, Washington sent soldiers over the mountains to quell the resistance and ensure that federal taxes were paid.

As for foreign policy, he was one of those wimps who kept America from taking sides in the dispute between France and England.

So it's hard to see how George Washington could have received any modern party's support, just as we must wonder about the wisdom of Lincoln's holding the Union together 150 years ago.

Maybe that's why their birthdays are no longer celebrated in popular culture, but have instead devolved into a generic Presidents Day.

Acknowledgments

Deeper into the Heart of the Rockies is a team effort, and I'm grateful for the contributions of the following people:

Cohen Peart, Letters Editor at *The Denver Post*, helped immeasurably with column selection, retrieval, and editing. He was also a great source of inspiration and support throughout the process.

Aaron Thomas helped with the final selection of columns, designed the cover and book interior, and managed our Kickstarter campaign.

Allen Best helped select columns and wrote the foreword. You can find more of Allen's writing at http://mountaintownnews.net

Martha Quillen helped with column selection.

Hal Walter's stunning photo graces the cover of the book. You can find more of his work at http://hardscrabbletimes.com

Bill Hays helped with column selections and had a knack for finding the most humorous ones.

Finally, the book would not have been published without our generous supporters, especially:

Charles Downing	David Blair
Bill Hays	Dorothy Quillen
Mark Emmer	George Sibley
Andrea Fay Thomas	Curtis Imrie
Jeff Donlan	Trish Rose
Kevin Quillen	Ralph Taylor
Justin Rae	L. Carter Butts
Anthony Galassini	Doug Brady
Ann Parker	Richard Doxtator
Judith Kinzie	Tom Purvis
Amy and Mike Dugan	Susan J. Tweit
Robert and Carol Allison	JD McFarland
Kendall Keene	Anna Ward
Rich Price	Beth Wood
Forrest Whitman	Jane R. Carpenter

ABOUT THE AUTHOR

Ed Quillen was a regular contributor in *The Denver Post*'s Perspective section for 26 years. His was the longest-running column in the paper's history, according to Curtis Hubbard of *The Denver Post*. He wrote about history, politics, water issues, computers and small town living in his weekly dispatches, which he transmitted to the paper from his home in the mountains. He founded *Colorado Central Magazine* in 1994 with his wife Martha Quillen, and they published it for fifteen years. He also regularly wrote for *High Country News* and his work appeared in various other publications, including *Colorado Homes and Lifestyles*, the *Los Angeles Times*, and *Utne*. A long bio and his full archives are available at edquillen.com.

ABOUT THE EDITOR

Abby Quillen writes fiction and magazine articles. Her work has appeared in *YES! Magazine*, *The Christian Science Monitor*, and on *Common Dreams*, *Nation of Change*, *The Daily Good*, *Truthout* and *Shareable.net*. She lives in Eugene, Oregon with her husband, two sons, two cats and three chickens. You can find her online at abbyquillen.com